Black Samson

Black Samson

The Untold Story of an American Icon

NYASHA JUNIOR AND JEREMY SCHIPPER

OXFORD
UNIVERSITY PRESS

OXFORD
UNIVERSITY PRESS

Oxford University Press is a department of the University of Oxford. It furthers
the University's objective of excellence in research, scholarship, and education
by publishing worldwide. Oxford is a registered trade mark of Oxford University
Press in the UK and certain other countries.

Published in the United States of America by Oxford University Press
198 Madison Avenue, New York, NY 10016, United States of America.

Library of Congress Cataloging-in-Publication Data
Names: Junior, Nyasha, author. | Schipper, Jeremy, author.
Title: Black Samson : the untold story of an American icon / Nyasha Junior and Jeremy Schipper.
Description: New York : Oxford University Press, [2020]. |
Includes bibliographical references and index.
Identifiers: LCCN 2019047199 (print) | LCCN 2019047200 (ebook) |
ISBN 9780190689780 (hardback) | ISBN 9780190689803 (epub) | ISBN 9780190936853
Subjects: LCSH: African American men—Race identity. | Samson (Biblical judge)—In literature. |
Samson (Biblical judge)—Art. | African American men in literature. |
African American men in popular culture. | Bible. Judges—Criticism, interpretation, etc.
Classification: LCC E185.625 .J85 2020 (print) | LCC E185.625 (ebook) |
DDC 305.38/896073—dc23
LC record available at https://lccn.loc.gov/2019047199
LC ebook record available at https://lccn.loc.gov/2019047200

1 3 5 7 9 8 6 4 2

Printed by Sheridan Books, Inc., United States of America

We dedicate this book to the memory of Matthew Ewing, Sr.

Contents

Acknowledgments

Several colleagues provided helpful feedback on drafts of this work, including Timothy Beal, Douglas R. Egerton, Herbert Marbury, Ellen Muehlberger, Justin Reed, Stephen Russell, Love Sechrest, Jeffrey Stackert, Linn Washington, and our colleagues in the Department of Religion at Temple University. We would like to thank Carly Crouch and Christopher Hayes for inviting us to present portions of our work as part of the David Allan Hubbard Old Testament Lecture Series at Fuller Theological Seminary in January 2019. We appreciate the tireless assistance of the staff of the Charles L. Blockson Afro-American Collection at Temple University and Temple University librarian Fred Rowland. This book was funded in part by Temple University's Presidential Humanities and Arts Research Program.

Black Samson

Introduction

What We Talk about When We Talk about Samson

> If the world fails to give you consideration, because you are black men, because you are Negroes, four hundred millions of you shall, through organization, shake the pillars of the universe and bring down creation, even as Samson brought down the temple upon his head and upon the heads of the Philistines.
>
> —Marcus Garvey, 1923[1]

The United States has never existed without a Black Samson. His story begins before the Declaration of Independence or the Constitution. Mid-eighteenth-century court records in colonial America reveal that a number of enslaved African men were named after the biblical hero Samson (sometimes spelled "Sampson"). Samson is a popular subject in biblical scholarship on the use of the Bible in art, literature, and popular culture, although this scholarship tends to focus on Samson in White European and White American art and literature.[2] Scholars have paid little attention to the many interpretations of Samson as a Black man.[3] In this book we seek to rectify this neglect and to demonstrate how Americans from various racial and ethnic backgrounds have used the story of Samson to talk frankly about race for over two hundred years. By invoking this controversial figure, they developed a vocabulary to address race alongside myriad political issues, including slavery, education, patriotism, organized labor, civil rights, and gender equality. Our goal for this book is not simply to catalogue references to Black Samson in American art and literature as a corrective to a gap in the scholarly literature. Rather, by investigating legal documents, narratives by enslaved people, speeches, sermons, periodicals, poetry, fiction, and visual arts, we seek to tell the unlikely story of how a flawed biblical hero became an iconic figure in

America's racial history.[4] In telling the story of Black Samson we are telling a story of race in America.[5]

Like any story of race in America, the story of Black Samson is not linear. The first three chapters of this book cover Black Samson traditions mostly in the nineteenth century. The last four chapters focus primarily on the twentieth and twenty-first centuries. We will move back and forth at times in order to link various uses of Black Samson in different historical periods. In this chapter, we discuss physical descriptions of Samson in the Bible, provide examples of the use of Black Samson in America, and consider why the biblical story of Samson may have become associated with African Americans.

The Bible covers Samson's entire life story in only four short chapters (Judges 13–16). The King James Version of the Bible, which is the version we quote throughout this book, needs barely over three thousand words to translate these chapters into English (consult the appendix).[6] In contrast, the story of Abraham and Sarah occupies thirteen chapters in the book of Genesis. Joseph also gets thirteen chapters in Genesis and a lavish Broadway musical. Queen Esther gets ten chapters and an entire biblical book named after her. The story of King David spans three books of the Bible and then is recapped in 1 and 2 Chronicles. Moses's story spans four lengthy books: Exodus, Leviticus, Numbers, and Deuteronomy. Compared with other major biblical figures, Samson's story receives relatively little attention. Outside of the book of Judges, he appears only one other time in the Bible, in a passing reference to him buried in a laundry list of ancient heroes of faith in the New Testament (Hebrews 11:32). He is never mentioned in any ancient Egyptian or Mesopotamian literature outside of the Bible, and there is no archeological evidence of his existence.

Moreover, nothing in the few biblical descriptions of Samson's appearance accounts for his later racialization as Black. The Bible never describes his eye color, skin color, hair texture, or phenotype.[7] Despite later artistic interpretations of a pale-skinned Samson with a chiseled, muscular physique, biblical texts do not discuss his body. They mention only his hair styled in "seven locks" (Judges 16:13–14, 17) and that the Philistines "put out his eyes" after his capture (Judges 16:21, 30). In contrast to Samson, biblical texts describe the future King Saul as tall and handsome (1 Samuel 9:2) and the future King David as a handsome lad with beautiful eyes (1 Samuel 16:12). Although we might imagine Samson as tall and muscular because he performs feats of superhuman strength, biblical texts do not describe his physical frame or even his height. In contrast, when introducing Goliath, the Philistine giant who battles David, the biblical text provides his height and describes his heavy armor and thick weaponry (1 Samuel 17:4–7).[8]

Despite this lack of physical description, the name Samson became linked with enslaved and free African Americans as early as the eighteenth century. For example, a document from the session of the Council of Maryland held on May 17, 1738, requests a pardon for "Negro Sampson a slave belonging to John Rider Esq now under Sentence of Death in Dorchester Country."[9] Also, a document from the session of South Carolina's Commons House of Assembly held on January 31, 1754, describes a slaveholder named Mr. Robert Hume as "the Negro Sampson's master" and includes a resolution to pay three hundred pounds to Hume "for the Negro man named Sampson, upon the said Negroes discovering the Remedy for the Bites of Snakes."[10] On February 5, 1788, the Council of Virginia issued a pardon "to Negro Sampson, belonging to Mary Dickson, under Sentence of death by the judgment of James City County Court for burglary."[11] The name Sampson also appears in reference to presumably free persons of African descent in the eighteenth century. For example, Richard Allen, the founding bishop of the African Methodist Episcopal Church, and Absalom Jones, the first bishop of African descent in the Episcopal Church, mention a man named Sampson in their book on people of African descent during Philadelphia's yellow fever epidemic of 1793. Regarding this Sampson, they wrote, "A poor black man, named Sampson, went constantly from house to house where distress was, and no assistance without fee or reward; he was smote with the disorder, and died, after his death, his family were neglected by those he had served."[12]

It is not surprising to find references to free and enslaved men of African descent named Samson in these eighteenth-century documents. In colonial America, free and enslaved people were often named after characters from biblical texts or from Greek or Roman classical literature. There are records of enslaved and free persons of African descent named Abraham, Hagar, Hercules, Moses, Sarah, and many other names. Yet, while many of these names come from the Bible, when slaveholders gave these names to the persons whom they enslaved, they did not necessarily intend to connect the enslaved person to the biblical stories about their namesakes.[13] For example, when a slaveholder named an enslaved woman Hagar, it was probably not meant to invoke memories of the biblical story about the enslaved Egyptian who ran away from Abram and Sarai (Genesis 16:6–14).[14] Likewise, naming an enslaved man Samson was not meant to connect him to the story of how the biblical Samson killed thousands of his captors after they imprisoned him and forced him into labor (Judges 16:21–30). Biblical names are not always meant as allusions to biblical stories.

Nevertheless, by the early nineteenth century, opponents of slavery had enlisted the biblical Samson in their cause. Although these early anti-slavery advocates did not necessarily interpret the biblical character as a Black man, they applied parts of Samson's story to racially charged issues in the United States. A memoir published in 1810 provides the earliest evidence of an enslaved African's interpretation of the Samson story. In this memoir, Boyrereau Brinch, nicknamed Jeffrey Brace, recalled how he was forced to fight in the Revolutionary War in 1777 when his slaveholder Benjamin Stiles was drafted.[15] Brace noted the irony of an enslaved man fighting for his oppressors' independence. He recounted:

> I also entered the banners of freedom. Alas! Poor African Slave, to liberate freeman, my tyrants. I contemplated going to Barbadoes [where he was first enslaved] to avenge myself and my country, in which I justified myself by Samson's prayer, when he prayed God to give him strength that he might avenge himself upon the Philistines, and God gave him the strength he prayed for.[16]

Brace refers to Samson's dying plea for vengeance moments before he brings the Philistine temple down. Samson prays, "O Lord GOD, remember me, I pray thee, and strengthen me, I pray thee, only this once, O God, that I may be at once avenged of the Philistines for my two eyes" (Judges 16:28). Although Brace does not necessarily interpret Samson as a Black man, he finds biblical support for avenging his enslavement by linking it with Samson's desire for revenge, which Samson expresses throughout his battles with the Philistines (Judges 15:7–8, 11).[17]

Another early reference to the biblical story of Samson appears in an 1822 letter that mentions Denmark Vesey's plans for an uprising in Charleston, South Carolina. This letter provides indirect evidence that the organizers of the uprising invoked Samson in connection with their cause. Mary Lamboll Beach, a White slaveholding widow from Charleston, wrote a letter, dated July 5, 1822, to her sister Elizabeth Gilchrist in which she discussed Denmark Vesey, a formerly enslaved man of African descent. Vesey is best known for allegedly conspiring to lead what could have been the largest revolt against slaveholders in US history.[18] The plan was suppressed before it could be carried out. Vesey was tried and hanged with five others on July 2,

1822. According to court records, Vesey used several biblical texts to justify the revolt.[19] Although no references to Samson appear in any of the trial
transcripts, Beach's letter, dated three days after Vesey's execution, claims
that "the voluminous papers found [in connection to Vesey's plans for in-
surrection] . . . speak of their deliverance from the hand of the Philistines."[20]
Before Samson is born, an angel informs Samson's mother that "he shall
begin to deliver Israel out of the hand of the Philistines" (Judges 13:5). While
there are many instances of Israelites fighting the Philistines in the Bible, in
the context of an uprising, the revolt's organizers may have been referring
to Samson's role as a deliverer. Beach's letter suggests that some people of
African descent may have used the story of Samson to justify militant action
against slaveholders early in US history.

In 1834, Margaretta Matilda Odell, a White New Englander who claimed
to be a descendant of Phillis Wheatley's slaveholders, associated the experience of enslaved persons with Samson when discussing the possibility of
the enslaved taking revenge on their slaveholders. In her best-selling book,
Memoir and Poems of Phillis Wheatley, a Native African and a Slave, written
three years after Nat Turner's well-publicized rebellion in 1831, Odell cautioned that southern plantations were not filled with the singing and dancing
of happy enslaved persons but with their cries for vengeance.[21] She wrote:

> We have been told of the happiness of the Negro in his bondage; how
> blithely he joins in the dance, and how joyously he lifts the burthen of the
> song, and how free he is from all care for the morrow. . . . [Yet,] Make him
> acquainted with the wealth of his own spirit—his own strength—and his
> own rights—and the white man would strive to bind him as vainly as the
> Philistines strove against Sampson. Even now, in his day of darkness, how
> often has he made the hearts of his keepers to quail, and their cheeks to
> blanch with fear, when they have looked on their wives and little ones, and
> heard the cry of vengeance fill their plantations with dismay.[22]

Odell alludes to the Philistines' capture of Samson at Lehi when the Spirit of
the Lord rushes upon him: "and the cords that were upon his arms became as
flax that was burnt with fire, and his bands loosed from off his hands. And he
found a new jawbone of an ass, and put forth his hand, and took it, and slew a
thousand men therewith" (Judges 15:14–15).[23]

Eventually, anti-slavery advocates began to use the name Samson as short-
hand for African Americans collectively. Austin Steward was born into

slavery in 1793 in Prince William County, Virginia, and in 1857, he published his autobiography. The book begins with several letters of recommendation that endorse its publication.[24] In one of the letters, dated July 1, 1856, Edwin Scrantom of Rochester, New York, wrote, "Your book may be humble and your descriptions tame, yet truth is always mighty; and you may furnish the sword for some modern Sampson, who shall shout over more slain than his ancient prototype."[25] Scrantom suggested that books like Steward's autobiography would serve as weapons to inspire contemporary Samson-like revolutionaries who would kill more of their oppressors than the thousands of Philistines who were slain by the biblical Samson (Judges 14:19; 15:8, 15; 16:30).

In an 1859 book titled *Roving Editor: Or, Talks with Slaves in Southern States*, James Redpath, a Scottish-born journalist and outspoken abolitionist, documented his travels to the southern states, which he began in 1854.[26] At one point, he provided a detailed narrative of a slave auction held by Dickinson, Hill and Company that he witnessed in Richmond, Virginia.[27] He was horrified when several enslaved women and men were stripped naked and closely examined. Redpath concluded his chapter about this auction by quoting in its entirety a poem by an unidentified author titled "A Curse on Virginia."

> Curses on you, foul Virginia,
> Stony-hearted whore!
> May the plagues that swept o'er Egypt—
> Seven and seventy more,
> Desolate your homes and hearths,
> Devastate your fields,
> Send ten deaths for every birth-pang
> Womb of wife or creature yields;
> May fever gaunt,
> Protracted want,
> Hurl your sons beneath the sod,
> Send your bondsmen back to God!
> From your own cup,
> Soon may you sup,
> The bitter draught you give to others—
> Your negro sons and negro brothers!
> Soon may they rise,

As did your sires,
And light up fires,
Which not by Wise,
Nor any despot may be quenched;
Not till Black Samson, dumb and bound,
Shall raze each slave-pen to the ground,
Till States with slavers' blood are drenched![28]

The poem curses the state of Virginia and proposes that slaveholders will reap the bitterness that they have sown. It describes those involved in a slave insurrection collectively as "Black Samson" and suggests that these enslaved persons will rise up against their oppressors.

In 1866, John Townsend Trowbridge, a White northern writer, claimed that during "a tour of the old negro auction rooms" in Richmond, Virginia, his unnamed guide told him, "I've seen many a Black Samson sold; standing between those posts; and many a woman too, as white as you or I."[29] Albion W. Tourgée, a White lawyer who served as the lead attorney for Homer Plessy in the landmark Supreme Court case *Plessy v. Ferguson*, used the term "Black Samson" and "ebony Samson" to describe enslaved African Americans multiple times in his 1880 novel *Bricks Without Straw*.[30] In the same year, Timothy Thomas Fortune, who was Booker T. Washington's ghostwriter and the editor of the highly influential African American newspaper the *New York Age*, described the comfortable economic conditions that the southern plantation owner enjoyed before the Civil War. He wrote, "Their vast landed estates and black slaves were things that did not fluctuate; under the effective supervision of the viperous slave-drivers the black Samson rose before the coming of the sun."[31]

In August 1885 in Chautauqua, New York, William Henry Crogman delivered a lecture entitled "The Negro Problem."[32] Crogman was a professor of Greek and Latin at Clark University in Atlanta, Georgia, and, in his lecture, he debunked the paternalistic idea that African Americans would "die out" if left to care for themselves without their enslavers.[33] Noting failed efforts to institute voluntary or involuntary colonization of formerly enslaved persons, Crogman highlighted the growth in the African American population since the abolition of slavery with the ratification of the Thirteenth Amendment.[34] He exclaimed, "Black Samson had just begun to grow, and that under freedom he has attained a growth unequaled in any similar period of his bondage."[35] Although it may appear to be an obscure reference today, in 1885, Crogman's audience would have understood his use of "Black Samson" as referring to the social and political advancement of African Americans.

Church manuals and bulletins from that era included speeches and sermons that also referred to Black Samson.[36] An article in the African American newspaper *Savannah Tribune* summarizes an 1899 lecture on Black Samson delivered by Dr. W. P. Thirkeild, who was the president of Gammon Theological Seminary, a historically Black seminary in Atlanta.[37] In an 1899 *Saint Louis Sun* article, reprinted in Topeka's *Plain Dealer*, the author assumed that the audience was familiar with Black Samson as a representation of African American progress. In considering the prospects for African Americans in the twentieth century, the author asked, "What is there to discourage his going forth but the old adage, 'A lion in the way'? If he be a black Sampson, as most of our writers have pictured and denominated him, let the Negro, like the giant of old, procure the jawbone of an ass and slay the king of the forest, which figuratively lies in his pathway."[38] The writer uses a rhetorical question to claim that no reasonable obstacle will prevent African Americans from achieving progress and that they can overcome any impediment through Samson-like strength.

By the late nineteenth century, the term "Black Samson" was not used only as a reference to the collective strength of African Americans. Physically gifted African Americans were also described as "Black Samsons." An 1874 article titled "Black Sampson—Fall of the Chair Factory Ruins" reports that a "colored" man named Daniel Young quickly brought down a wall of a ruined chair factory that local firefighters had been working on for quite some time.[39] In 1880, the term "Black Samson" was used to describe Tom Molineaux, an African American heavyweight boxer, in a racist account of his European boxing tours written decades after the fact. The article explained, "The Black, like most of his race, had a childish propensity for gaiety, and a strong passion for dress, was amorously inclined, and devoted himself by turns to Bacchus and Venus. Of course, the Black Samson met with many mercenary Dalilahs."[40] Another article published in the *Boston Daily Globe* in 1908 discusses a local "beef lugger," born into slavery, named Jimmy Golden. The article, titled "Marvels of Strength: 'Jimmy' Golden is Called the 'Black Samson,'" reported that Golden was known for "the heavy lifting and carrying that made him famous in the district as a marvel of strength."[41] In 1910, the *Baltimore Afro-American* reprinted an article from the *Philadelphia*

JOHN ARTHUR JOHNSON.

The black Samson as he looked when he entered the ring July 4, at Reno, Nevada, and looked James J. Jeffries in the eye, while dealing him some sledge hammer blows.

Figure I.1

Tribune about a title fight between Jack Johnson (born John Arthur Johnson), the first African American world heavyweight champion (figure 1.1), and the former champion James J. Jeffries.[42] The article about the fight stated:

> The black Samson slithered and knocked out the white Goliath at Reno, July 4th. . . . The white philistines throughout the country bet on their Goliath and when he was done up they got sore in the head as they were in the pocket and began to maltreat black people. . . . There may be no more legalized prize fighting in this country. In that case the championship of physical prowess will remain with the black Samson and his people.[43]

Although Johnson's most popular nickname was the "Galveston Giant" because he was born and raised in Galveston, Texas, a number of other African American publications referred to him as "black Samson."[44]

Finally, in 1921, the African American newspaper the *Broad Ax* published a poem titled "Black Sampson" that tells the story of a "plain black fellow" named Sam who "could lift surprising weights which seemed light to him."[45]

So how can we account for the myriad associations of Samson with African Americans? Among the many biblical characters, Samson may seem to be a curious choice for expressing ideas about race in America. Although descriptions of Samson's appearance in the Bible cannot explain why he became closely linked with African Americans, biblical stories about him may provide some clues. Many interpreters noticed a small, easily overlooked detail. After his dramatic capture by the Philistines, the text notes that the Philistines "bound him with fetters of brass; and he did grind in the prison house" (Judges 16:21). As we discuss throughout this book, generations of American interpreters understood Samson as an enslaved man forced into labor. His death became a final act of resistance against his oppressors. For some interpreters, it represents the ultimate sacrifice of a heroic martyr. For others, it is the foolish consequence of a selfish vendetta. In the end, however, there is no clear victor amid the rubble of the Philistine temple. The story does not leave us with the triumph of a shepherd boy over a giant or a victory dance of the formerly enslaved on the banks of the Red Sea. Samson's story is not one of liberation but of continued struggle against oppression in a morally complicated world. When read against the backdrop of American history, the Samson story becomes a haunting analogue for the hope and horror of race relations in the United States.

1

Black Samson in the Temple of Liberty

The last stanza of "The Warning" seems almost like a prophecy.
—Juliet M. Bradford, 1909[1]

In 1776, Thomas Paine, an outspoken advocate for colonial America's independence from England, published a poem titled "Liberty Tree" in the *Pennsylvania Magazine*. Written under a pseudonym, Paine's poem mythologized the colonies as a divinely established "temple of liberty." It describes how "the goddess of liberty" descends with a plant that takes root and grows. Its fame attracts "the nations around, / to seek out its peaceable shore, / Unmindful of names or distinctions they came . . . and their temple was Liberty Tree."[2] Over the next several decades, the metaphor of America as a temple called Liberty Tree shifted to America as a "temple of liberty." The term "Temple of Liberty" has been used to refer to the capital of the United States since at least 1795. In an anonymous letter from Philadelphia dated January 4, 1795, the author writes, "The Federal city, situated in the centre of the United States, is a temple erected to liberty; and towards this edifice will the wishes and expectations of all true friends of their country be incessantly directed."[3]

In the nineteenth century, prominent writers and politicians invoked the Temple of Liberty in debates over slavery. Both pro- and anti-slavery advocates had concerns regarding the stability of the nation's democracy due to the enslavement of African peoples. The idea of Black Samson in the Temple of Liberty became an important element within anti-slavery efforts. Henry Wadsworth Longfellow's 1842 poem "The Warning" popularized the image of a blinded Black Samson figure. In this chapter, we analyze how nineteenth-century American writers used Samson to address not only slavery but also other issues related to race. In doing so, these writers created a lasting link between the biblical Samson and the plight of African Americans that helped to generate a uniquely American Black Samson figure.

In 1834, Margaretta Matilda Odell highlighted the hypocrisy of the nas-cent American democracy in her *Memoir and Poems of Phillis Wheatley, a Native African and a Slave*. Odell wrote, "How can a free people be a slave-holding people? Surely in that social community, where man is claimed as the property of his fellow, the cornerstone of the Temple of Liberty must be laid in the sand; and whither shall we flee when such a frail foundation is un-settled?"[4] In this quote, Odell alluded to Jesus's warning that those who do not act on his words are like a fool who "built his house upon the sand: And the rain descended, and the floods came, and the winds blew, and beat upon that house; and it fell: and great was the fall of it" (Matthew 7:26–27). Odell warned that the practice of slavery is an equally frail foundation for the Temple of Liberty. She implied that, like the proverbial house built on sand, the Temple will crumble when the inevitable storm arises. As we discussed in the introduction, Odell associated enslaved African Americans with Samson in the same book. Also, she linked the United States with the Temple of Liberty, although she did not connect the two images by placing a Black Samson figure in the Temple of Liberty.

Four years after Odell's book was first published, a twenty-eight-year-old Abraham Lincoln delivered what became known as the "Lyceum Address" to the Young Men's Lyceum of Springfield, Illinois, on January 27, 1838. The address condemns mob violence as a means of suppressing anti-slavery efforts, asserting it was not "necessary, justifiable, or excusable."[5] Lincoln cited examples of mob violence, including the lynching of a mixed-race man named Francis McIntosh in St. Louis, Missouri, on April 28, 1836. Also, he referred specifically to a suppressed slave revolt planned for July 4, 1835, in Natchez, Mississippi. He stated, "Negroes, suspected of conspiring to raise an insurrec-tion, were caught up and hanged in all parts of the State [of Mississippi]: then, white men, supposed to be leagued with the negroes."[6] He warned that mob rule undermines the respect for law and the nation's political institutions.

Lincoln contrasted such violence with his idealized view of the founders of the United States. Metaphorically, he identified those involved in the War for Independence as "the pillars of the temple of liberty."[7] He contended that new patriots must take their place. He charged that "now, that they have crumbled away, that temple must fall, unless we, their descendants, supply their places with other pillars, hewn from the solid quarry of sober reason."[8] Lincoln did not explicitly compare the older pillars to the pillars of the temple that Samson brought down. Instead, he argued that terrorist tactics against African Americans operate outside the law and thus threaten the pil-lars of the Temple of Liberty. Yet, eventually the idea of the United States as a Temple of Liberty threatened by the oppression of African Americans became linked to the idea of enslaved and formerly enslaved persons as Samson figures. This combination formed the powerful image of Black Samson as an internal threat to the Temple of Liberty.

Black Samson and the Temple of Liberty were not linked until the publication of "The Warning," a poem by Henry Wadsworth Longfellow in 1842. Longfellow was an internationally known poet and Smith Professor of Modern Languages at Harvard University. This poem was one of nine that appeared in a small collection of his anti-slavery poetry titled *Poems on Slavery*. It popularized the image of Black Samson as one who shakes the pillars of American democracy. Although the poem does not identify Samson as Black directly, it refers to him as a "poor, blind Slave." Then, it alludes to enslavement in the United States by stating "there is a poor, blind Samson in this land." Thus, the poem depicts enslaved persons collectively as a Samson figure. While Longfellow was not the first to invoke Samson as an African American in an anti-slavery context, his poem transformed the Temple of Liberty into the Philistine temple of Dagon with Samson poised to bring it crashing down. "The Warning," in its entirety, reads:

> Beware! The Israelite of old, who tore
>   The lion in his path,—when, poor and blind,
> He saw the blessed light of heaven no more,
> Shorn of his noble strength and forced to grind
> In prison, and at last led forth to be
> A pander to Philistine revelry,—
>
> Upon the pillars of the temple laid
>   His desperate hands, and in its overthrow
> Destroyed himself, and with him those who made
>   A cruel mockery of his sightless woe;
> The poor, blind Slave, the scoff and jest of all,
> Expired, and thousands perished in the fall!
>
> There is a poor, blind Samson in this land,
>   Shorn of his strength and bound in bonds of steel,
> Who may, in some grim revel, raise his hand,
>   And shake the pillars of this Commonweal,
> Till the vast Temple of our liberties.
> A shapeless mass of wreck and rubbish lies.[9]

Often, Longfellow's *Poems on Slavery* present enslaved persons as long-suffering or tragic figures.[10] This is typical of abolitionist literature that resorted to sentimentalized depictions of slavery as epitomized in Harriet Beecher Stowe's classic novel *Uncle Tom's Cabin; or, Life among the Lowly.*[11] This strategy aimed to create sympathy for enslaved persons and to emphasize the moral injustice of slavery as an institution. "The Warning" plays up the image of the mighty Israelite who had once torn apart a lion as now blinded, shorn of his strength, forced into hard labor, and mocked by the Philistines. These reversals in fortune emphasize the tragic nature of Samson's present circumstances. The repeated and stereotypical use of "poor, blind" amplifies this sentimentalized portrait.

Following the initial publication of *Poems on Slavery*, Longfellow seemed to have doubts about whether his anti-slavery poems could sway public opinion after a man named Isaac Appleton Jewett wrote to him praising the book. Jewett explained that he enjoyed hearing enslaved persons sing and invited Longfellow to a slave auction in New Orleans where they could see enslaved persons dance.[12] Realizing that Jewett had profoundly misunderstood his intentions, Longfellow responded in a letter dated May 23, 1843. He acknowledged that his poems were "so mild that even a Slaveholder might read them without losing his appetite for breakfast."[13] Yet, despite Longfellow's concerns, "The Warning" became an anthem for many supporters of abolition. His short poem facilitated the use of the biblical hero as a potent symbol for a wide variety of African American experiences. Over the next century, this Black Samson figure developed in ways that Longfellow could not have imagined.

In the decades following its publication, many writers and speakers quoted or paraphrased "The Warning." The 1851 book *The Natural History of Man; or Popular Chapters on Ethnography* quotes the entirety of Longfellow's poem. The author introduced the poem as follows: "The nation which possesses at present the unenviable pre-dominance as slaveholder and taskmaster would do well to hear the voice of one of her own sons."[14] The poem was also reprinted in the second volume of *The Garland of Freedom; a Collection of Poems, Chiefly Anti-Slavery* published in London in 1852.[15]

Frederick Douglass, a formerly enslaved abolitionist who became an iconic orator and voice for social reform, alluded to "The Warning" in his landmark address originally titled "The Meaning of July the Fourth for the American Negro." Popularly known as "What to the Slave Is the Fourth of July?," Douglass delivered this address on July 5, 1852, to the Rochester

Anti-Slavery Sewing Society at Corinthian Hall in Rochester, New York. The audience included President Millard Fillmore. In his speech, Douglass offered a searing critique of the hypocrisy of celebrating American independence while slavery continued. He compared himself to Samson and borrowed from Longfellow's "The Warning," when he declared:

> I am not included within the pale of this glorious anniversary! Your independence only reveals the immeasurable distance between us. . . . This fourth [of] July is yours, not mine. You may rejoice, I must mourn. To drag a man in fetters to the grand illuminated *temple of liberty*, and call upon him to join you in joyous anthems, were inhuman mockery and sacrilegious irony. If so, there is a parallel to your conduct. And let me warn you that it is dangerous to copy the example of a nation whose crimes, lowering up to heaven, were thrown down by the breath of the Almighty, burying that nation in irrecoverable ruin![16]

Douglass was invited before the president and other dignitaries at an event to commemorate the anniversary of the signing of the Declaration of Independence. He compared this invitation to the demand that Samson entertain the Philistine elites at the temple of Dagon (Judges 16:25). He paralleled his experience with that of a chained and mocked enslaved man in the "temple of liberty." Although Douglass did not refer to Samson by name or quote from "The Warning" directly, his language reworked the Samson imagery from Longfellow's poem. Like Longfellow, Douglass warned his audience of the dangers of following the example of the Philistines.

Other publications from the mid-1850s also quote "The Warning." An 1855 article in the *New Englander* warned, "And there is, most dangerous of all, the 'poor, blind Samson in our land,' untamed by civilization, untaught and ignorant, degraded and despised, who may yet, in his wrath, rise up and shake the pillars of the state, and mingle all in a common destruction."[17] *Leaven for Doughfaces; or, Threescore and Ten Parables*, an 1856 collection of anti-slavery parables, contained another clear reference to Longfellow. Within this collection, a parable titled "Free Trade" discussed how capitalist systems can reduce people to "slaves," who "thenceforward, like a blind Samson shorn of his strength, staggered on toward poverty and despotism."[18] An 1857 book, *Incidents of a Southern Tour: Or the South, as Seen with Northern Eyes* reprinted "The Warning" as the book's epilogue, although it did not attribute it to Longfellow.[19]

Even pro-slavery advocates invoked Longfellow's poem. Robert Toombs, a politician from Georgia, reworked "The Warning" in a speech to the US Senate in January 1860. Toombs served as both a US congressman and senator before becoming the Confederacy's first secretary of state. In his speech, he declared, "Never permit this Federal government to pass into the hands of the Black Republican party. It has already declared war against you and your institutions. . . . Defend yourselves; the enemy is at your door; wait not to meet him at your hearthstone,—meet him at the doorsill, and drive him from the Temple of Liberty, or pull down its pillars and involve him in a common ruin."[20] Toombs warned his fellow senators to drive away what he understood as the Republican threat to the nation or else destroy the entire Temple of Liberty in Samson-like fashion.

In 1861, as the Civil War intensified, Harriet Beecher Stowe wrote an essay in favor of allowing African Americans to serve in the Union army. She noted the contributions of African Americans to the war effort and acknowledged that African American forces could determine the outcome of the war. In citing "The Warning," she cautioned, "The poor blind Samson in our land is still an awful and a fatal power—and all the horoscope of our destiny is affected by him. Let everyone ponder this."[21] Stowe may have used Longfellow's poem to discuss African Americans as well as the fateful consequences of slavery for the nation.[22] In 1862, Douglass returned to the Samson imagery from the closing lines of Longfellow's "The Warning" to describe the tenuous state of the Republic. In a speech on the Civil War, he declared, "Every pillar of the national temple is shaken."[23]

While Longfellow's poem was an anti-slavery poem, its influence outlived the legal abolition of slavery with the ratification of the Thirteenth Amendment. In the late nineteenth century, writers and speakers cited "The Warning" when addressing other social ills facing African Americans and the nation as a whole. In particular, African American authors, clergy, and activists used Longfellow's poem in appeals for better educational opportunities, in anti-lynching campaigns, in poetry celebrating social progress for African Americans, and in calls for Black nationalism.

Examples of such uses of "The Warning" occurred during the National Education Assembly conference that was held in Ocean Grove, New Jersey, in 1883. At this meeting a variety of Christian educators gave speeches on the current state of education, including the limited educational opportunities for African Americans. The speakers included Professor S. B. Darnell, who was the pastor of Ebenezer Methodist-Episcopal Church in Jacksonville, Florida, and the founder of the Cookman Institute, the first institution of higher education for African Americans in Florida.[24] In his speech, Darnell used Longfellow's poem to criticize the United States for not adequately educating African Americans. He understood education as essential for "the safety of the whole body politic, the future stability of our great government."[25] He paraphrased the last stanza of Longfellow's poem to reinforce the societal danger that he believed uneducated African Americans posed to the stability of the Republic. He wrote:

> A poor, blind Samson is in our land,
> Bound hand and foot and prone upon his back,
> But, who knows, that in some drunken revel,
> He may rise and grasp the pillars,
> Of our temples' liberties, shake the foundations,
> Till all beneath its broken columns lie in ruins.[26]

By paraphrasing Longfellow's poem about a "poor, blind Samson," Darnell's speech contrasts a man whose education equips him with a solid Christian character to a poor, uneducated man whose drunken actions could threaten the Republic.

Another speaker at the National Education Assembly was Reverend John Braden, the pastor of Clark Memorial Methodist Church, the oldest African American Church in Nashville, Tennessee, and the first president of the short-lived historically Black Central Tennessee Methodist Episcopal College. Like Darnell, Braden alludes to Longfellow's poem. But, unlike Darnell or Longfellow, Braden made explicit use of the term "black Samson" along with the biblical description of Samson's forced labor in Judges 16:21 to describe slavery in the United States. He argued that the Civil War made White Christians realize that the institution of slavery had almost destroyed "the fair fabric of our national existence."[27] He wrote, "Christians saw how nearly black Samson, grinding in our prison-house, had pulled down the pillars of our temple of liberty; and that, instead of being an enemy to national progress, he might be made a friend."[28] Braden also claimed that White Christians became aware of the necessity of providing educational opportunities for African Americans after realizing that the Civil War almost brought about the national collapse about which Longfellow's poem had warned.

As the nineteenth century ended, the use of Black Samson continued in the works of African American poets, novelists, and journalists. Arguably the most influential contribution came from a Philadelphia poet named Josie D. Heard. Born Josephine Henderson, she was the daughter of formerly enslaved parents in North Carolina. Heard became a schoolteacher and later married an African Methodist Episcopal minister in Philadelphia.[29] Many of the poems in her only published collection of poetry, *Morning Glories*, focus on African American upward social mobility and self-determination.[30] A section of *Morning Glories* titled "The Race Problem" begins with a poem called "Black Sampson." In this poem, Heard transformed the image of Black Samson by reworking Longfellow's poem into a celebration of uncompromising African American self-empowerment. The entire poem reads:

> There's a Samson lying, sleeping in the land,
> He shall soon awake and with avenging hand,
> In an all unlooked for hour,
> He will rise in mighty power;
> What dastard can his righteous rage withstand?
>
> E'er since the chains were riven at a stroke,
> E'er since the dawn of Freedom's morning broke,
> He has groaned, but scarcely uttered,
> While his patient tongue ne'er muttered;
> Though in agony he bore the galling yoke.
>
> O, what cruelty and torture has he felt?
> Could his tears, the heart of his oppressors melt?
> In his gore, they bathed their hands,
> Organized and lawless bands—
> And the innocent were left in blood to welt.
>
> The mighty God of Nations doth not sleep,
> His piercing eye, its faithful watch doth keep,
> And well-nigh His mercy's spent,
> To the ungodly lent;
> "They have sown the wind, the whirlwind they shall reap."
>
> From his nostrils issues now the angry smoke,
> And asunder bursts the all oppressive yoke;
> When the prejudicial heel
> Shall be lifted, we will feel,
> That the hellish spell surrounding us is broke.

The mills are grinding slowly, slowly on,
And till the very chaff itself is gone;
Our cries for justice louder
'Till oppression's groan to powder—
God speed the day of retribution on!

Fair Columbia's filmy garments all are stained;
In her courts is blinded justice rudely chained;
The Black Samson is awaking,
And his fetters fiercely breaking;
By his mighty arm, his rights shall be obtained.[31]

The opening of Heard's poem—"There's a Samson lying, sleeping in the land / He shall soon awake and with avenging hand"—alludes to the lines in the "The Warning," which read: "There is a poor, blind Samson in this land . . . Who may, in some grim revel, raise his hand." Yet, unlike the Samson in Longfellow's poem, Heard's Black Samson is not a tragic or sentimental figure who is "poor" or "blind." Instead, he is asleep. Conversely, the United States, personified as Columbia, is no longer the divine champion of liberation that Phillis Wheatley celebrated in her poem "To His Excellency, George Washington" over one hundred years earlier.[32] Rather, Columbia has become blinded and chained by its oppression of African Americans. By contrast, Black Samson is awakening. Although Longfellow's poor, blind Samson is "shorn of his strength," Heard's Black Samson will break his fetters and obtain his rights "by his mighty arm." Grinding in the mills calls to mind Samson's forced labor for the Philistines, but Heard used it to refer to the work of justice that grinds away at African American oppression.[33]

Frances Ellen Watkins Harper's classic *Iola Leroy, or Shadows Uplifted* offers a more sentimentalized portrait of Samson.[34] In *Iola Leroy*, the titular character is the daughter of a wealthy slaveholder named Eugene Leroy and his wife Marie. Marie is mixed race but could pass for White. As an enslaved woman, she serves Eugene and nurses him back to health when he becomes ill. Harper depicts the relationship between the enslaved Marie and her slaveholder Eugene in sentimental terms. At one point in Harper's novel, Eugene explains, "I not only pitied her, but I learned to respect her. . . . I thought of this beautiful and defenseless girl adrift in the power of a reckless man . . . she, with simple, childlike faith in the Unseen, seemed to be so good and pure that she commanded my respect and won my heart."[35] Eugene sends Marie

North to educate her, frees her, and marries her after she graduates at the top of her class. At the graduation ceremony, Marie delivers an impassioned speech on the theme "American Civilization, Its Lights and Shadows." In her speech, Marie alludes to Longfellow's poem. The narrator describes the graduation speech and ceremony:

> Graphically she portrayed the lights, faithfully she showed the shadows of our American civilization. Earnestly and feelingly she spoke of the blind Sampson in our land, who might yet shake the pillars of our great Commonwealth. . . . Strong men wiped the moisture from their eyes, and women's hearts throbbed in unison with the strong, brave words that were uttered in behalf of freedom for all and chains for none. Generous applause was freely bestowed, and beautiful bouquets were showered upon her.[36]

Harper's use of Longfellow's "blind Sampson in our land" contributed to her moving appeal for freedom and her sentimentalized depiction of the horrors of slavery.[37]

Journalist Ida B. Wells-Barnett also employed the sentimental aspect of Longfellow's Samson but reworked it creatively. Wells-Barnett was a journalist, an activist. and a founding member of the National Association for the Advancement of Colored People (NAACP). She is probably best known for her landmark documentation of the lynching of African Americans. In her 1892 pamphlet *Southern Horrors: Lynch Law in All Its Phases*, she argued that lynching is not a response to criminal activity by African Americans but a means of enforcing White supremacy in the face of African American political and economic advances. Wells-Barnett focused on how false allegations of rape by White women were used to justify lynching African American men.[38] She labeled such women "white Delilahs," which characterizes the White women not as innocent victims of rape but as co-conspirators with male White supremacists. Wells-Barnett referred to African American men as "poor blind Afro-American Sampsons." She explained that her intention was to

> give the world a true, unvarnished account of the causes of lynch law in the South. This statement is not a shield for the despoiler of virtue, nor altogether a defense for the poor blind Afro-American Sampsons to be betrayed by white Delilahs. . . . I feel that the race and the public generally should have a statement of the facts as they exist. They will serve at the same

time as a defense for the Afro-American Sampsons who suffer themselves to be betrayed by white Delilahs.[39]

The phrase "poor blind Afro-American Sampsons" invokes the line from Longfellow's poem, "There is a poor, blind Samson in this land" with the specification of his race. Wells-Barnett's use of Longfellow's sentimental description of Samson as a victim helped to recast African American men not as those who assault White women but as those who are victimized by White women.

Despite the popularity of anti-lynching campaigns, the allegations of rampant sexual assaults of White women by African American men persisted. In 1904, Thomas Nelson Page, a White southern lawyer and popular author, published an essay that defended lynching as an appropriate response to his thoroughly unfounded claim that there was a recent increase in the "ravishing and murdering of women and children" by African American men.[40] Page credited this alleged rise "to racial antagonism and to talk of social equality that inflames the ignorant Negro. . . . The intelligent Negro may understand what social equality truly means, but to the ignorant and brutal young Negro, it signifies but one thing: the opportunity to enjoy, equally with white men, the privilege of cohabiting with white women."[41]

In 1907, the *Colored American* acknowledged Page's essay when it reprinted Heard's "Black Sampson," seventeen years after her poem's initial publication. The African American newspaper introduced her poem with a quotation by John Mitchell, Jr., the editor of the African American newspaper the *Richmond Planet*: "A full realization of Dr. Thomas Nelson Page's fear as to the Negro . . . is admirably portrayed in Mrs. Josie D. Heard's 'Black Sampson.'"[42] Mitchell's statement reminds the reader that Heard's poem boldly celebrates the economic and social advances of African Americans, which was what Page and others feared. By placing her poem in the context of the anti-lynching campaign, the editors of the *Colored American* used Heard's work to support the argument that lynching was not a punishment for sexual assaults by African Americans as much as a tool for social control of African Americans.

Nearly twenty years later, Heard's "Black Sampson" was once again recast within the context of the emerging Black Nationalism of the early twentieth century. For the actor and activist Henrietta Vinton Davis, whom Marcus Garvey once described as "the greatest woman of the Negro race today," Heard's poem epitomized the collective strength of Black Nationalism.[43]

Davis was at one time a prominent member of Garvey's Universal Negro Improvement Association. In 1924, he traveled to Liberia as part of a delegation seeking to establish a colony for the association in hope of achieving Black self-governance independent of European influence. Upon their return, members of the delegation, of which she was the only woman, presented a report to the Universal Negro Improvement Association. Davis gave an optimistic assessment of the trip, which included a modified quotation of the first stanza of Heard's poem. She stated, "But I want to say here, that in the land of Africa, there is a Sampson lying sleeping who will soon awake, and with an avenging hand and an unlooked-for hour he shall rise in might and power. What dastard can his mighty strength withstand?"[44] For Davis, Heard's poem spoke of the potential of Black self-determination personified as a Samson figure.

Although popularized by Longfellow's anti-slavery poem "The Warning," the iconic image of a Black Samson in the Temple of Liberty provided more than a biblically inspired cautionary tale about the dangers of slavery. Throughout the nineteenth century, the legacy of this image extended into many politically charged discussions about race in America, including abolition, educational opportunities, and anti-lynching campaigns. It would help generations of Americans, including prominent nineteenth-century writers such as Frederick Douglass, Frances Harper, Harriet Beecher Stowe, and Ida B. Wells-Barnett, among many others, voice their own warnings concerning a wide variety of racially charged issues. This powerful image would become deeply engraved in the American literary imagination over the next century.

2

Black Samson of Brandywine

The rugged Americanism of the Black Sampson has never failed
Uncle Sam and never will!

—Madison C. Peters, 1918[1]

Henry Wadsworth Longfellow was not the only writer to popularize a Black
Samson figure. Moving away from treating Samson as an abolitionist hero,
other writers continued to develop this uniquely American Samson figure
within folklore, fiction, and poetry. For example, Black Samson became
immortalized in Paul Laurence Dunbar's "Black Samson of Brandywine,"
which transformed Samson into a symbol of African American achievement.
In this chapter, we highlight the writers who offered new understandings of
Samson as a loyal American patriot.

George Lippard was born into a family of German descent in Pennsylvania
and lived most of his life in Philadelphia. Living in the city raised Lippard's
awareness of the difficulties facing urban laborers, which led to his work as
a labor organizer and social reform advocate. In the 1840s, around the same
time that Longfellow published "The Warning," Lippard gained immense
fame as a writer of legends about early American history. Lippard did not
claim that his legends were strictly factual accounts of historical events.[2]
He freely acknowledged that he embellished historical events with colorful
scenery, eloquent dialogue, and even the inner thoughts of some characters.
As part of his labor-reform efforts, Lippard often focused his legends on poor
laborers and their real or imagined contributions to the formation of the
United States. For example, he produced extensive folklore about the Battle
of Brandywine, where the British general William Howe defeated George
Washington's forces outside Philadelphia on September 11, 1777.[3] Lippard's
writings about Brandywine were serialized in the Philadelphia newspaper
Saturday Courier and reprinted in his 1846 book, *Blanche of Brandywine*.
The next year, they were expanded in his 1847 book, *Washington and His*

Generals, which was also first published serially in the *Saturday Courier*. In his narration of the battle, Lippard introduced several fictional patriotic characters who fought against the British and their loyalists at Brandywine, including poor laborers of various ethnicities such as, among others, Tom O'Dilworth, a blacksmith; Hirpley Hawson, from the Dutch community in Pennsylvania; Gottlieb Hoff, a German immigrant; and Ben Sampson, who is described as "the Negro, Sampson" and "a giant Negro."[4] Ben Sampson is called Black Sampson, Negro Sampson, or Black Hercules at several points in Lippard's narratives.

In contrast to the uses of Samson by Longfellow and other abolitionists, Lippard's Samson is not necessarily modeled after the biblical hero or his story in the book of Judges. His name was not meant to evoke the specifics of the biblical story of Samson beyond a possible general reference to his legendary strength. Although he is held as a slave by a kindly old schoolteacher named Jacob Mayland in Lippard's earlier work, *Blanche of Brandywine*, in *Washington and His Generals*, Black Sampson is a freeman working as a poor laborer. A passionate advocate of labor reform, Lippard used Black Sampson not as a polemic against slavery, but as an argument that poor laborers have been loyal American patriots since the nation's beginnings. In *Washington and His Generals*, immediately after Lippard introduced Black Sampson as "a Negro and yet a Hero!," he emphatically distanced himself from the abolitionists. Using the term factionist rather than abolitionist, Lippard insisted:

> I am no factionist, vowed to the madness of treason . . . who in order to free the African race, would lay unholy hands upon the American Union. . . . The man that for any pretence, would lay a finger upon one of its pillars, not only blasphemes the memory of the dead, but invokes upon his name the Curse of all ages yet to come.[5]

Lippard's imagery served to counter the depiction of Black Samson in abolitionist literature and characterized abolitionists as laying hands upon the American Union and a finger upon its pillars. These images invoke Longfellow's description of how Samson, representing enslaved African Americans, destroys the temple, representing the Union, with lines such as "Upon the pillars of the temple laid, His desperate hands . . . raise his hand, / And shake the pillars of this Commonweal" in his poem "The Warning."[6] In Longfellow's poem, Samson threatens to bring down the Union as long as slavery exists. In Lippard's folklore, Sampson helps secure the Union's existence by fighting the British and their loyalists at Brandywine. In order to depict Sampson as a patriotic laborer, Lippard distanced his Sampson from the image of the enslaved person who may destroy the Temple of Liberty. To rebrand Black Samson as a member of Lippard's ethnically diverse band of early patriots at Brandywine, it was important to negate the idea that he posed a threat to the American Republic. Thus, Lippard developed an alternative view of Samson: furiously loyal to his fallen White slaveholders (in *Blanche of Brandywine*) and his benefactors (in *Washington and His Generals*), while valiantly fighting the British forces to avenge their deaths.[7]

In *Blanche of Brandywine*, Sampson's slaveholder, Jacob Mayland, is burned alive by the British. After Mayland's murder, Sampson rallies poor laborers of various ethnicities to fight the British and their loyalists to help him avenge Mayland's death. Using a racially stereotyped dialect, he declares, "Revenge for his murder—all Sampson lib, for all Sampson die for! Revenge!"[8] Sampson's desire to avenge his slaveholder's murder fuels his massacre of British troops at the Battle of Brandywine. Thus, Lippard recast Black Sampson as a loyal patriot. This figure was not a militant champion of African Americans who, following the biblical example, challenged the White Philistines. Instead, he fought willingly in the Revolutionary War to avenge his White slaveholder.

In the opening scene of *Blanche of Brandywine*, Lippard used racially stereo-typed dialect to introduce Black Sampson as a passionate supporter of George Washington and the American Revolution.[9] Sampson's first line comes during a debate between the patriotic Mayland and the British loyalist Gibert Gates. During the conversation, Sampson injects, "Washington berry good . . . Better nat say he haint Massa Gates."[10] Earlier in the story, Lippard described Sampson's physical features in heavily racialized terms. He wrote, "His head— with the face of African features, the protruding eyes, the flat nose, somewhat aquiline in contour, the lips thick and large, yet determined or expressive, and the prominent chin—was slightly turned aside, while the jet black skin glis-tened in the light."[11] In a detailed description of Sampson's fighting style during the Battle of Brandywine, Lippard resorted to these stereotypes again, in-cluding the description of an African American man as a demon.[12]

And there, striding forward with immense paces, foaming like some caged tiger, suddenly let loose from his cage the Negro Sampson came on. . . . The negro's brawny arms. His feet, his iron chest, all were bare; the glittering scythe swung aloft, guided by the impulse of his giant strength. He rushed forward, a Black Hercules, his aquiline nose with its quivering nostrils, his thick lips whitened with foam, his massive forehead topped by short wooly hair, all turned to lurid red by flashes of battle-light. He came on, looking in very truth like a demon from the fabled hell. . . . "This for Massa!" thundered the negro whirling his scythe around his head, and cutting down redcoat soldiers, one by one, like wheat stubble in a harvested field.[13]

Lippard expanded and modified his Sampson character in *Washington and His Generals*. In this version, Sampson was a prince of the Ashantees before he was enslaved. Jacob Mayland is not Sampson's slaveholder. He is a kindly, old Quaker schoolteacher who takes Sampson in after Sampson first went to Brandywine having escaped from slavery. After Sampson arrives in Brandywine, he becomes a laborer. Like other laborers, he is "a poor man . . . who had toiled from dawn to dusk, with the axe and spade."[14] Lippard changed Sampson from an enslaved man to a free but poor laborer who fought alongside Tom O'Dilworth, Hirpley Hawson, and Gottlieb Hoff. In doing so, Lippard idealized the American Revolution as a time of labor solidarity for a patriotic cause.[15]

While far less celebrated than Lippard's work, Augustine Duganne's novels from the 1840s and 1850s also addressed the plight of poor urban laborers in northern cities. Duganne, who was a contemporary and friend of Lippard, lived in Boston, Philadelphia, and New York City. In 1857, Duganne published *The Tenant-House: Or, Embers from Poverty's Hearthstone*.[16] Although both Lippard and Duganne were concerned about urban labor conditions, it is not solidarity among poor workers as in Lippard's legends that bridges racial divides in *Tenant-House*. Instead, it is common religious practice that brings people together from different racial and economic backgrounds. In *Tenant-House*, religion rather than class creates solidarity.[17]

Set in New York City, the novel's protagonist, Mr. Granby, is accompanied by his African American servant named Samson. Like Lippard's Sampson, this character is "an old negro man of herculean proportions."[18] An encounter with a homeless orphan named Bob inspires Granby to launch a campaign for Protestant Christian reform by establishing schools in the tenant houses to provide religious instruction for the children, who will then have a positive moral influence on their parents and the adults in the community. Samson helps Granby come up with the idea for the schools, which becomes a major part of the novel's subsequent plot. Although Granby is Samson's slaveholder,

Granby refers to Samson as "my old friend" and treats him as a valued confidant.[19] Like Lippard, Duganne characterized Samson by using the stereotype of the African American who is extremely loyal to his slaveholder. In fact, Samson refuses Granby's offer of freedom when given the opportunity. An emotional Samson uses racist stereotypes to explain that the love in his heart is the only thing that chains him to his "kind massa." He exclaims:

> "Yes massa! what harm in de word slave, when my heart only be chained un lubbing a kind massa? Samson rather be slave ten thousand times, dan part from Massa Granby." He bent his head, as he spoke, kissing the old man's hand. "And have you never, indeed, regretted the choice you made, when, twenty years ago, I offered you freedom and competence?—never repented following your old friend?"
>
> "Nebber! Nebber!" sobbed the negro. "Samson hab a white heart in his black bosom, and close down dere is de face ob massa, jes' like a lookin'-glass, forebber and ebber. Bress de Lord, dat put sense in de nigger's head."[20]

Both men are portrayed as Christians who are so similar that Samson's "white heart" mirrors Granby's heart. This helps erase the distance in race and social status that separates the two men. The notion that religion can overcome the differences between a wealthy White philanthropist and an enslaved African American provides an implicit justification for the religious education of the disadvantaged children living in the tenant houses.

Through his emphasis on the reforming power of religion and specifically Protestant Christianity, Duganne continued Lippard's depiction of a Black Samson as a loyal patriot of the United States. In *Tenant-House*, the British and their loyalists are not the national threat. Rather, it is Jews and Italian Catholic immigrants, such as Mordechai Kolephat, the indifferent Jewish landlord of the tenant houses, and an Italian Catholic woman named Monna Maria, whom Duganne describes as a "slave to the tenets and dogmas of her Church," a "bigot and fanatic," and a person who practiced "superstitious devotions" that threaten "the great [Protestant] Christian city of New York."[21] Duganne published *Tenant-House* three years before the Civil War at a time when Longfellow's Black Samson was quickly becoming an abolitionist icon. Yet, unlike the Catholic immigrants and Jews throughout most of the novel, the Black Samson that Duganne imagines is a loyal American citizen. He represents Christian piety rather than a harbinger of revolution like Longfellow's Samson.

In Samuel Fletcher's 1867 novel, *Black Samson: A Narrative of Old Kentucky*, set prior to the American Revolution, the protagonist is a loyal enslaved man who seems to be modeled after Lippard's Sampson rather than the biblical Samson.[22] Although Fletcher observed that, in battle, Samson "exhibited the strength of four ordinary men," Fletcher made only two passing references to the biblical Samson in his novel.[23] He described the head of his Samson as "covered with a luxuriant growth of black wool, which—not having been cut for a long time—hung down upon his shoulders."[24] Toward the close of the novel, he wrote, "Among the darkeys Samson was a real hero, eclipsing even his namesake of the olden time."[25]

Fletcher's Samson is just as fiercely devoted to his slaveholders as Lippard's or Duganne's Samson. Fletcher's novel begins with Samson recounting how he and young "Massa Clem," the son of Samson's slaveholder Squire Scuyler, were captured by Native Americans. Although Samson has opportunities to escape, he remains by Clement's side until Clement tells him to go get help. Later, Samson leads multiple rescue missions to save Clement and other members of his slaveholder's family who are captured by Native Americans. At the end of the novel, Scuyler rewards Samson's heroism by freeing him and giving him a cottage and a garden of his own on the condition that he marry Polly, an African American chambermaid, who would be freed if Samson agrees to do so. Samson, who has feelings for Polly, replies, "The Lor' bress you, Massa Scuyler!"[26] Despite its significant differences in plot with Lippard's legends and Duganne's novel, Fletcher's novel continues to characterize Samson with heavily racialized stereotypes, including Samson's dialect and his intense loyalty to his slaveholders.

Another version of the Black Samson legend appeared in the Boston-based journalist Charles M. Skinner's 1896 multivolume collection of American folklore, *Myths and Legends of Our Own Land*.[27] Skinner wanted to collect examples of America's folklore to show that the nation had a legitimate, emerging literary tradition. His first volume includes an abbreviated version of Lippard's legend of the Battle of Brandywine under the title "Father and Son."[28] Following the version in *Washington and His Generals* rather than the version in *Blanche of Brandywine*, Skinner focused on the fate of Gilbert Gates, a British loyalist who arranged the death of Samson's benefactor Jacob Mayland in revenge for Mayland's involvement in the death of Gates's father.

In Skinner's abbreviated legend, Samson is mentioned only once, and his role is limited to a single paragraph.

> In the fight at Brandywine the next day, Black Samson, a giant Negro, armed with a scythe, sweeps his way through the red ranks like a sable figure of Time. Mayland had taught him; his daughter had given him food. It is to avenge them that he is fighting. In the height of the conflict he enters the American ranks leading a prisoner—Gilbert Gates.[29]

Unlike Lippard, Duganne, and Fletcher, Skinner's version of the Battle of Brandywine does not refer to Samson's enslavement or use racial stereotypes to describe him. The description of Samson as a "sable figure of Time" compares him to a personification of death, possibly because a scythe is his weapon of choice.[30] Although Skinner's discussion of Samson is brief, the details that he includes reinforce the notion of Black Samson as an early American patriot who is loyal to his White benefactors. He highlights Samson's massacre of "the red ranks" and specifies that Samson captures Gilbert and delivers him to the American forces at the Battle of Brandywine.

Skinner's version of the Black Samson legend became the source for Paul Laurence Dunbar's landmark poem, "Black Samson of Brandywine." The poem was included in Dunbar's 1903 collection of poetry, *Lyrics of Love and Laughter*.[31] Born in Dayton, Ohio, to parents who were formerly enslaved, Dunbar achieved international fame and became known as the "Poet Laureate of the Negro Race."[32] He would transform Black Samson of Brandywine into a powerful symbol of African American achievement for future generations. In *Lyrics of Love and Laughter*, Dunbar introduced his Black Samson poem by quoting a line from Skinner's account of the Battle of Brandywine with a citation of Skinner. Dunbar's introduction and his entire poem read:

> "In the fight at Brandywine, Black Samson, a giant negro armed with a scythe, sweeps his way through the red ranks . . . " C. M. Skinner's "Myths and Legends of Our Own Land."

> Gray are the pages of record,
> Dim are the volumes of eld;
> Else had old Delaware told us
> More that her history held.

Told us with pride in the story,
Honest and noble and fine,
More of the tale of my hero,
Black Samson of Brandywine.

Sing of your chiefs and your nobles,
Saxon and Celt and Gaul,
Breath of mine ever shall join you,
Highly I honor them all.
Give to them all of their glory,
But for this noble of mine,
Lend him a tithe of your tribute,
Black Samson of Brandywine.

There in the heat of the battle,
There in the stir of the fight,
Loomed he, an ebony giant,
Black as the pinions of night.
Swinging his scythe like a mower
Over a field of grain,
Needless the care of the gleaners,
Where he had passed amain.
Straight through the human harvest,

Cutting a bloody swath,
Woe to you, soldier of Briton!
Death is abroad in his path.
Flee from the scythe of the reaper,
Flee while the moment is thine,
None may with safety withstand him,
Black Samson of Brandywine.

Was he a freeman or bondman?
Was he a man or a thing?
What does it matter? His brav'ry
Renders him royal—a king.
If he was only a chattel,
Honor the ransom may pay

Of the royal, the loyal black giant
Who fought for his country that day.

Noble and bright is the story,
Worthy the touch of the lyre,
Sculptor or poet should find it
Full of the stuff to inspire.
Beat it in brass and in copper,
Tell it in storied line,
So that the world may remember
Black Samson of Brandywine.[33]

Dunbar's poem retains several elements from earlier legends about Black Samson of Brandywine. As in Lippard's and Skinner's accounts, Samson fights the British. Like his predecessors, Dunbar highlighted Samson's physically imposing frame, referring to him as "an ebony giant" and a "loyal black giant." A scythe is his weapon of choice, which, like Skinner, Dunbar compares to the Grim Reaper's blade. As in Skinner's account, Dunbar's poem does not include some of the racial stereotypes that Lippard uses when describing Samson. Nor does Dunbar's poem mention Samson's enslavement directly but leaves open the possibility that Samson could have been free or enslaved.

As in previous versions of the Black Samson of Brandywine legend, Dunbar's Samson is motivated by loyalty. The speaker praises Samson as "the loyal Black giant who fought for his country that day." Yet, Samson's loyalty is to America rather than to his slaveholder or White benefactor. Dunbar did not include any of the characters in Lippard's multi-ethnic band of patriots that fought at the Battle of Brandywine. Nor did Dunbar mention the treachery and capture of Gilbert Gates. Instead, Dunbar stressed the isolated valor of Black Samson. By focusing on Samson's heroism, Dunbar transformed the legend of the Battle of Brandywine from Lippard's story about the contribution to the war effort by poor laborers of various ethnicities into an unadulterated celebration of African American achievement and patriotism. Dunbar depicted Samson as a loyal American patriot from the very founding of the nation.[34] To those who may doubt the full humanity or citizenship of African Americans, Dunbar asks rhetorically, "Was he a freeman or bondman? Was he a man or a thing?" and responds, "What does it matter? His brav'ry / Renders him royal—a king." Dunbar's poem celebrates Black

Samson's commitment to the revolutionary cause.[35] At the conclusion of the poem, the speaker exhorts, "Tell it in storied line / So that the world may remember / Black Samson of Brandywine." Dunbar framed the poem as a call to memorialize Black Samson as a hero within the canon of great American patriots.[36]

Over the next several decades, a multitude of writers would respond to Dunbar's call to remember Black Samson of Brandywine. In 1917, the poem was reprinted in the NAACP's magazine, *The Crisis*.[37] In 1922, Alice Dunbar Nelson, Dunbar's widow and an accomplished poet, teacher, and activist, argued that the poem could help African American schoolchildren learn about the contributions of African Americans to American history.

> The child mind must have concrete examples, for it is essentially poetic and deals in images. It is not enough to say that black men fought in the Revolutionary War to the extent of so many regiments. . . . It is not enough to say that black slaves, from Massachusetts to Maryland, stood by the Nation when red-coated Tories overran the land. Dunbar's spirited ballad of "Black Samson of Brandywine" will fix the idea in the youthful mind, even as "Paul Revere's Ride" has fixed the date of Concord and Lexington in the minds of generations of young Americans, white and black, from Maine to California.[38]

According to Dunbar Nelson, students will not fully appreciate the history of African American military accomplishment if it is taught via a series of dry numbers and statistics. They will only internalize it if it is brought to life through vivid images such as those found in Dunbar's poem.

Although fictional, Dunbar's Black Samson became a celebrated war hero over time. A White member of the Sons of the American Revolution, a national organization for descendants of those who served in the Revolutionary War, admitted that he did not know of any African American participants in the Revolutionary War until he heard Dunbar's poem recited during an address that he gave at a local high school. Some African American newspapers circulated this story, which contributed to the spread of the legend of Black Samson of Brandywine.[39] Various publications, including prominent African American newspapers, would frequently list him among a catalogue of African American military heroes such as Crispus Attucks, William Harvey Carney, Salem Poor, and Peter Salem as well as the poet Phyllis Wheatley.[40] Since Samson was listed routinely alongside these historical persons, the lines began to blur between Samson as a legendary figure and a real-life military hero.[41]

The association of Black Samson with military accomplishment was not limited to African American writers and orators. During the First World War, Madison Clinton Peters, a White minster in Philadelphia, included a section on African American military involvement in his book, *The Distribution of Patriotism in the United States*.[42] Beginning with Crispus Attucks, he recounted several of the same stories of African American military participation found throughout African American publications. Peters does not mention the Battle of Brandywine directly, but he concludes his discussion of African American military service by noting that "more than 600 Negroes have received commissions in the Great Army that will go to France."[43] He describes these African American soldiers as "Black Sampsons."[44] Several years earlier, an article in the *Christian Observer* quoted Peters as saying, "With our tide of immigration, bringing in the vices of Europe, eating like cancers at the vitals of our nation, we need the strong arm and rugged Americanism of the black Samson."[45] Peter's anti-European immigrant sentiment assumes that African Americans are fully American. Although Peters referred to African Americans collectively rather than to a specific individual, his connection of Black Samson with rugged Americanism fits with the emphasis on African American patriotism popularized by Dunbar's poem.

Unlike his biblical counterpart, Black Samson of Brandywine had always been associated with American loyalty and patriotism. Distinct from Black Samson's legacy as an abolitionist icon, Lippard's folklore gave birth to a separate mythology of Black Sampson as a loyal American patriot. This Black Samson represents African Americans not as threats that could topple the United States but as full citizens who could build it up. Dunbar's passionate tribute, which emphasizes Black Samson's heroism in battle and downplays the racial stereotypes in earlier descriptions of him, helped pave the way for African Americans in the early twentieth century to claim a part of US history as their own. While Lippard's legends about the Battle of Brandywine appear in Skinner's collections of folklore, it was Dunbar's poem that began the transformation of Black Samson of Brandywine into a significant figure in American literature.

Folklore about the Battle of Brandywine developed a less revolutionary and more conciliatory image of Black Samson than the ones modeled after the biblical story that were developing at the same time. Lippard intended his Sampson to curb the abolitionist warning that Samson may tear apart the fabric of a nation in which slavery was practiced. Yet, the idea that a Black Samson figure could represent both an American patriot and a national threat epitomizes how African Americans are often viewed in the United States. The tension of Black Samson as a patriot and as a threat has never been resolved. Moreover, as we will find in the next chapter, the mythology of Black Samson as an American war hero could not stop the increased association of Samson with historical figures who fought and often died in the struggle against racial oppression and terror in America.

3

Samson and the Making
of American Martyrs

Last Friday morning, when John Brown was swung from the gallows, American Slavery felt that pinioned hand strike a blow to its
very heart. . . . He was content to "Die with the Philistines," when he
could slay more of them at his death than in all his life.
                                        —Fales Henry Newhall, 1859[1]

On December 2, 1859, John Brown, a militant White abolitionist, was hanged
in Charlestown, Virginia, after leading a failed attempt to seize a federal armory at Harpers Ferry, Virginia.[2] Brown believed the end of slavery would
require an armed revolt. He planned to seize the federal armory, which
contained 100,000 firearms, to provide enslaved persons with weapons to
create an army. Brown and an interracial group of twenty-one other men
began the raid on October 16, 1859. Initially Brown took control of the armory, but he was captured two days later by the US Marines led by Robert
E. Lee. Two of his sons, Oliver and Watson, along with eight others from
Brown's force were killed during the brief conflict. Brown was imprisoned
and tried for murder, conspiracy with African Americans to produce insurrection, and treason against the Commonwealth of Virginia. On November
2, he was found guilty on all three charges.

Despite George Lippard's efforts to promote a more patriotic version of
Black Sampson in his writings about the Battle of Brandywine, by the 1850s,
some abolitionists had begun to use the term "Samson" to refer to those involved in insurrections by enslaved persons.[3] By the dawn of the Civil War,
they extended that term to describe real-life persons who fought to end
slavery. While Longfellow's "The Warning" likens African Americans as a
collective to Samson, later comparisons with Samson served to mythologize
specific individuals as icons in the struggle for liberation.[4] In the last half of

the nineteenth century, poets, clergy, scholars, and other intellectuals began to identify the biblical Samson with historical individuals who challenged racial oppression in America. The biblical hero had already become a potent symbol of African Americans' collective strength in the fight against slavery and other barriers to social advancement. Eventually, he became associated with those who took up this struggle through passionate rhetoric, violence, and, at times, political compromise. In the process, persons like John Brown, Fredrick Douglass, Gabriel Prosser, Nat Turner, and Booker T. Washington became memorialized as larger-than-life Samson figures.

Two days after Brown's conviction, *The Liberator*, a weekly Boston-based newspaper founded in 1831 by White abolitionists William Lloyd Garrison and Isaac Knapp, introduced a poem titled "Song, Supposed to be Sung by Slaves in Insurrection" with the preface that it "was written many years ago by the late William J. Snelling, Esq. of Boston and is full of prophetic warnings to Southern oppressors at this solemn crisis."[5] Since Snelling died in 1848, his poem does not mention Brown's raid directly. Yet, the poem targets Virginia, the state in which Brown was executed, and the opening stanzas refer to African Americans who fight against their oppressors as a collective Samson. In 1859, the *Liberator* recasts Snelling's poem as a prophecy concerning the "solemn crisis" surrounding John Brown and his raid on Harpers Ferry.

> See, tyrants, see! Your empire shakes!
> Your flaming roofs the wild winds fan;
> Stung to the soul, the negro wakes;
> He slept, a brute—he woke, a man!
> His shackles fall!
> Erect and tall,
> He glories in his new-found might;
> And wins with bloody hand his right.
> Just Heaven! And can it be,—the strong
> With mind to think, the heart to feel,
> He borne upon his neck so long
> A weak and cruel tyrant's heel:
> When one brave stroke
> Had burst his yoke!
> Day dawns at last on mental night,
> And Samson girds him for the fight.[6]

Direct comparisons of Brown with Samson may have originated with Brown himself as he identified with the biblical hero explicitly in various letters written shortly before his death. In a letter published posthumously to his friend and benefactor Franklin Benjamin Sanborn dated February 24, 1858, over a year before his raid on the armory, Brown wrote, "I expect to effect a mighty conquest, even though it be like the last victory of Samson."[7] Brown continued to compare himself to Samson in letters that he wrote from prison while awaiting execution. On November 15, 1859, he wrote to his former schoolmaster, Reverend H. L. Vaill. He declared, "Had Samson kept to his determination of not telling Delilah wherein his great strength lay, he would probably have never overturned the house. I did not tell Delilah but I was induced to act very contrary to my better judgment; and lost my two noble boys, and other friends, if not my two eyes."[8] Brown compared his own capture to Samson's capture to argue that his was necessary to achieve a larger, if not costly, victory in the struggle against slavery. He interpreted Samson as a flawed instrument who was nevertheless used to accomplish a divine plan. Ten days later, Brown expressed this sentiment more explicitly in a letter to Reverend Doctor Heman Humphrey. Although Brown did not mention Samson by name, he quoted directly from Judges 13:5:

> "He shall begin to deliver Israel out of the hand of the Philistines." This was said of a poor erring servant [Samson] many years ago, and for many years I have felt a strong impression that God had given me powers and faculties, unworthy as I was, that He intended to use for a similar purpose. This *most unmerited honor* He has seen fit to bestow, and whether like the same poor frail man to whom I allude my death may not be of vastly more value than my life is, I think, quite beyond all human foresight.[9]

The biblical quotation that Brown uses comes from the angel's announcement to Samson's mother that she will have a special child set apart for a unique mission. Brown casts his own struggle against slavery as a divinely endorsed campaign by applying the angel's announcement to his own life. Yet, the line that Brown quotes does not indicate that Samson will complete the task of delivering Israel from Philistine oppression. Instead, the angel only promises that he will begin the struggle. Unlike other leaders in the book of Judges, the story of Samson ends without indicating that Samson's actions served to liberate his people. In this respect, Brown may have understood his life and death as beginning this process of liberation even if he did not complete it.

At Brown's trial, his court appointed attorney entered a plea of insanity. Brown objected to this plea and told the court, "I am perfectly unconscious of insanity, and I reject, so far as I am capable, any attempts to interfere in my behalf on that score."[10] In defense of Brown's sanity, Frederick Douglass published an editorial titled "Captain John Brown Not Insane" in the November 1859 edition of his newspaper *Douglass' Monthly*.[11] Douglass justified Brown's tactics as rational and wrote, "Moral considerations have long since been exhausted upon slaveholders. It is vain to reason with them. One might as well hunt bears with ethics."[12] He concluded his editorial by praising the sacrifice that Brown made. Douglass declared, "His daring deeds may cost him, but priceless as is the value of that life, the blow he has struck, will, in the end, prove to be worth its mighty cost. Like SAMSON, he has laid his hands upon the pillars of this great national temple of cruelty and blood, and when he falls, that temple will speedily crumble to its final doom, burying its denizens in its ruin."[13] This Samson comparison assisted Douglass in portraying Brown as a sane abolitionist martyr whose actions were completely rational.

On December 4, 1859, two days after John Brown was hanged, Reverend Fales Henry Newhall preached a sermon at the Warren Street Methodist Episcopal Church in Roxbury, Massachusetts.[14] His text that Sunday morning was Judges 16:30: "And Samson said, Let me die with the Philistines. And he bowed himself with all his might; and the house fell upon the lords, and upon all the people that were therein. So the dead which he slew at his death were more than they which he slew in his life." In his sermon, Newhall re-examined Brown's last days in light of the Samson narrative. He described Brown's earlier military victory over pro-slavery forces in Osawatomie, Kansas, as Brown slaughtering the enemy "heaps upon heaps." This is the same phrase used to describe Samson's slaughter of a thousand Philistines with the jawbone of an ass (Judges 15:16). When recounting Brown's capture at Harpers Ferry, he invoked several images from the biblical account of Samson's capture and death (Judges 16:19–30).

[F]or a moment that keen, wakeful eye slumbered, and they stole behind him and sheared his locks. . . . [They] cried, "Ha! it is he! it is Samson of Ossawattomie! Praised be Baal! Glory to Dagon!" and they bound him and led him away. They shouted through Gath and Ascalon, "we have caught the terrible Samson! . . . It is he! the old Samson of Ossawattomie, caged at last." But O! how the old hero's locks grew in that dusky prison air! Every moment they kept him there, the strength of a thousand Samsons was gathering in his thews and sinews. . . . And so they hurried him forth to die; but in the blindness of their fear and passion they did not see that when they placed him on the scaffold, they had set him between the very pillars of their idol's temple. And he looked up and prayed, "Avenge me now for my two eyes." He threw his arms around those pillars and bowed himself; "Let me die with the Philistines," cried Samson of Ossawattomie. Ah! see the vast fabric totter! hear the Philistines shriek! To-day there are dropping over all the land the first falling fragments from the great crash of American Slavery.[15]

Newhall compared Samson's death and the collapse of the Philistine temple to Brown's death and abolitionist efforts as signaling the eventual demise of slavery in the United States.

In addition to Newhall, other clergy referred to Brown as Samson on December 4, 1859, the Sunday following Brown's death.[16] Also, the week after Brown's execution, the *Liberator* printed a poem memorializing Brown that mentions Samson directly in the following stanzas:

> And through the future untold years
> The weak and blasted life ye take
> Shall rise a Samson to your fears,
> And make each proud oppressor quake.
> And History's faithful pen shall trace
> A line of light around his name,
> Who, by his death, hath gained a place
> For Truth this life could never claim.[17]

Following his execution, a number of biographies of Brown were published over the next fifty years.[18] In his biography of Brown, the German academic Hermann von Holst quotes from Brown's letter to Reverend H. L. Vaill in which he compares himself to Samson.[19] Several other biographers quote Brown's comparison between his death and "the last victory of Samson" in his letter to Sanborn.[20] Probably the most extensive comparisons between Brown and Samson occur in the biography by the outspoken journalist James Redpath. Published in 1860, the year after his death, it was the first book-length biography of John Brown. Redpath made clear early in the biography that he supported Brown's raid when he wrote, "I think that John

Brown did right in invading Virginia and attempting to liberate her slaves."[21] Throughout the book, he characterized Brown's opponents as the Philistines. In the preface, he compares Brown's raid on the armory to Samson's massacres of the Philistines in Judges 15.[22] Also, he titles the section of the book that deals with Brown's imprisonment, trial, and execution as "Book Four: Among the Philistines" and combines parts of Judges 15:8 and 16:21, 23, 24, 30 into the epigraph for this section. The epigraph reads:

> 8. And he smote them hip and thigh with a great slaughter. (Chapter xv).

> 21. But the Philistines took him, and put out his eyes, and brought him down to Gaza.

> 23. Then the lords of the Philistines gathered them together to offer a great sacrifice unto Dagon their god, and to rejoice: for they said, Our god hath delivered Samson our enemy into our hand.

> 24. And when the people saw him, they praised their god: for they said, Our god hath delivered into our hands our enemy, and the destroyer of our country, which slew many of us.

> 30. And Samson said, Let me die with the Philistines. And he bowed himself *with all his* might; and the house fell upon the lords, and upon all the people that *were* therein. So the dead which he slew at his death were more than *they* which he slew in his life. —*Book of Judges*, Chapter xvi.[23]

This epigraph is a selective quotation of the biblical text, and it skips over any details about Samson's hair to focus attention on the verses that emphasize his slaughter of the Philistines—an aspect of the biblical story that is more relevant to Redpath's interpretation of John Brown's life.

Redpath concludes his biography by quoting a poem titled "John Brown, Samson Agonistes." The poem was written by the White American poet Rose Terry Cooke shortly after Brown's execution.[24] Although part of the title of Cooke's poem comes from John Milton's epic poem, "Samson Agonistes," the title also makes a specific reference to John Brown. In its entirety, Cooke's poem reads:

You bound and made your sport of him, O Philistia!
You set your sons at him to flout and jeer;
You loaded down his arms with heavy fetters;
Your mildest mercy was a smiling sneer.

One man amidst a thousand who defied him—
One man from whom his awful strength had fled—
You brought him out to lash him with your vengeance,
Ten thousand curses on one hoary head!

You think his eyes are closed and blind forever,
Because you seared them to this mortal day;
You draw a longer breath of exultation,
Because your conqueror's power has passed away.

Oh fools! His arms are round your temple-pillars;
Oh blind! His divine strength begins to wake;—
Hark! the great roof-tree trembles from its centre,
Hark! how the rafters bend and swerve and shake![25]

Employing imagery of Samson's captivity and the presumably unnoticed growth of Samson's hair during his imprisonment (Judges 16:22), Cooke turns Samson's blindness into a stereotypically negative metaphor for the failings of Brown's opponents. In her poem, the pro-slavery forces may think that they have permanently blinded the resistance by executing Brown, but they are ones who are blind to the inevitable consequences of their actions.[26]

The association of Brown with Samson would endure for over a century. In his 1929 biography of John Brown, the Pulitzer Prize–winning author Robert Penn Warren reconsidered Brown's use of Samson. Warren argued that in the letters Brown wrote from prison he "built up the outlines of the new conception of himself—the role of the martyr and the Samson now, and not that of the conqueror."[27] In the biblical story, it is not as clear that Samson martyrs himself on behalf of his people's freedom because with his dying breath he seeks revenge for his lost eyesight (Judges 16:28; cf. 15:7–8, 11). Nevertheless, the "new conception" of Brown as a Samson-like martyr for the abolitionist cause quickly caught on. In American literature, Brown was imagined as a martyr, and comparisons between Brown and Samson deemed Brown's morally complex mission to be divinely endorsed and the fulfillment of prophecy

(Judges 13:5; 14:4). In 1960, Jan Willem Schulte Nordholt, a Dutch poet and historian who wrote extensively on racial issues in the United States, declared, "John Brown became a legend and after his death he defeated more enemies than he had during the whole of his life. This Samson had shaken the pillars of the Union, and soon the whole building would collapse."[28]

By the end of the nineteenth century, memorials that compared the deceased with Samson were not limited to John Brown. The comparison appears in memorials for prominent African American orators like Fredrick Douglass and Booker T. Washington. At Douglass's funeral, Reverend Dr. Jeremiah Rankin, the president of Howard University from 1890 to 1903, interpreted Douglass's life as a divinely commissioned abolitionist mission:

> I believe that the birth of Frederick Douglass into slavery was the beginning of the end. And that this was just as needful to his anti-slavery associates as to himself. God planted a germ there, which was to burst the cruel system apart. It was as though he said, "Go to, ye wise men of the Great Republic; ye Websters and Clays, miserable physicians are ye all. I will set this Samson of Freedom in your temple of Dagon, and his tawny arms shall yet tumble its columns about the ears of the worshipers."[29]

Rankin's belief that Douglass's birth was the "beginning of the end [of slavery]" alludes to the angel's prophecy to Samson's mother that her son "shall begin to deliver Israel out of the hand of the Philistines" (Judges 13:5). Similarly, in his letter from prison to Heman Humphrey, Brown applies the same verse to his own life in support of his longstanding view "that God had given me powers and faculties, unworthy as I was, that He intended to use for a similar purpose." Yet, Rankin does not compare Douglass's moment of death with Samson's fatal destruction of the Philistine temple. Douglass did not die as a martyr in the way that Brown is often remembered as having died.[30] Instead, Rankin imagines that Douglass's entire career as an advocate for reform is what brought down the columns of the temple of Dagon.[31]

Like Douglass, educator Booker T. Washington was also likened to Samson. At the end of the nineteenth century, Washington was among the most influential African American writers, educators, and lecturers. He served as president of the Tuskegee Institute, where he was buried after his death resulting from poor health on November 14, 1915. Washington is known not as a militant but as an accommodationist. On September 18,

1895, he delivered a famous speech at the Cotton States and International Exposition in Atlanta, Georgia, that called for Whites to provide greater employment, due legal process, and education for African Americans if the latter agreed not to challenge the White social and political power structure.[32] Nevertheless, at Washington's funeral on November 17, 1915, Reverend J. F. Anderson, a former principal of the Hearne Academy, which was an African American school outside Hearne, Texas, stated:

> It is not too much to say that Dr. [Booker T.] Washington died a martyr to his race. It is true that no assassin's bullet pierced his body; no knife of the bloody homicide pieced his breast. Still he fell a martyr to the race. . . . His life was ever an inspiration to us, and we trust his death will be a still greater . . . like Samson, he may have accomplished more in his death than in his life.[33]

Reverend Anderson acknowledged that Washington was not a martyr in the traditional sense but still viewed him as a martyr because he hoped that Washington's death would inspire "some boy in this audience . . . to make an effort to take his place."[34] In other words, he hoped that future generations of African Americans would respond to Washington's death with a resolve to continue and grow his work. This hope led Anderson to draw a comparison to Samson's death. As noted in Judges 16:30, a verse often applied to John Brown's death, Samson killed more Philistines in his death than he had during his lifetime. Anderson used this biblical assessment of the significance of Samson's death to imagine Washington as a martyr because of what his death might accomplish in the future. Also, this focus on the work left to be done acknowledges that, like Samson, Washington's work is only the beginning of the struggle against oppression (Judges 13:5). Although the circumstances of Douglass's and Washington's deaths are vastly different than Brown's death, the use of Samson imagery to memorialize them places their work on a prophetic and biblical scale in the radical tradition of John Brown.

Upon their deaths, Brown, Douglass, and Washington were memorialized as Samson figures immediately. For others, the mythologies that compared them to Samson developed slowly in the decades, or even centuries, after they died. In 1800, a twenty-four-year-old man named Gabriel planned to carry out an insurrection with possibly twenty-five other enslaved persons in Richmond, Virginia. He was commonly referred to as Gabriel Prosser because he was held as a slave by Thomas Henry Prosser. Gabriel and his brothers, Martin and Solomon, were born into slavery in Virginia and trained as blacksmiths. The rebellion was suppressed before it could begin because slaveholders and Virginia's governor and future president James Madison were warned of the plan. Gabriel, his brothers, and the other enslaved people were captured and tried. Gabriel was hanged in Richmond on October 7, 1800.

Over time, a mythology linking Gabriel and Samson developed that suggested Gabriel wore his hair long in imitation of Samson and that he had messianic aspirations. Yet, the historian Douglas R. Egerton has shown that the transcripts of Gabriel's trial and other historical documents from the early nineteenth century do not mention Gabriel's religious beliefs or associate him with Samson or messianic aspirations.[35] In fact, his slaveholder Thomas Henry Prosser described Gabriel as having "*short* black knotty hair" in the Richmond newspaper *Virginia Argus* on September 23, 1800.[36] Also, early scholarship on Gabriel in the nineteenth century does not connect him with Samson.[37] According to Egerton, the earliest known association with Samson and messianic aspirations appears more than eight decades after Gabriel's death in an 1883 novel titled *Judith*, which Egerton characterizes as "an astonishingly racist epic" even by the standards of the late nineteenth century.[38] The novel was written by a Virginian author named Mary Virginia Terhune under the penname Marion Harland. The novel's narrator describes Gabriel as follows:

> He had persuaded the negroes that the Lord had made him on purpose to deliver them, as He had Samson to deliver the Israelites. His hair was long and thick, and had never been cut. He wore it generally in a cue [*sic*], like a gentleman's, but this night he let it hang loose on his shoulders, to remind his men of Samson's hair "wherein his great strength lay."[39]

Harland's description may be the genesis of the view of Gabriel as a Samson-like figure.

Twentieth-century scholars have amplified the connections between Gabriel and Samson. In 1936, Arna Bontemps, a prominent writer during the Harlem Renaissance, published a historical novel about Gabriel's insurrection titled *Black Thunder*. The novel does not refer to Samson or his hair. Nor does it depict Gabriel has having messianic aspirations.[40] Nonetheless, in his introduction to the 1992 edition of Bontemps's novel, literary scholar Arnold Rampersad wrote, "The real Gabriel identified with Samson, another figure of great strength who died for freedom, but Bontemps's Gabriel does not offer himself as a mystic instrument of God."[41] Rampersad's claim reflects the popularity and longevity of the idea that Gabriel saw himself as a messianic Samson figure. In 1938, historian Joseph C. Carroll's study of insurrections by enslaved persons in the United States described Gabriel as "a careful student of the Old Testament, where he believed that he found his own prototype in the picturesque and legendary figure of Samson."[42] As Egerton observes, Carroll does not provide documentation for this claim.[43] In 1982, Cornel West, a leading public intellectual and professor at Union Theological Seminary at the time, wrote, "In 1800, a young twenty-five-year-old black prophetic Christian named Gabriel Prosser appealed to the Samson story in the Old Testament, understood himself as the divinely elected deliverer of black people, and subsequently engaged in the first thoroughly planned and overtly revolutionary attempt to liberate black people from slavery."[44] In 2000, seven years after the publication of Egerton's book, Dwight N. Hopkins, a theologian and professor at the University of Chicago wrote, "Like his hero, Samson, Prosser wore his hair long and believed firmly that God had set him aside since childhood to liberate his fellow slaves."[45]

Outside of academia, the claim that Gabriel meant to imitate Samson in the way he wore his hair appears periodically in African American newspapers. For example, a 1968 article in the *Philadelphia Tribune* describes Gabriel as "an impressive figure who stood over six feet, two inches tall and wore his hair in the manner of Samson, his biblical idol."[46] The claim that Gabriel was over six feet tall is similar to that of his slaveholder Thomas Henry Prosser's description in the *Virginia Argus* from 1800.[47] Yet, as we mentioned earlier, he also described Gabriel's hair as short rather than long.[48] Likewise, the columnist Willie Dixon, Jr. described Gabriel as a "Black giant who wore his hair long like Samson, who was his idol" in an October 1986 issue of *Chicago Metro News*.[49] Despite the lack of historical evidence, popular and scholarly literature perpetuated the idea that Gabriel emulated Samson's hairstyle as if this were a historical fact. Like John Brown's raid on Harpers Ferry, this connection with Samson imbued Gabriel's insurrection plot with biblical significance.

Like Gabriel, Nat Turner was linked with Samson. Yet, these connections were made not during his lifetime but more than a century after his death in controversial novels written during the heart of the Civil Rights Era in the late 1960s. Nat Turner was held as a slave by Samuel Turner in Southampton County, Virginia, and, in 1830, was sold to Joseph Travis. Turner, who was literate, could read the Bible and reportedly preached and had visions like the biblical prophets. Beginning on August 21, 1831, Turner led a revolt against slaveholders in Southampton, which resulted in the deaths of between fifty-five and sixty-five White persons, the most fatalities of White persons from a slave revolt in American history. Although the rebellion was suppressed within a few days, Turner was not captured until October 30, 1831. After a quick trial, he was hanged on November 11, 1831. Altogether, fifty-six persons were executed, although as many as two hundred African Americans were killed in White retaliatory violence in the bloody aftermath of Turner's revolt.

Soon after Turner's capture and execution, a lawyer named Thomas Ruffin Gray published *The Confessions of Nat Turner: The Leader of the Late Insurrection in Southampton, Virginia*. This document was allegedly based, in part, on Gray's conversations with Turner during his brief imprisonment.[50] It quickly became a bestseller, although scholars later questioned the accuracy of Gray's work.[51] While Gray's book does not make any comparisons to Samson, it served as one of the key sources for two novels about Turner's revolt that invoked the biblical hero.[52] In 1967, well over one hundred years after the revolt, the White American authors William Styron and Daniel Panger each wrote novels about Nat Turner that were published during the Civil Rights Era. Although the authors worked independently, both novels were written as if they were Turner's first-person account.[53]

Styron's novel, *The Confessions of Nat Turner*, won the Pulitzer Prize in 1968. Yet Styron faced criticism that he employed racist stereotypes by portraying Turner as an emasculated Sambo-like figure who longs to sleep with White women.[54] At the same time, Styron cast Turner as a Black Samson figure in the tradition of Longfellow's "The Warning." During Thomas Gray's first visit with Turner in the novel, the lawyer comments on the extent of Turner's restraints. Gray says, "Those chains there around your neck and them quadruple leg irons, and that big ball of iron they hung onto your ankle there. Lord God Almighty, you'd think they'd figure you was old Samson himself, fixing to break down the place with one mighty jerk."[55] This comparison of Turner to Samson articulates a fear not that Turner will escape from his captors but that he will destroy the structures that support them. While Gray views the heavy restraints as excessive, he acknowledges that they betray a concern that Turner could "break down the place." Turner's captors fear that he has the ability to bring down the political structure that upholds the institution of slavery. If not heavily restrained, Turner could become a

Samson, who, in the words on Longfellow, "may, in some grim revel, raise his hand, And shake the pillars of this Commonweal."

In contrast to Styron's novel, some critics have found a stronger and more competent version of Turner in Panger's *Ol' Prophet Nat*.[56] In this novel, Turner understands himself in the tradition of the biblical prophets. At one point, Turner compares not only himself but also his entire army to Samson when describing the revolt. He declares, "Never before was such an army of black people seen in all this land. The shadows of my people, like terrible giants, were thrown against the woods by the gushing fire. We were a band of Samsons, doing vengeance for all the terrible sins committed against all black people. My sword was like the jawbone of the ass as were the other weapons in my people's hands."[57] In Panger's novel, Turner invokes several aspects of the biblical story of Samson. The well-known image of "the jaw-bone of the ass" comes from Judges 15:15, when Samson is a captive of the Philistines for the first time. After he breaks his bondage, "He found a new jawbone of an ass, and put forth his hand, and took it, and slew a thousand men therewith."

Panger did not use Samson imagery to portray Turner and his army as martyrs for the abolitionist cause as others did with portrayals of John Brown as a Samson-like figure. Rather, Panger invoked the biblical Samson's motivation when he depicts them as "a band of Samsons, doing vengeance for all the terrible sins committed against all black people." As we noted earlier, revenge—albeit personal rather than for his people—is the primary motivation that inspires Samson's battles against the Philistines in the Bible (Judges 15:7–8, 11; 16:28). In keeping with the widespread use of Samson as a collective representation of African Americans, Panger uses the term "a band of Samsons" to describe "an army of black people" who have risen up in vengeance against their oppressors in Panger's novel. Unlike John Brown, links between Turner and Samson in Styron's and Panger's novels are not thought to have originated with Turner himself. Instead, they are a literary flourish that occurs in historical novels about his revolt written over one hundred years later that connect Turner with a tradition of historical figures who displayed militant resistance to slavery.

Beginning in the last half of the nineteenth century, Samson imagery was used to describe specific historical individuals, including John Brown, Frederick Douglass, Booker T. Washington, Gabriel Prosser, and Nat Turner, and their controversial actions. This association lent a divine endorsement to what were often viewed as morally complex actions in the struggle against racial injustice. Samson imagery helped elevate these historical individuals into martyrs as future generations compared their actions to that of the equally morally complex biblical character. In other words, Samson comparisons could help turn a man into a biblical icon. As we discuss in the next chapter, the image of a Black Samson would become associated with other radical political causes in the early twentieth century.

4

Black Samson and Labor Movements

White northern laborers find killing Negroes a safe, lucrative employment which commends them to the American Federation of Labor.

—W. E. B. Dubois, 1917[1]

The 1917 race riots in East St. Louis, Illinois, illustrated the close connection between race, ethnicity, and labor issues.[2] Beginning with responses to this riot, we track developments in the use of Samson imagery by African American writers who examined the complex and often contentious relationship among African Americans, labor movements, and the Communist Party. From the early twentieth century through the Harlem Renaissance, the Great Depression, and toward the Civil Rights Era, we document how many leading African American intellectuals used Black Samson imagery to voice various opinions about the close relationship of racial oppression and economic exploitation.

Pulitzer Prize–winning journalist Isabel Wilkerson describes what has become known as the "Great Migration" of millions of African Americans from the rural South to the urban centers in the North as "perhaps the biggest underreported story of the twentieth century."[3] From roughly 1910 to 1970, the Great Migration reshaped the racial map of the United States and the makeup of its cities as African Americans searched for better living conditions and economic opportunities in the North. These changes expanded the labor force available in northern cities. In the early twentieth century, thousands of African American workers poured into cities such as Philadelphia and New York each week.

In early 1917, the Aluminum Ore Packing Company in East St. Louis sought to break a strike of workers of predominantly European descent who were members of the Central Trades and Labor Unions. Management hired replacement workers, including more than four hundred African Americans.

The unionized laborers filed complaints against the African American workers with local government officials. Racial tensions built throughout the spring and into the summer. These tensions turned violent on May 28, 1917, and they came to a head on July 2. On the evening of July 1, shots were fired at African Americans from a car with White men in it. Later that evening, African Americans fired at another car killing two White police officers. What followed became known as the East St. Louis Massacre. It was one of the deadliest race riots in American history. In protest of the massacre, W. E. B. Dubois and the NAACP organized a massive demonstration in New York City. On the morning of July 28, 1917, thousands of African American men, women, and children marched silently down 5th Avenue carrying protest signs in what became commonly referred to as the "Silent Parade." A congressional report on the East St. Louis Massacre determined that at least thirty-nine African Americans and eight White people were killed in the riots.[4] Yet, Ida B. Wells-Barnett, a founding member of the NAACP, interviewed several survivors of the riot and reported that the African American death toll was more than two hundred persons along with three million dollars' worth of property damage.[5] Wells-Barnett concluded that in the wake of these riots "the labor unions which have this country by the throat, which paralyze its industries, dynamite its buildings and murder men at their own sweet will— refuse to let Negroes work with them and murder them if they work anyway, in what they call 'white men's jobs.'"[6]

Following the massacre, Jessie Redmon Fauset, an accomplished novelist, poet, and the literary editor for the *Crisis*, the flagship magazine of the NAACP, wrote a powerful editorial titled "A Negro on East St. Louis."[7] In keeping with Wells-Barnett's findings, Fauset argued that law enforcement enabled "the East St. Louis mob to expel from their homes 6,000 working men, burn down the dwellings of several thousands, and butcher and burn upwards of 200 helpless men, women, and children."[8] Fauset explained that these riots revealed "the absolute conviction on the part of the labor leaders that no Negro has the right to any position or privilege which the white man wants."[9]

Fauset emphasized this point by closing her editorial with a reference to Samson's death in the Philistine temple. She distinguished African American laborers and African American professionals, or what she called "two classes, the trained and the untrained."[10] Her editorial asserts that the riots make clear to the African American laborer migrating to the North that "he is damned if he stays South and he is damned if he doesn't."[11] In regard to

African American professionals, Fauset wrote, "We are becoming fatalists; we no longer expect any miraculous intervention of Providence. We are perfectly aware that the outlook for us is not encouraging."[12] Fauset concluded with allusions to the biblical stories of both Esther and Samson. The final lines of the editorial explain, "We, the American Negroes, are the acid test for occidental civilization. If we perish, we perish. But when we fall, we shall fall like Samson, dragging inevitably with us the pillars of a nation's democracy."[13]

The line, "If we perish, we perish" alludes to Queen Esther's appeal to the Persian king without being summoned by him in order to plead for her people's safety. Esther resolves, "I go in unto the king, which is not according to the law: and if I perish, I perish" (Esther 4:16). This allusion reinforces Fauset's fatalistic view regarding the limited choices for African Americans in the North and the South. She follows this allusion by comparing the fate of the American democracy to the Philistine temple that Samson destroyed. The haunting conclusion of her editorial is in keeping with earlier warnings that as the African American community goes, so goes the fate of the United States as a whole. Fauset's reference to Samson's destruction of the temple suggests that the use of Samson imagery in the nineteenth century as a warning that the fate of African Americans could bring down the entire democratic project had established a firm foothold among African American intellectuals by the early twentieth century.

Despite a national outcry over the East St. Louis Massacre, racial tensions persisted within labor movements in the years to come. The summer of 1919 was dubbed the "Red Summer" due to race-related riots across the nation that resulted in the deaths of hundreds of African Americans. The writings of Dubois, Fauset, and Wells-Barnet regarding the East St. Louis Massacre reflected a deep suspicion of organized labor movements among leaders in the NAACP. In contrast, other Harlem Renaissance intellectuals, like Claude McKay, were more sympathetic toward organized labor. McKay and several other leading figures of this era used Samson imagery to promote socialist and communist ideas among African Americans.

Claude McKay was a prominent Jamaican-born poet, novelist, and essayist who immigrated to the United States in 1912. From 1919 to 1923 he had extended stays in England and Russia. While in London, he wrote for *Workers' Dreadnaught,* a self-identified socialist British weekly newspaper. In the January 31, 1920, issue, he published an essay titled "Socialism and the Negro." The essay sharply criticized the NAACP as an elitist organization that did not represent the political and economic concerns or needs of the Black working class. After referring to Dubois and the NAACP by name, McKay wrote:

> A group of wealthy and socially and politically influential bourgeois of the North helped to launch the movement [the NAACP] and became its directing spirit. . . . This group [is] palpably ignorant of the fact that the Negro question is primarily an economic problem. . . . Strangely, it is the professional class of Negroes that is chiefly opposed to Socialism, although it is the class that suffers and complains most bitterly. Dr. Dubois has flirted with the Socialist idea from a narrow, opportunist—racial standpoint; but he is in spirit opposed to it.[14]

For McKay, the NAACP represented the professional class and did not fully appreciate the economic factors contributing to African American oppression. He argued that the solidarity among laborers that he found in socialist and communist ideas could better address what he referred to as the "Negro question."

McKay acknowledged the difficulties in convincing African Americans to embrace socialist and communist ideas in light of the racial tensions within labor movements. In 1922, he wrote:

> The blacks are hostile to Communism because they regard it as a "white" working-class movement and they consider the white workers their greatest enemy, who draw the color line against them in factory and office and lynch and burn them at the stake for being colored. Only the best and broadest minded Negro leaders who can combine Communist ideas with a deep sympathy for and understanding of the black man's grievances will reach the masses with revolutionary propaganda. There are few such leaders in America today.[15]

In the January 10, 1920, issue of *Workers' Dreadnaught*, a few weeks before "Socialism and the Negro" appeared in the same newspaper, McKay used the image of Black Samson in an effort to achieve this combination of "Communist ideas" and "sympathy for and understanding of the black man's grievances." McKay published two short poems in that issue. The first poem, titled "Travail," does not address the economic situations of laborers of African descent specifically, but it does celebrate the idea of a worldwide workers' revolution.[16] The second poem is titled "Samson." The entire poem reads:

> Samson, the chosen Nazarite, who ruled
> The Jews for twenty years and judged their sins,
> Snared in the web of flesh, by woman fooled,
> Was captured by the hated Philistines.
> But God remembered him in his downfall
> And, in his blindness, gave him back his power,
> Which nobly used he, at his gaoler's call,
> To save his soul in one grand crowning hour.
> O sable Samsons, in white prisons bound,
> Wounded and blinded, in your hidden strength
> Put forth your swarthy hands: the pillars found,
> Strain mightily at them until at length
> The accused walls, reared of your blood and tears,
> Come crashing, sounding freedom in your ears.[17]

McKay's "Samson" poem addresses people of African descent and shares several themes and motifs with other racialized uses of Samson. The structure of McKay's poem is similar to Longfellow's poem "The Warning." The first half of the poem recounts the biblical story of the Israelite hero with attention to his capture, blinding, and destruction of his oppressor's temple. The second half compares the biblical hero to people of African descent by stating, "O sable Samsons, in white prison bound" and "Put forth your swarthy hands." While Longfellow wrote to sway opinions of an often-White antebellum readership toward the abolitionist cause, McKay emphasized the idea of self-determination by addressing people of African descent directly. Also, McKay promoted ideas of strength and self-liberation in the tradition of Josie D. Heard's poem "Black Samson." McKay's poem "Samson" does not address communism, socialism, or labor movements as overtly as his poem, "Travail" or his essay, "Socialism and the Negro." Nevertheless, by publishing "Samson" in the socialist newspaper *Workers' Dreadnaught* alongside his poem "Travail," McKay combined communist ideas with a biblical image familiar to African Americans as representing resistance to the current oppressive social and political order.

Nonetheless, in the 1920s, many African Americans remained suspicious of organized labor. For example, in 1925, an article titled "What Is a

Communist?" in the *New York Amsterdam News*, a prominent African American newspaper at the time, used the familiar image of Samson destroying the temple to predict the inevitable failure of communism among African Americans. Invoking Longfellow's image of Samson in the Temple of Liberty, the article concludes that the "remnants of white communism, if they are tampering with American's loyal colored citizens, are, like a drowning man, grasping a straw, a straw which is far too weak to perform the Samson feat of pulling down the pillars of the temple of freedom to the destruction of self and of Government."[18] Considering McKay's awareness that many African Americans were suspicious of socialist or communist organizing, his use of Samson reflected a strategy to gain a hearing for these ideas within their communities.

Claude McKay's views and his use of Samson imagery were not unique among prominent writers during the Harlem Renaissance. In 1923, Jean Toomer, a poet and playwright, published *Cane*, a Harlem Renaissance literary classic. Beginning on July 19, 1919, the deadly race riots of the "Red Summer" spread to Toomer's native city of Washington, DC. In early August, Toomer published an article titled "Reflections on the Race Riots" in the *New York Call*, a daily newspaper associated with the Socialist Party of America. Like McKay's "Socialism and the Negro," this article is critical of the NAACP. Although Toomer did not mention Dubois or the NAACP by name, he seems to critique the NAACP's focus on legislative solutions. He disparaged a "group which limits its suggestions to the worn-out method of 'constitutional rights for the Negro,' who seem to believe that therein lies the sole solvent of racial antagonisms."[19] Toomer argued that an economic structure based on socialist ideas rather than capitalist competition offers a better means of addressing racism in the United States. He wrote:

> It is generally established that the causes of race prejudice may primarily be found in the economic structure that compels one worker to compete against another, and that furthermore renders it advantageous for the exploiting classes to inculcate, foster, and aggravate that competition. If this be true, then it follows that the nucleus of race co-operation lies in the substitution of a socialized community for a competitive one.[20]

Toomer employed Samson imagery in his short story "Box Seat," which appeared in his book *Cane*. Set in Washington, DC, the two-part story engages issues of class differences and critiques the values of the emerging

African American professional class. The story's protagonist is Dan Moore, who describes himself as "a poor man out of work."[21] The story recounts the courtship of Moore with a schoolteacher named Muriel, who desires acceptance in the city's African American professional class. In part one, Dan visits Muriel's home, but she dismisses his advances because she is concerned about what her landlady and others might think about her love for Dan. Throughout the story, Toomer represents the African American professional class as rigid. Even their chairs and their homes are described as "stiff," "bolted," and "locked."[22] In part two, Dan follows Muriel to the Lincoln Theatre, which served the African American community.[23] The imagery of enclosure continues as Dan refers to Muriel's theater seating as a "brass box."

The performance that evening involves a boxing match between dwarfs, but the audience of professionals, collectively referred to as "the house," wants more. After the narration of the boxing match, the text continues, "The house applauds. The house wants more. Must give the house something."[24] Like the Philistines in the temple of Dagon, the audience in the theater demands to be entertained (Judges 16:25). The attendant announces to the audience that the winner of the fight, Mr. Barry, will sing "one of his own songs for your approval."[25] As he sings his "sentimental love song," Mr. Barry uses a mirror to flash light on members of his audience. As Toomer describes it, "Dan's eyes are half blinded" by the light from the mirror.[26] Some scholars have interpreted this description as a subtle allusion to the blinding of Samson because it comes shortly after a more explicit connection between Dan and Samson.[27] Revolted by the evening's performance and by the audience's reaction, Dan Moore's actions recall the biblical hero from the Israelite tribe of Dan who stays outdoors (Judges 15:8) and destroys the city gates of Gaza and later its temple (Judges 16:3, 30). Dan imagines himself destroying "the house" in Samson-like fashion. When Mr. Barry sings his song, Dan thinks to himself, "I am going to reach up and grab the girders of this building and pull them down."[28] Yet, in the end, Dan does not attempt to destroy the theater but disrupts the performance by jumping up and shouting. He has a physical confrontation with an audience member who demands that Dan step outside to fight him. The house follows the men outside. Yet, once outdoors, Dan forgets about his opponent and walks away.

In "Box Seat," Toomer invoked Samson's destruction of the Philistine temple to describe a poor, unemployed African American man's fantasy of bringing down the professional class that rejects him. Like McKay, Toomer used this powerful biblical scene to critique class differences and elitism as he promoted what he called "the substitution of a socialized community for a competitive one." In a creative twist, however, Toomer mobilized this image to indict African American professionals for embracing an economic system rooted in exploitation and competitive practices that prevent racial cooperation. Unlike previous writers who used Samson imagery to counter racial divisions, Toomer stressed that economic inequality and class difference are also corrosive forces in African American communities.

The use of Samson to translate socialist and communist ideas to African American communities also appears in the works of Langston Hughes, one of the best-known poets of the Harlem Renaissance. Like McKay, Toomer, and other permanent writers and artists of this era, Hughes published in newspapers affiliated with socialism and communism. In 1932, Hughes traveled to the Soviet Union, and in 1953 he was called to testify before the Permanent Subcommittee on Investigations during Senator Joseph McCarthy's investigations into alleged communist infiltration in the United States. Beginning in 1931, Hughes published several poems in the Marxist magazine *New Masses*, including a short poem titled "Union."[29] Considering the political leanings of the magazine in which this poem was published, the title "Union" could be understood on multiple levels. It could refer to the labor movements and the trade unions that Hughes viewed as instrumental in ending what the poem refers to as the "rule of greed" defended by the current capitalist structure. The title could also refer to the racial solidarity among the working poor required to bring down a system of economic oppression. Rather than using Samson imagery as a symbol of African Americans alone, Hughes asserted in his poem that it would take both "the whole oppressed, poor world, Black and white" to help bring about this change. In "Union," he employed an image that had been used for resistance to racial oppression to call for resistance to economic oppression. He states that the poor, regardless of race, must "put their hands with mine, / To shake the pillars of those temples." In contrast to earlier poetry associating Samson with African Americans, here, the "temples" represent worldwide capitalist greed rather than the United States government. For Hughes, the current economic structure had become a Philistine temple that upholds the rule of greed. As with other writings from the Harlem Renaissance, Hughes's poem "Union" uses Samson imagery to frame racial oppression as closely related to economic exploitation.

As the Great Depression intensified during the 1930s, Hughes returned to Samson imagery to explore themes of race and class in his fiction. In January

1935, *Esquire* magazine published his short story, "On the Road."[30] The story is about Sargeant, an African American man who attempts to find shelter on a snowy night. Sargeant is a Black Samson figure who illustrates the combined complexities of oppression due to both race and class. Initially, the text describes Sargeant as a down-on-his-luck man during the Depression. He has been traveling by freight train, a common mode of transport for those unable to afford a rail ticket. He is "too hungry, too sleepy, too tired" to even notice the snow.[31] His race becomes apparent only when Reverend Dorset turns on his porch light, and Sargeant is identified as "a big black man" who is "obviously unemployed."[32]

Sargeant's efforts to find assistance highlight the failure and hypocrisy of White institutions. Dorset, a minister, refers Sargeant to the relief shelter, but Sargeant's previous experience tells him that the shelter has a "color line" and does not provide services to African Americans.[33] When Dorset turns him away from the parsonage, Sargeant finds a church next door with "two high arched doors with slender stone pillars on either side."[34] When Sargeant knocks on the church door, he finds it closed and locked. This is not the openness advocated by Jesus who says, "Knock, and it shall be opened unto you" (Matthew 7:7; Luke 11:9). He tries to break down the locked doors of the church in order to spend the night there, but his efforts attract the attention of several townspeople. Sargeant pushes against the door grunting "like a chaingang song," which links his effort to seek refuge with racialized and dehumanizing prison labor.[35] When the White onlookers confront him as he lunges against the door, Sargeant explains to them, "I know it's a white folks' church, but I got to sleep somewhere."[36] For Sargeant, his basic need for shelter overrides their segregationist religion.

When the police arrive, Sargeant grabs one of the stone pillars while the police and passersby attempt to pull him away. The church members do not help Sargeant in finding shelter but assist the police trying to pull Sargeant away from the church. The narrator shares their thoughts: "'A big black unemployed nigger holding on to our church!' thought the people. 'The idea.'" Also, as the police beat Sargeant, the narrator notes, "Nobody protested." The church members are concerned for their building and not for the person seeking refuge on a cold snowy night. Despite being beaten by the police, Sargeant pulls the church down covering both the police and the people there. The building that was the subject of concern for the church members has been destroyed. The narrator describes the destruction, "Gradually, the big stone front of the church fell down, the walls and the rafters, the crucifix and the Christ. Then the whole thing fell down, covering the cops and the people with bricks and stones and debris. The whole church fell down in the snow."[37] What Sargeant refers to as a "white folks' church" has become a Philistine temple whose destruction crushes his oppressors.

Sargeant walks away from the rubble but discovers that he is not alone as Christ begins to walk with him. Sargeant's destruction of the church had dislodged Christ from the crucifix in the church, creating a symbolic distinction between Christ and the "white folks' church." Christ tells Sargeant that the White church members had kept him on the cross, but Christ is now free.[38] After a brief conversation, Christ leaves for Kansas City, while Sargeant chooses to spend the night in a makeshift camp of homeless people.[39] Sargeant finds shelter in this "hobo jungle," which, unlike the parsonage, the church, and the relief shelter, does not have doors or a color line. He finds some brief respite with others who are suffering. He realizes that Christ is not found within a building but on the road with other out-of-work hobos. As a Black Samson, Sargeant frees Christ from the White religious institutions that exclude and oppress others on the basis of race and class. Ultimately, however, Sargeant awakens to discover that his destruction of the church had been a fantasy and that the police had arrested him when he tried to break down its doors. The story ends with Sargeant in jail threatening to break down the door of the jail. Although Sargeant has a Samson-like fantasy of destruction, in the end, he remains imprisoned.

Like Hughes, the celebrated author Richard Wright also addressed issues of race, class, and religion. In his short story "Fire and Cloud," he detailed the political evolution of a fictitious African American minister named Reverend Daniel Taylor, who leads a congregation in a small town in Mississippi. In 1938, *Story* magazine printed "Fire and Cloud," after it won first prize in the magazine's nationwide Writer's Project contest.[40] Similar to Hughes, Wright was a vocal advocate of communism who published poetry in the Marxist magazine *New Masses*. In 1933, Wright joined the Communist Party while living in Chicago.

Like authors discussed earlier, Wright used Samson to connect communist ideas to the concerns of many African Americans. When invoking the image of Samson, he reinforces this connection by using vernacular prose, a style of writing that intends to represent oral forms of expression of particular dialects, groups, or regions. For example, in "Fire and Cloud," Wright uses a traditional song about Samson and Delilah that has its roots in earlier African American spirituals.[41] On December 3, 1927, an African American preacher and blues singer from Texas known as Blind Willie Johnson recorded arguably the most influential version of the song under the title "If I Had My Way I'd Tear the Building Down."[42] The lyrics to Johnson's version read:

Well, if I had my way
I had-a, a wicked mind
If I had-a, ah Lord, tear this building down
Weh-ell!
Delilah was a woman fine an' fair
Her pleasant looks-a, her coal black hair
Delilah gained old Samson's mind
A-first saw the woman that looked so fine
A-well went Timnathy, I can't tell
A daughter of Timnathy, a-pleased him well
A-Samson told his father, "I'm goin a-a-a"
Help me Lord
If I had my way
Well, if a had-a, a wicked world
If I had-a, ah Lord, tear this building down
Weh-ell!
Samson's mother replied to him
"Can't you find a woman of your kind and kin?"
"Samson, will you please your mother's mind?"
Go'd and married that-a Philistine
Let me tell you what, old Samson
Well, he roared at the lion, the lion run
Samson was the first man the lion attack
He caught the lion and got upon his 'ack
A-written that he killed a man with his
And Samson had his hand in the lion's jaws
If I had my way
If I had-a, a wicked world
If I had-a, ah Lord, tear this building down
"Well, your riddle please, a-tell it to me"
"A-how an eater became forth meat?"
"Well, your riddle please, a-tell it to me"
"A-how strong of it came forth sweet?"
Deliah, got his army after him

Well, the bees made-a honey in the lion hair
Well, if I had my way
Well, if I had-a, a wicked world
If I had-a, ah Lord, tear this building down
Sewed me tow knot, an' formed a plot
Not many days 'fore Samson was caught
A-bind this hands whilst a-walkin' along
A-looked on the ground and found a lil' jawbone
He moved his arm ropes, a-pop like thread
Dropped those threads free, three thousand were dead
Lord, If I had my way
Well, if I had a, a wicked world
If I had a, ah Lord, tear this building down
Weh-ell!
Samson's trick though they never found out
'Till they began to wonder about
A-'till his wife sat up upon his knee
"A-tell me where your strength lie, if you please?"
Samson's wife she a-talked so fair
Told his wife cut off-a his hair
"Shave my head, clean as your hand
'Till I become a natural man!"
Lord, If I had my way
Well, if I had a, a wicked world
If I had a, ah Lord, tear this building down.[43]

According to legend, Blind Willie Johnson was arrested for nearly inciting a riot when he played his version of the song outside of the historic United States Customs House at 423 Canal Street in New Orleans, Louisiana. Whether the legend is true or not, it reflects the belief that the song could serve as a powerful and politically dangerous protest song. Since the 1920s, many writers and artists have recognized the political undertones of the song.

A decade after Blind Willie Johnson recorded "If I Had My Way I'd Tear the Building Down," Wright alluded to this song when narrating a pivotal moment in the political evolution of Reverend Taylor. In "Fire and Cloud," Reverend Taylor, an influential figure in the local African American community, is torn between two opposing parties. Communist organizers, referred to as "Reds" in the story, ask him to march in a demonstration and allow them to include his name on literature promoting the protest. While Reverend Taylor has concerns over the deep poverty and hunger in his community, the White mayor, chief of police, and others discourage him from participating in the demonstration or publicly endorsing it. In an effort to ensure that he does not participate in the march, local White men kidnap him, drive him into the woods, brutally beat him, and force him to walk home on his own. The narrator describes Reverend Taylor's feelings as he walks through a White neighborhood on his way home.

> Like a pillar of fire he went through the white neighborhood. Some days theys gonna burn! Some days they gonna burn in Gawd Amightys fire! How come they make us suffer so? The worls got too mucha everything! Yit they bleed us! They fatten on us like leeches! There ain no groun yuh kin walk on that they don own! N Gawd knows tha ain right! . . . Gawd, ef yuh gimme the strength Ahll tear this ol buildin down! Tear it down Lawd! Tear it down like ol Samson tore the temple down![44]

This experience leads to Reverend Taylor's political transformation. He decides to participate in the march despite the danger that he and his fellow demonstrators would face from local officials. As he walks through the White neighborhood, Reverend Taylor's prayer, "Gawd, ef yuh gimme the strength Ahll tear this ol buildin down!" is similar to Samson's prayer for strength before he brings the temple down: "O Lord GOD, remember me, I pray thee, and strengthen me, I pray thee, only this once, O God, that I may be at once avenged of the Philistines for my two eyes" (Judges 16:28). Yet, when Reverend Taylor finally commits to march with the communists, he does not quote from Samson's prayer in the Bible. Instead, his prayer comes from the chorus of Blind Willie Johnson's "If I Had My Way I'd Tear the Building Down." By quoting this song instead of the biblical text, Taylor expresses his commitment to the communist cause by comparing himself to Samson as sung about in his own vernacular tradition.

Wright uses a similar technique with another biblical image when he signals Taylor's new resolve by comparing him to a "pillar of fire" as he makes his way through the White neighborhood. This image alludes to the Israelites' journey to the land of Canaan: "And the LORD went before them by day in a pillar of a cloud, to lead them the way; and by night in a pillar of fire, to give them light; to go by day and night: He took not away the pillar of the cloud by day, nor the pillar of fire by night, from before the people" (Exodus 13:21–22). Wright returns to this image in the story's final scene. As the interracial march begins under Reverend Taylor's leadership, a person described only as a "fat black woman" starts to sing,

> So the sign of the fire by night
> N the sign of the cloud by day
> A-hoverin oer
> Jus befo
> As we journey on our way . . .[45]

While these lyrics refer to the pillars of cloud and fire in Exodus 13:21–22, they do not quote the biblical text directly. Instead, the lyrics come from a hymn titled "The Cloud and Fire," written by a White man named Charles Austin Miles in 1900. Wright renders the hymn's lyrics in the vernacular.[46] Wright recast this popular hymn as a song protesting the economic exploitation of poor laborers. Others in the interracial crowd begin to join the woman in singing this hymn as the demonstration progresses. The concluding scene of "Fire and Cloud" depicts Reverend Taylor leading a "sea of black and white faces" in the demonstration. When Reverend Taylor and other African Americans in the story choose to join the communist demonstration, Wright uses hymns and spirituals, rendered in the vernacular, to signal their resolve. The interracial demonstrators transform the chorus of "The Cloud and Fire" into a labor protest song. Similarly, Wright uses the chorus of "If I Had My Way I'd Tear the Building Down" to express Reverend Taylor's outrage at an economic structure in which the White community owns everything. In the early 1920s, Claude McKay had called for leaders who could combine communist ideas with a deep appreciation of the concerns of the African American working class. With his employment of vernacular language, Wright develops previous writers' use of Samson imagery to create this combination.[47]

Over time, Claude McKay, Richard Wright, and other influential African American writers of the era became increasingly disillusioned with the Communist Party. While not necessarily abandoning socialist ideas, they suspected that the Communist Party's interest in African American labor was opportunistic. In September 1938, McKay wrote, "I do not accept the basic political ideology of Communism. I reject absolutely the idea of government by dictatorship, which is the pillar of political Communism."[48] Six

years later, in August 1944, Wright published an article in *Atlantic Monthly* titled "I Tried to Be a Communist."[49] Yet no one signaled this change as clearly
as the literary giant Ralph Ellison.

Ellison first met Langston Hughes and Richard Wright in New York in
the 1930s. Like Hughes and Wright before him, he published in the Marxist
magazine *New Masses* in the late 1930s and early 1940s.[50] Yet, in August
1945, Ellison wrote in a letter to Wright: "We've got to do something, to offset
the C. P. [Communist Party] sell-out of our people; and I mean by this, both
Negroes and labor."[51] Like his predecessors, Ellison used Samson imagery
when exploring the relationship of African Americans with communism in
his novel *Invisible Man*, which won the National Book Award in 1953, a year
after its publication. Yet, the Samson imagery in this novel reflects dramatic
shifts in opinion regarding the Communist Party when compared with earlier uses of the biblical hero in the writings of McKay, Hughes, Wright, and
others.

At one point in *Invisible Man*, the unnamed African American protagonist
is working in a paint factory. On his first day, another employee tells him that
management is "firing the regular guys and putting on you colored college
boys. . . . That way they don't have to pay union wages. . . . It's not your fault.
You new guys don't know the score. Just like the union says, it's the wise guys
in the office. They're the ones who make scabs out of you."[52] This strategy by
management reflects the decades-old practice of hiring African American
workers to break strikes by unionized workers in cities like East St. Louis
during the Great Migration. This contributed to many African Americans
being suspicious of organized labor. At the factory, the protagonist works
as an assistant to an older African American man named Lucius Brockway,
whose opinions reflect these suspicions. During his lunch break, the protagonist accidentally interrupts a meeting of unionized workers in the locker room.
When he tells Brockway what happened, Brockway is furious and accuses
him of belonging to "that bunch of troublemaking foreigners!"[53] As the argument between the two men intensifies, Brockway exclaims, "That *damn*
union! They after my job! I know they after my job! For one of us to join
them damn unions is like we was to bite the hand of the man who teached us
to bathe in a bathtub!"[54] In Brockway's opinion, unionized labor would cost
African American workers their jobs.

The argument between the protagonist and Brockway turns into a physical
altercation. As they fight, they neglect the factory's machines and the tanks of
paint under their care. Eventually, the unattended equipment explodes. The

narrator invokes Samson's destruction of the temple when the protagonist describes how the factory's machinery collapsed on top of him. The unnamed protagonist explains, "Then a great weight landed upon me and I seemed to sprawl into an interval of clarity beneath a pile of broken machinery, my head pressed back against a huge wheel, my body splattered with a stinking goo."[55] After the explosion, the protagonist passes out. The narrator makes a more explicit reference to Samson in the next chapter when the protagonist thinks about destroying other machinery in the factory's hospital.

After the accident, the protagonist regains consciousness in the factory's hospital. Once again, he is trapped by a machine. Members of the hospital staff are performing electronic shock experiments on him without his consent. During his confinement, he debates whether to destroy the machine that administered the electronic shocks. He states, "I fell to plotting ways of short-circuiting the machine. Perhaps if I shifted my body about so that the two nodes would come together—No, not only was there no room but it might electrocute me. I shuddered. Whatever else I was, I was no Samson. I had no desire to destroy myself even if it destroyed the machine; I wanted freedom, not destruction."[56] When he was hired, the factory had used him to undermine unionized labor. When he was hospitalized, the factory's medical staff used him to conduct experiments. Yet, Ellison's protagonist declares that he is no Samson when he decides that he is not willing to sacrifice himself in the struggle against the structures that exploit African American labor. The destruction of the factory machines injured him, and the potential destruction of the hospital machine could kill him. He decides that he will not bring the machine down if it means risking his own life in the process.

Later in the novel, the machinery image returns when the protagonist joins a fictitious organization called the Brotherhood, which presumably represents the Communist Party in the novel. The Brotherhood sends him to Harlem to promote the organization's objectives among African Americans. He quickly rises through the ranks of the Brotherhood but insists, "I'm no hero and I'm far from the top; I'm a cog in a machine. We here in the Brotherhood work as a unit."[57] The machine now represents the Brotherhood and its communist politics, which the protagonist embraces initially. Yet, the protagonist feels betrayed when a White member of the Brotherhood tells him that the organization plans to abandon its work in Harlem because "all of us must sacrifice for the good of the whole. Change is achieved through sacrifice."[58] The protagonist thinks, "Suddenly I saw the hospital machine, felt as though locked in again."[59] He realizes that the Brotherhood is like the machine at the factory's hospital in which he was trapped. Ellison portrays the protagonist as a Samson figure trapped in the machinery of a capitalist factory and, later, in the machinery of a communist-like organization, both of which exploit his labor.

At this point, the protagonist becomes determined to destroy the machine. He understands that members of the Brotherhood only see what they want to see in their encounters with him. Realizing that they do not see him as a person but only a yes-man, he declares, "I now recognize my invisibility."[60] He decides that he can use his invisibility to his advantage by following his grandfather's deathbed advice given in the opening pages of the novel. His grandfather instructs him, "I want you to overcome 'em with yess, undermine 'em with grins, agree 'em to death and destruction, let 'em swoller you till they vomit or bust wide open."[61] In a 1958 article in the *Partisan Review*, Ellison explained that the grandfather advises the protagonist to become a different type of Samson figure than the one that the protagonist had rejected while in the hospital.

> [The grandfather is not] so much a "smart-man-playing-dumb" as a weak man who knows the nature of his oppressor's weakness . . . the strategy he advises is a kind of jujitsu of the spirit, a denial and rejection through agreement. Samson, eyeless in Gaza, pulls the building down when his strength returns; politically weak, the grandfather has learned that conformity leads to a similar end, and so advises his children. Thus, his mask of meekness conceals the wisdom of one who has learned the secret of saying the "yes" which accomplishes the expressive "no."[62]

Although Samson is "eyeless in Gaza," the Philistines do not see him.[63] They do not seem to notice that his hair begins to grow back while he is in prison (Judges 16:22). Instead, they see him only as their vanquished enemy who is there for their entertainment (Judges 16:24–25). This mistake costs them their lives. When the protagonist finally understands his grandfather's cryptic advice, he launches into a diatribe against the Brotherhood that echoes his grandfather's dying words.

> Let them [the Brotherhood] gag on what they refuse to see. Let them choke on it. . . . Saying "yes" could destroy them. . . . All they wanted of me was one belch of affirmation and I'd bellow it out loud. Yes! Yes! Yes! That was

all anyone wanted of us, that we should be heard and not seen, and then heard only in one big optimistic chorus of yassuh, yassuh, yassuh! . . . They wanted a machine? Very well, I'd become a supersensitive confirmer of their misconceptions. . . . And if I got hurt? Very well again. Besides, didn't they believe in sacrifice? They were subtle thinkers—would this be treachery? Did the word apply to an invisible man? Could they recognize choice in that which wasn't seen?[64]

Ellison presents the protagonist's plan to bring down the Brotherhood through a twist on the traditional use of the story of Samson. He embraces his grandfather's strategy that Ellison associates elsewhere with Samson-like behavior. Moreover, the Brotherhood behaves like the Philistines in Ellison's comparison. Since they choose not to see the protagonist as a person capable of determining his own fate, they will mistake his affirmations of their plans as his sacrifice for the good of the whole instead of an act of treachery that will lead to their destruction. Earlier in the novel the protagonist associated Samson with self-destruction rather than freedom. Now, he concludes that "if I got hurt," it would be because he could freely choose to pull the building down.

Ellison's use of Samson imagery to critique communism's relationship with African Americans rather than to promote communist ideas among African Americans signals a change from earlier uses of this imagery in the works of McKay, Toomer, Hughes, and Wright. The strained relationship of African Americans and organized labor generated a wide variety of opinions among African American writers in the early twentieth century. Some saw organized labor as a threat to African American social and economic progress, while others saw socialism and communism as a vehicle for it. As the nation moved toward the Civil Rights Era, attention to the uses of Samson imagery will continue to allow us to track the nuances and developments in national discourses over politics, economics, religion, and racial uplift.

5

The Samson Complex

His remembrance shall perish from the earth, and he shall have no
name in the street.

—Job 18:17 (King James Version)

On May 17, 1954, the Supreme Court's ruling in *Brown v. Board of Education*
declared that segregation in public schools was unconstitutional. Over the
next several years, the NAACP sought to register African Americans in all-
White schools. In September 1957, nine African American students enrolled
in Central High School in Little Rock, Arkansas. Yet, despite the legislative
progress that the NAACP made in the 1950s, their strategy was not without
its detractors. Some critics viewed it as too accommodating to racist power
structures and called for militant direct action regardless of the cost. A letter
by a reader identified only as L. W. Collins published on June 26, 1959, in the
African American newspaper *Los Angeles Tribune* exemplifies this critique.

> The NAACP leaders seem to forget that there is no substitute for militancy
> in the struggle for freedom. Legal technicalities and hairsplitting pig-Latin
> cannot take the place of mass action inspired by a determination to sacrifice
> even life itself in the attainment of an objective. . . . Away forever, with non-
> resistance philosophy. It was meant for slaves, and will be embraced only by
> slaves. . . . We must be like blind Samson, willing to pull away the pillars of
> authority, and bring down the whole temple of greed and corruption that
> would hitch us to the treadmill of inferiority and degradation.[1]

The letter uses "blind Samson" as a model for African American resistance
that Collins understands as more radical than the NAACP's legislative strategies. As campaigns for civil rights intensified over the next decade, interpretations of Samson's climactic action in the Philistine temple would continue
among parties calling for more militant approaches in the struggle against

racial injustice. At the same time, this racially charged image sparked controversy among African American intellectuals and activists as some claimed that the younger activists had a "Samson complex" that would ultimately result in nothing but self-destruction. Disagreements between African American intellectuals and activists over strategies of resistance during the Civil Rights Era are evident in their different perspectives regarding the wisdom of Samson's actions.

While the 1959 letter from Collins praises Samson's determination to sacrifice life itself, Ralph Ellison, in a publication from 1960, points out that Samson also sacrifices potentially innocent lives when he destroys the temple. Although Ellison had not completed or given a title to his second novel at the time of his death in 1994, he began to publish excerpts from it in the early 1960s.[2] The substantial drafts that Ellison left behind indicate that the novel focuses on a fictional character named Alonzo Hickman. Hickman, an itinerant African American preacher, tries and fails to prevent the assassination of a race-baiting senator named Adam Sunraider, whose race is unspecified. Framed by conversations at the politician's deathbed, the novel reveals that Hickman served as a ministerial mentor for the future politician, who was called "Bliss" as a child. After a long estrangement, Bliss surfaces in New England as Sunraider. One excerpt, written in the first person and published under the title "The Roof, the Steeple and the People," involves a conversation between Bliss as a young man and his boyhood friend Body. During the conversation, Body, who refers to Bliss as "Rev," raises difficult questions about the collateral damage during Samson's destruction of the temple.

Say Rev, Body said.

Can't you hear? I said do you remember in the Bible where it tells about Samson and it says he had him a boy to lead him up to the wall so he could shake the building down?

That's right, I said.

Well answer me this, you think that little boy got killed?

Killed, I said, who killed him?

What I mean is, do you think old Samson forgot to tell that boy what he was fixing to do?

I cut my eyes over at Body. I didn't like this idea. Once Daddy Hickman had said: Bliss, you must be a hero just like that little lad who led blind Samson to the wall, because a great many grown folks are blind and have to be led toward the light. . . . The question worried me and I pushed it away.[3]

Body's question is troubling because the Bible mentions the boy in only one verse, which reads, "And Samson said unto the lad that held him by the hand, Suffer me that I may feel the pillars whereupon the house standeth, that I may lean upon them" (Judges 16:26). The text does not indicate that the boy survived the temple's collapse. Despite Bliss's dismissal of this question, Body does not let it go. Later in the conversation, Body says, "I wanted to talk about Samson and you didn't want to." Bliss continues to dodge the question, replying, "Forget about Samson, man."[4] After Bliss accuses Body of lying about another matter, Body responds, "Listen, Bliss, a little while ago you wouldn't tell me whether that boy who led Samson got killed or not, so now dont come preaching me no sermon."[5] In a portion of the novel not published during Ellison's lifetime, Ellison elaborates on why Bliss is so troubled by Body's questions about the lad's fate. During an exchange with Bliss, Hickman explains how the slave trade stripped enslaved women and men of their identity.

> Without personality, without names, Rev. Bliss, we were made into nobody and not even *mister* nobody either, just nobody. They left us without names. Without choice. Without the right to do or not to do, to be or not to be. . . .
>
> You mean without faces and without eyes? We were eyeless like Samson in Gaza? Is that the way, Rev. Hickman?
>
> Amen, Rev. Bliss, like baldheaded Samson before that nameless little lad like you came as the Good Book tells us and led him to the pillars whereupon the big house stood. Oh, you little black boys, and oh, you little brown girls, you're going to shake the building down! And, then, oh, how you will build in the name of the Lord!
>
> Yes, Reverend Bliss, we were eyeless like unhappy Samson among the Philistines—and worse.[6]

Prompted by Bliss, Hickman extends the comparison of African Americans to a blinded and bald Samson to include the important role played by the lad in bringing down the Philistine temple. The lad's actions represent the leadership role that younger African Americans can play for their people. Although Hickman imagines the next generation building a new structure after the present edifice crumbles, Body's question forces Bliss to confront the grim implications of this plan for "little black boys" and "little brown girls." If the younger generation led Samson in shaking the building down, they may very well die when it collapses.

Despite Ellison's innovative uses of Black Samson imagery, more militant associations with Samson continued. Nothing illustrates this as clearly as the controversial comments made in 1962 and 1963 by Malcolm X, who was a high-ranking minister in the Nation of Islam at the time. His comments connect the crash of Air France Flight 007 with the killing of Roland Stokes, a member of the Nation of Islam in Los Angeles. During a confrontation between Los Angeles police officers and members of the Nation of Islam in the early morning hours of April 27, 1962, officers shot Stokes in the back and killed him. Stokes's death troubled Malcolm X deeply, but Elijah Mohammed, the leader of the Nation of Islam, instructed him not to retaliate or organize against the Los Angeles police department. Just over a month later, on June 3, Air France Flight 007 was scheduled to fly from Paris, France, to Atlanta, Georgia. Passengers on the chartered flight included over one hundred patrons of the Atlanta arts scene returning from a European tour sponsored by the Atlanta Arts Association. Malcolm X, who was in Los Angeles at the time, immediately connected the two seemingly unrelated events while speaking to a large audience.

> I would like to announce a very beautiful thing that has happened. As you know, we have been praying to Allah. We have been praying that He would in some way let us know that He has the power to execute justice upon the heads of those who are responsible for the lynching of Ronald Stokes on April 27. And I got a wire from God today, wait, all right, somebody came and told me that he really had answered our prayers over in France. He dropped an airplane out of the sky with over 120 white people on it because the Muslims believe in an eye for an eye and a tooth for a tooth. But thanks to God, or Jehovah, or Allah, we will continue to pray, and we hope that every day another plane falls out of the sky.[7]

Malcolm X's statements were recorded and appeared on the front page of the *Los Angeles Times* a few days later. The next year, he elaborated on his comments during an interview with Louis Lomax, an acclaimed African American journalist whose 1959 series of television specials, *The Hate That Hate Produced*, brought national attention to the Nation of Islam. During the 1963 interview, Malcolm X explained the theological reasoning behind Elijah Muhammad's call for racial separation rather than integration.[8]

> The Honorable Elijah Muhammad teaches us that God now is about to establish a kingdom on this earth based on peace and brotherhood, and the

white man is against brotherhood and the white man is against peace. . . .
Since his own history makes him unqualified to be an inhabitant or a citizen
in the kingdom of brotherhood, the Honorable Elijah Muhammad teaches
us that God is about to eliminate that particular race from this earth. Since
they are due for elimination we don't want to be with them.[9]

Lomax followed up by asking Malcolm X if "the American white establishment will come to a bitter end, perhaps be destroyed?"[10] His lengthy response
to this question invokes a number of biblical images, including a comparison
of the crash of Flight 007 with the destruction of the Philistine temple.

God is going to punish this wicked devil for his misdeeds toward black
people. Just as plagues were visited on Pharaoh so will pestilences and
disasters be visited on the white man. Why, it has already started: God has
begun to send them heat when they expect cold; he sends them cold when
they expect heat. . . . Not only that, God has started slapping their planes
down from the sky. . . . When the plane fell, I said it was God's way of letting
his wrath be known. . . . What's so wrong when a black man says his God
will protect him from his white foe? If Jehovah can slay Philistines for the
Jews, why can't Allah slay crackers for the so-called Negro.[11]

Then, Lomax continued, "You spend much of your life getting on and off air-
craft. Don't you fear that you might just be aboard when God sees fit to slap
down a jet and kill a few score white people?"[12] Malcolm X responded, "But if
I am aboard one of these vessels, I will be happy to give my life to see some of
those white devils die. Like Samson, I am ready to pull down the white man's
temple, knowing full well that I will be destroyed by the falling rubble."[13] This
comparison imagines the White establishment as the Philistine temple of
Dagon. Invoking a similar image as Collins's 1959 letter in the *Los Angeles
Tribune*, Malcolm X imagined himself as a Samson-like martyr willing to
sacrifice his life for this divine cause. His use of the familiar comparison of
the biblical hero with African Americans reinforces his interpretation of recent events as representing a divine plan.

In 1962 Martin Luther King, Jr. condemned Malcolm X's initial comments
about Flight 007 in statements that were also printed by the *Los Angeles
Times* a week later. King said, "I knew many of the people who were killed.
Many of them believed in progress. Some of them who lost their lives were to
have attended a concert only last week at which Harry Belafonte sang. If the

Muslim leader said that, I would certainly disagree with him."[14] King's use of Samson imagery when addressing African American resistance to White supremacy contrasts sharply with Malcolm X's reference to Samson. At some point between July 1962 and March 1963, King drafted a version of the sermon "Love in Action" for inclusion in a collection of sermons published as *Strength to Love*.[15] "Love in Action" focuses on the nature of forgiveness and Jesus's statement from the cross: "Father, forgive them; for they know not what they do" (Luke 23:34). King's sermon uses blindness as a negative metaphor to describe the human condition that Jesus's prayer addresses. He explained that Jesus's prayer from the cross "is an expression of Jesus' awareness of man's intellectual and spiritual blindness. 'They know not what they do,' said Jesus. Blindness was their trouble. Enlightenment was their need. We must recognize that Jesus was nailed to the cross not simply by sin but by blindness."[16]

King contrasted Jesus's prayer for divine forgiveness with two biblical examples of how the desire for revenge "blinds" humanity. The first example comes from the story of Samson's death. King explained, "One can only see the greatness of this [Jesus's] prayer by contrast. . . . Man is slow to forgive. We live by the philosophy that life is a matter of getting even and saving face. We genuflect before the altar of revenge. Samson, eyeless at Gaza, prays fervently for his enemies, but only for their utter destruction."[17] King's reference to Samson's dying prayer for revenge on the Philistines (Judges 16:28) touches on a theme developed throughout the biblical story of Samson.[18] A blinded Samson serves as his example of humanity bowing at "the altar of revenge." Although the biblical text does not use Samson's blindness as a metaphor, King used stereotypes that associate blindness with ignorance to interpret Samson's physical blindness as an indication that he was spiritually compromised. King did not make a direct comparison of this blinded Samson with African American resistance to racial oppression or any specific endorsement of violent revenge by an African American leader. This sermon was probably written before Malcolm X's 1963 interview with Lomax in which Malcolm X refers to Samson's violent death approvingly. Nevertheless, considering that King addressed slavery and racial segregation in the same sermon, it is very likely that King was alluding to the well-established tradition of Black Samson imagery and its use in calls for more violent responses to racial oppression.

For King's second biblical example of revenge that he contrasted with Jesus's prayer, he cited the legal principle of an eye for an eye.[19] King countered the principle of revenge, which he suggested Samson followed, with an allusion to Jesus's command from the Sermon on the Mount to turn the other cheek: "Ye have heard that it hath been said, An eye for an eye, and a tooth for a tooth: But I say unto you, That ye resist not evil: but whosoever shall smite thee on thy right cheek, turn to him the other also" (Matthew 5:38–39). King referred to these verses when he wrote that Jesus "knew that the old eye for an eye philosophy would end up leaving everybody blind." Instead of lifting up Samson as a heroic martyr for a divine cause and affirming the belief in an eye for any eye as Malcolm X did, King turned Samson's death into an example of the consequences of the eye for an eye philosophy. It is a failed strategy which shows that only radical love can overcome evil. For King, Samson's death served as a cautionary tale about what happens when, in his mind, we are "blinded" by the desire for revenge.

King's nonviolent approach was derided by some of the younger more militant Black activists.[20] He engaged the growing Black Power movement directly in his final book before he was assassinated on April 4, 1968.[21] In his 1967 book *Where Do We Go from Here: Chaos or Community?*, King critiqued White liberals for overestimating racial progress made on the basis of recent legislative victories during President Lyndon Johnson's administration. After citing a survey indicating that 80 percent of White Americans still objected to miscegenation and 50 percent objected to integration in their neighborhoods, King wrote, "Most whites in America in 1967, including many persons of goodwill, proceed from the premise that equality is a loose expression for improvement. White America is not even physiologically organized to close the gap—essentially it seeks only to make it less obvious but in most respects to retain it."[22] Despite King's analysis of the state of race relations in America, he did not believe the tactics and strategies espoused by the Black Power movement provided the answer. He concluded that the rejection of nonviolence and racial integration is ultimately self-defeating for African Americans.[23]

A brief editorial by an unidentified author titled "Modern Day Samson," which was broadcast on the radio station WDIX in Orangeburg, South Carolina, on August 2, 1967, misrepresented King's position by conflating it with the positions of advocates of Black Power. Although *Where Do We Go from Here* does not contain any references or allusions to Samson, the editorial implies that King argues that African Americans will tear society down in Samson-like fashion if White America does not change. It claims, "Mr. King says that the white community must change itself, or—like

Samson—the Negro will bring down the roof of Western civilization on their mutual heads."[24]

The editorial focuses on the survey that King cites in his book. In response, it concludes that King and advocates of Black Power seek to blame others rather than take responsibility for their own circumstances. For example, the editorial claims inaccurately that attitudes about miscegenation reflect the fact that African Americans have not made themselves into desirable candidates for marriage. Referencing the race-related riots in multiple cities across the United States in the summer of 1967, the editorial mischaracterizes King's followers as "stone-age savages" who resort to violence in the face of antimiscegenation attitudes. The editorial compares this violence to Samson's destruction of the temple, which is the tragic climax to a chain of events that began when Samson, an Israelite, attempted to marry an unnamed Philistine woman (Judges 14:1–15:8). The editorial declares, "Until Black Power and Martin Luther King Negroes understand that they must earn a desirability as marriage prospects, they are in the position of saying, if you don't marry me I'll kill you—which is what some white people do. Martin Luther King, Jr. displays the mind of a stone-age savage. It is stone-age savagery that moves the Negro to this ten-city riot. Samson brought down the temple on his own head—but the community prevailed." The editorial implies that Samson died in vain. After he dies, the Philistines are still in power. Despite the large number of Philistines that Samson kills, the Israelites remain in conflict with them until well after his death.[25] In fact, the Israelites are still fighting the Philistines in 1 Samuel 17 when David kills Goliath. The editorial compares this situation to the 1967 "ten-city riot" that the author believes is nothing more than an exercise in African American self-destruction. It will not bring down the current political structure on anyone's head other than those who provoke the riots.

In contrast to this editorial, others understood the 1967 riots as the emergence of a new brand of leadership in the struggle for racial justice that fits the particular historical moment. Albert B. Cleage, Jr., who later changed his name to Jaramogi Abebe Agyeman, was a fiery minster in Detroit in the late 1960s where he emerged as a leading figure in Black theology. At a time when biblical characters were often interpreted as White, Cleage's sermons reinterpreted them as Black revolutionaries. In a 1967 sermon titled "No Halfway Revolution," he recast Samson as a young, Black militant whose unconventional form of leadership was exactly what was needed at that moment. Cleage declared:

Normally people would have frowned on him. They would have called him a hoodlum. They wouldn't have listed him in their religious scriptures as a "judge" of Israel. But during this particular time, he had what everyone wanted. He wasn't afraid, he didn't mind dying, he was emotional, he struck out against oppression. So everyone called him a judge of Israel. . . . [A] hundred years from today we may remember as heroes some of these very individuals we call hoodlums today, who are striking out for freedom.[26]

Cleage saw similarities between those involved in the 1967 multi-city riots and Samson. History may one day remember those who violently resist racial oppression in the United States as heroes just as Samson was eventually remembered as a champion of his people. Rather than dismissing the violence as illogical acts of self-destruction, Cleage asserted that it could be understood as analogous to Samson's resistance against his oppressors. He explained:

All over the country we have young men now who are aware of the problems, who are participating in a rebellion, who understand what the nature of the rebellion is. They fight one way here and another way some place else. . . . Sometimes you wonder, "What are they trying to do, what do they hope to accomplish?" Remember when Samson was in the Temple and the Philistines were all around, making fun of him, robbing him of his dignity. . . . You have to understand that indignation, anger, hatred, all of them stemming from systematic oppression, can develop to the point where an individual says, "I am willing to die if I can take a whole bunch of them with me." That is what Samson said. I am not quoting from anybody in Detroit or Newark. That is in the Bible. "Let me die with the Philistines."[27]

For Cleage, the multi-city riots were not random acts of violence. Rather, they were an understandable response to systematic oppression by those who had a full grasp of the nature of racial problems in the United States.

Some interpretations of the 1967 riots hearken back to Longfellow's warning to antebellum America in 1842. The August 18, 1967, issue of *Life* magazine published a letter to the editor regarding the six-day riots in Newark, New Jersey, that took place on July 12–17, 1967. In this letter, a woman identified only as Grace H. McPherson from Globe, Arizona, expressed her concern over yet another outbreak of race-related violence. She alluded to the race-related civil unrest in the Watts section of Los Angeles on

August 11–17, 1965. For McPherson, the Newark riots were a "new Watts." Her entire letter reads:

> Every time I read about a new "Watts" I think of these lines from Longfellow's "The Warning" written over a hundred years ago:
> *... There is a poor, blind Samson in this land,*
> *Shorn of his strength and bound in bonds of steel,*
> *Who may, in some grim revel, raise his hand,*
> *And shake the pillars of this Commonweal,*
> *Till the vast Temple of our liberties*
> *A shapeless mass of wreck and rubbish lies.*[28]

As we discussed in chapter 1, although Longfellow's poem was originally composed in support of the anti-slavery movement, its warning was applied to many other social injustices facing African Americans in the late nineteenth and early twentieth centuries. McPherson's letter continues this tradition by extending the warning into the 1960s. She regarded the urban unrest as a result of America's failure to heed Longfellow's warning. Although slavery had been legally abolished over one hundred years earlier, African Americans remain Samson-like prisoners in the American temple of liberty. McPherson understood the uprisings in Watts and Newark as evidence that oppressed African Americans were beginning to shake the pillars of American society just as Longfellow warned.

A few months later, one of America's most prominent White clergy also interpreted the 1967 uprisings as a harbinger of things to come by using the image of Samson resting his hands upon the pillars of the Philistine temple. In early 1968, the *Atlanta Daily World*, an African American newspaper, carried a brief article on a speech delivered by the Reverend Franklin Clark Fry, the president of the Lutheran Church of America and one of the most influential Lutheran clergy in the United States during the twentieth century. Speaking to a group of fellow White Lutheran clergy in Cincinnati, Ohio, Fry called upon his church to recognize the gravity of the current situation.

> Unstop your ears and be startled. What is commonly called the "racial crisis"—until to some, I fear, it sounds hackneyed, is real. The grievances fomenting it are just. . . . Frighteningly outspoken Negro people are more and more expressing their willingness to die for what they believe is right, and they are not unwilling to have others die with them. . . . You understand,

I am speaking sympathetically of these people. If there is an explosive up-rising, the heaviest responsibility will rest on white society which did not act when there was still a chance. We must find a way to deal with the problem of racism in our white neighborhoods and churches.[29]

Although Fry did not refer to Longfellow's poem directly, he compared the willingness of what he calls "frighteningly outspoken Negro people" to die while taking others with them to Samson's willingness to die among the Philistines in the temple of Dagon (Judges 16:30). Fry continued, "The present situation is comparable to Samson when he destroyed the Temple of Dagon and himself along with it. Like him, many black brothers, blind with rage, have their hands posed on the temple pillars, ready to start pushing."[30] Whereas Longfellow's "poor, blind Samson" offered a sentimentalized view of the enslaved African American as worthy of our pity, Fry's Samson is "blind with rage." For Fry, the image of blindness did not draw attention to Samson's pitiful state but to the extent of his very justified rage. To reinforce the urgency of the "racial crisis," he compared the present moment to the moment when Samson rests his hands on the pillars of the temple. If White America continues to ignore the crisis, just as the Philistines seemed to ig-nore that Samson's hair grew back while he was their captive (Judges 16:22), it is moments away from having its social structure collapse. Fry used Samson imagery to warn White America that it must address racism in its communities directly and immediately. The association of Samson's destruction of the Philistine temple with more militant approaches in the struggle against racial injustice had reached mainstream White America.

At the same time, some African American artists and activists were sus-picious of African American intellectuals who worked closely with White liberal elites. In their view, if Black Samson were a true revolutionary, he would need to tear down the current temples completely and build a new temple of his own. In 1968, Larry Neal, a poet, playwright, and professor, and LeRoi Jones, a poet and literary editor who later changed his name to Amiri Baraka, co-edited *Black Fire: An Anthology of Afro-American Writing*.[31] This extensive collection of essays, poetry, fiction, and drama was one of the most influential works to emerge from the early years of what became known as the Black Arts movement—a movement that cre-ated a place for the arts within the Black Power movement of the 1960s and 1970s.[32] In his influential 1968 article "The Black Arts Movement," Neal explained, "This movement is the aesthetic and spiritual sister of the Black

Power concept. . . . The Black Arts and the Black Power concept both relate broadly to the Afro-American's desire for self determination and nationhood."[33] The close relationship of the movement to Black Power is readily apparent. For example, Jones and Neal reprinted in *Black Fire* the 1966 essay "Toward Black Liberation" by Stokely Carmichael, a leading voice in the Black Power movement who was the chairman of the Student Nonviolent Coordinating Committee when the essay was written but later joined the Black Panther Party.[34] In language similar to Neal's later article, "The Black Arts Movement," Carmichael declared that Black Power involves the "struggle for the right to create our own terms through which to define ourselves and our relationship to society, and to have these terms recognized."[35] The radical politics of the Black Arts movement contrasted sharply with those of civil rights leaders, such as King, who advocated nonviolent protest and supported racial integration.

A number of works in *Black Fire* discuss Malcolm X, his death, and his legacy. Welton Smith, a Houston-born poet and playwright, eulogized the fallen icon in one of the most memorable works on Malcolm X to come out of the Black Arts movement. Smith captures the anger, pain, and grief of the moment in a poem simply titled "malcolm." He divides the poem into two parts. The first part has four sections: "malcolm," "The Nigga Section," "interlude," and "Special Section for the Niggas on the Lower East Side or: Invert the Devisor and Multiple." The second part has two sections: "interlude" and "The Beast Section." Smith uses misogynistic and derogatory references to homosexual acts among other extremely graphic images of sexual violence to lash out against various parties that he views as responsible for Malcolm X's death. Smith does not direct his anger only toward the men who shot Malcolm X. For example, the section titled "Special Section for the Niggas on the Lower East Side or: Invert the Devisor and Multiple" targets African American intellectuals who, in Smith's opinion, undermined Malcolm X's revolutionary cause by ingratiating themselves to White liberals. At one point, he evoked Black Samson imagery to critique the alleged hollowness of their commitment to the cause of African American freedom.

> you are jive revolutionaries
> who will never tear this house down
> you are too terrified of cold
> too lazy to build another house.[36]

For Smith, African American intellectuals' talk of revolution is largely empty rhetoric. He contended that a meaningful commitment to African American self-determination would require tearing down the house built on a foundation of White liberal politics and building another house by and for African Americans. From Smith's perspective, these lazy intellectuals would rather stay in the comfortable house of White liberal politics than fully commit to the revolutionary cause of self-determination and governance. The line "who will never tear this house down" does not come from the biblical Samson story. Instead, it seems to allude to the song about Samson that we discussed in chapter 4 popularized under the title "If I Had My Way I'd Tear the Building Down" by the preacher and blues musician known as Blind Willie Johnson in 1927. Over the years, the song had been used to express revolutionary political positions by influential African American artists and intellectuals such as Richard Wright.[37] Smith invokes the song's version of the Samson story to expose the African American intellectual of his day as nothing like the biblical hero. In Smith's opinion, the contemporary intellectual is no Samson and will never tear this house down.

While the Black Arts movement began in Harlem, another influential expression of Black Power was emerging on the other side of the country. In October 1966, Huey P. Newton and Bobby Seale formed the Black Panther Party for Self Defense in Oakland, California. In his autobiography, *Revolutionary Suicide*, Newton explained the party's initial goal of using armed but legal patrols to monitor police activity in their neighborhoods.

> [The Party] would be based upon defending the community against the aggression of the power structure, including the military and the armed might of the police. We informed the brothers of their right to possess weapons. . . . Many community people could not believe at first that we had only their interest at heart. Nobody had ever given them any support or assistance when the police harassed them, but here we were, proud Black men, armed with guns and a knowledge of the law.[38]

The Black Panther Party was founded on a ten-point program. The first point reflects its overall political agenda. It reads, "We want freedom. We want power to determine the destiny of our Black Community. We believe that Black people will not be free until we are able to determine our destiny."[39] The other nine points flesh out what this freedom and self-determination would require, including reforms in employment, education, housing, and current economic, military, criminal justice, and police practices.[40] Newton's childhood heroes included the biblical Samson with King David as a close second.

> Both my parents are deeply religious, and when Melvin [Huey's brother] and I were small, my father often read to us from the Bible. My favorite was the Samson story, followed closely by David and Goliath. I must have heard those stories a thousand times. Samson's strength was impressive, as well as his wisdom and his ability to solve riddles put to him. . . . I liked David and Goliath because, despite Goliath's strength and power, David was able to use strategy and eventually gain the victory. Even then, the story of David seemed directed to me and to my people.[41]

Newton was impressed by Samson and David because they each possessed not only impressive strength but also wisdom. For Newton, Samson was not a reckless, destructive, force acting out of rage without regard for the consequences of his violent actions. The biblical hero displayed a formidable intellect by using riddles to engage his opponents.[42] Although some used the Samson figure to question the prudency of militant actions coming from the Black Power movement, Newton embraced Samson as a model of the strategic militancy necessary to achieve the goals of the party's ten-point plan.

By 1968, the Black Panthers had chapters in cities across the nation, including Boston, Chicago, Detroit, New York City, and Newark, among others. As the party grew, local and federal law enforcement increased its surveillance and harassment of the group. For example, on August 6, 1969, the Black Panthers held a rally in New Haven, Connecticut, that attracted members from Boston and New York City. Douglas Miranda, the defense captain for the Boston chapter of the party, was in attendance. According to an article in the *Black Panther* newspaper, Miranda and other Panthers traveling with him back to Boston were arrested because the car they were driving was allegedly rented on a stolen credit card.[43] All of the Panthers except one were bailed out of jail. Nevertheless, according to the article, they were not bailed out "before the sadistic fascist pigs got their thing off by shaving the incarcerated brothers' heads. The pigs, with their comic book mentality were probably caught up in the fable of Samson and thought they were sapping the brothers of their revolutionary strength. . . . Vamping on Panthers on such absurd and ridiculous pretense will not destroy the Black Panther Party and cutting off brothers' naturals will definitely not sap them of their revolutionary strength."[44]

As the arrested Panthers wore their hair naturally as an intentional cultural expression, the police officers probably cut their hair to humiliate them and to demonstrate their cultural dominance and control over the Panthers in their custody. Yet, the article invokes the association of Samson with African American revolutionaries to reframe the haircuts as an indication of the officers' naivety. It mocks the police officers for buying into the Black Samson mythology and, like their Philistine counterparts, believing that they could vanquish their enemies with a haircut. The police officers' abuse of the arrested Panthers would not dissuade their commitment to the revolutionary cause any more than Samson's haircut had stopped his actions against the Philistines.

Neither Newton's autobiography nor the article in the *Black Panther* newspaper alludes to Samson's fatal destruction of the Philistine temple. Nevertheless, some African American intellectuals continued to focus on Samson's self-destruction to characterize younger activists involved in the Black Power movement as reckless and illogical. John Gibbs St. Clair Drake was a distinguished anthropologist and sociologist who founded the African American studies program at Stanford University. He epitomized this attitude toward younger activists in comments made during what became known as the "Haverford Discussions."

Beginning in 1969, Kenneth B. Clark led a series of meetings at Haverford College, a Quaker school in Pennsylvania. Clark, a psychologist, is probably best known for the experiments he developed with his wife and fellow psychologist Mamie Phipps Clark based on her work using dolls to study children's understandings of race. Their research was used in *Brown v. Board of Education* to show the harmful effects of segregation on children. Clark brought together a number of prominent African American academics and intellectuals who supported racial integration to formulate a response to the growing Black Power movement and those advocating anti-integration positions. In addition to Drake and Clark, the participants included, among others, Ralph Ellison; Adelaide McGuinn Cromwell, a professor of sociology and co-founder of the African studies program at Boston University; Robert C. Weaver, who was the secretary of Housing and Urban Development and the first African American to hold a cabinet position; William Henry Hastie, Jr., a federal appellate judge who President Kennedy considered nominating as a Supreme Court justice; and John Hope Franklin, an acclaimed historian at the University of Chicago who would become a recipient of the Presidential Medal of Freedom in 1995.

In general, the group was dismissive of the younger, more militant activists. For example, during the initial meetings on May 30, 1969, Drake singled out H. Rap Brown, now known as Jamil Abdullah al-Amin. Brown was chairman of the Student Nonviolent Coordinating Committee, and he briefly served as minister of justice for the Black Panthers. Following the 1968 uprising in Detroit in the wake of Martin Luther King, Jr.'s assassination, Brown wrote, "There was a town called Motown; now it ain't no town. They used to call it Detroit, now they call it Destroyed. I hear ain't nothing left but Motown sound. And if they don't come around, you gon' burn them down."[45] According to Drake, Brown had a "Samson complex" that Drake thought was common among younger, more militant activists. He viewed Brown as epitomizing a dangerous, self-destructive attitude that he compared to Samson's death in the Philistine temple.

> [This is] what I call a Rap Brown Synonym. I used to call it the Samson complex. You may recall that after Samson's hair grew back out, when he got his strength back, the Philistines brought him to make sport of him. . . . He was blinded. And as Milton said, "Samson Agonistes, eyeless in Gaza, grinding at the mill with slaves." He has to know his place. They brought him to the hall and he said: "Where are the pillars?" And when he got them, he pulled them down, see, and Samson died. But while he was dying, he was probably saying, "Man, look at all these Philistines dying! Just look at them, see!" I call this the Samson Complex, or the Rap Brown complex. . . . I think we just have to write off that proportion of these people who feel this way. Isn't any use trying to talk to these fellows.[46]

Although Newton had praised Samson for his wisdom rather than the manner in which he died, Drake used the story of Samson's death to characterize Brown and like-minded revolutionaries as unreasonable. He dismissed those who held this extreme position as not worth debating. Yet, this dismissive attitude prevented the Haverford group from providing a robust response. Their plans to publish an intellectually rigorous rebuttal did not materialize.[47] In fact, the transcripts of the Haverford Discussions were not published until 2013.[48] As the political climate on Haverford's campus shifted under the influence of Black Power, the group left the campus, changed its named to the Hastie Group after William Hastie, and held its final meeting in New York City in 1975. The final meeting was not transcribed.

The 1960s ended without a clear resolution between the deep differences in opinions over how to confront racial injustice. The use of Samson imagery signaled the growing fault lines among African American leaders throughout the 1960s and into the early 1970s regarding how to achieve meaningful racial justice. Some imagined Samson as a model of militant resistance even at the cost of one's life. Others interpreted his death as a cautionary tale about the end results of imprudent reactionary strategies. In 1963, James Baldwin, the acclaimed writer and social critic, published his landmark memoir, *The Fire Next Time*, which urgently warned that if America did not address its "racial nightmare" it was headed full steam toward an apocalypse. He concluded this book with a haunting claim. He wrote, "If we do not now dare everything, the fulfillment of that prophecy, re-created from the Bible in a song by a slave, is upon us: *God gave Noah the rainbow sign, No more water, the fire next time!*"[49] The increasing race-related violence, uprisings, and assassinations throughout the 1960s made *The Fire Next Time* seem prophetic nine years later when Baldwin published a second memoir, *No Name in the Street*, in 1972.[50] America had not heeded his earlier warning and had crossed a point of no return. Whereas Baldwin's 1963 book closes with a traditional song about the biblical flood story as a warning, his 1972 book opens with another traditional song about Samson's destruction of the Philistine temple. One of the epigraphs at the beginning of *No Name in the Street* captures this despair over the present order of the world. It reads, "If I had-a-my way, I'd tear this building down. Great God, then, if I had-a- my way, little children, I'd tear this building down—Slave Song."[51]

For Baldwin, the late 1960s demonstrated that the fire he warned of could no longer be prevented. The old world must collapse for a new one to emerge. In the epilogue of *No Name in the Street*, Baldwin wrote, "An old world is dying, and a new one, kicking in the belly of its mother, time, announces that it is ready to be born."[52] Baldwin insisted that "we accept that our responsibility is to the newborn," although he admits that "many of us are doomed to discover that we are exceedingly clumsy midwives."[53] Over the next few decades, however, better skilled midwives for this new world would emerge through engagements with the Black Samson tradition in the writings of a new generation of African American women.

6

But Some of Us Are Strong Believers in the Samson Myth

Tell the world we are rising.

—Blanche Taylor Dickinson, 1907[1]

The March 1974 issue of *Ebony* magazine featured an article on a small conference held at Jackson State College, a historically Black college in Mississippi.[2] The conference brought eighteen African American women writers to campus to honor the eighteenth-century African American poet Phillis Wheatley. The article included biographical blurbs on each of the women. The conference included participants who would eventually secure a place among the giants of twentieth-century American literature such as the late Nobel laureate Toni Morrison and the Pulitzer Prize–winner Alice Walker. Others, such as Lucille Clifton and Nikki Giovanni, were among the most prominent poets to be associated with the Black Arts movement. There was nothing in the article to connect the conference with traditions about Black Samson. Nevertheless, some of the poets at this conference would take the Black Samson tradition in bold and exciting directions during the last decades of the twentieth century.

As discussed in earlier chapters, African American women writers such as Frances Harper, Josie Heard, and Ida B. Wells-Barnett made robust contributions to the burgeoning Black Samson tradition in the late nineteenth century. Such writers used Black Samson primarily to express opinions about race and various social issues. The women discussed in this chapter use the Black Samson tradition to focus more directly on the complex intersections of race and gender. With their engagement of Black Samson, these poets continue a rich legacy of African American women who direct attention simultaneously to race and gender issues as they advocate for social reform.[3]

Explorations of race and gender with references to Black Samson appear in an obscure book of poetry published in 1910 by a young woman living in Washington, DC, named Christina Moody. Moody was only sixteen years old when she first published her poetry in a volume titled *A Tiny Spark*.[4] In the book's first poem, "To My Dear Reader," the speaker asks the audience not to "criticize my writing Cause I ain't well trained you know." The speaker claims that some of the poems were written when she was "a little kid of thirteen years or so."[5] Often, Moody wrote in a vernacular style that may reflect the influence of popular African American poets of her day such as Paul Laurence Dunbar, discussed in chapter 2. Like Dunbar, some of Moody's poems celebrate the valor of African American soldiers on the battlefield.[6] Off of the battlefield, however, men do not play much of a role in Moody's poetry. Instead, her poems focus on the worlds of African American women and their relationships with each other.

Many of Moody's poems present African American women as capable, confident, and audacious. For example, after "To My Dear Reader," the book opens with a poem titled "The Love of a Slave Mother." This poem sets the tone for the book and tells the story of an enslaved woman who escapes after her slaveholder decides to sell her child. This notion of African American womanhood receives its boldest expression in the final poem in Moody's book, titled "Samson No. 2."

> I's brave as de bravest,
> I kin fight from sun to sun,
> I can lick Jack Johnson—
> Yes lick him till he runs.
>
> But my jints is kinder stiff,
> And I needs to limber up,
> And I need a bit more practice,
> On dem things called upper-cuts.
>
> Everybody says that Jack
> Is mighty powerfull strong,
> But I clair I could lick him
> If he ever catched me wrong.[7]

The reference to Samson in the title of Moody's poem probably refers to the heavyweight champion Jack Johnson rather than the biblical character. Moody published *A Tiny Spark* the same year as Johnson's epic title defense against James J. Jeffries in Reno, Nevada. As we discussed in the introduction, "Black Samson" became a commonly used nickname for Johnson, especially after he fought Jeffries. If Moody refers to herself as "Samson No. 2," the poem's title may suggest that she will displace Johnson's claim to the title "Black Samson." In doing so, she boasts audaciously, "I can lick Jack Johnson— / Yes lick him till he runs."[8] Furthermore, by imagining herself as the next Black Samson, she extends a heavily racialized image across gender lines to represent the strength and vitality of African American women. Moody ends her book of poetry that had praised capable African American women by staking her claim to the Black Samson tradition.

While Moody engages the Black Samson tradition by celebrating the capabilities of African American women, Blanche Taylor Dickinson uses the tradition to explore attempts of African American women to gain recognition in a world of men. Among African American writers active during the Harlem Renaissance, Samson was easily recognizable as a symbol of radical efforts to overturn the current racist status quo. Poets and writers such as Langston Hughes and Claude McKay utilized the image of Black Samson shaking the temple pillars in writings that addressed racial oppression. Although her male counterparts explored how racial injustice and economic exploitation mutually supported this status quo, Taylor Dickinson expanded the use of Black Samson to highlight the intersections of race and gender in critiques of the status quo.

Several of Taylor Dickinson's poems were anthologized in *Caroling Dusk*, a landmark collection of African American poetry published in 1927.[9] The anthology included six of her poems alongside poems by women for whom Taylor Dickinson expressed admiration, such as Georgia Douglas Johnson and Jessie Redmon Fauset.[10] In her poems, Taylor Dickinson invokes biblical images of walls crashing down to express a desire to break from restrictive racial and gender norms that regulate her behavior. Her poem "The Walls of Jericho" uses the image of the city's walls to express African Americans' desire to achieve social advancement. Referring to the city of Jericho, she writes, " 'We want in,' the dark ones cried, 'We will love it as the rest.' "[11]

Biblical walls feature prominently in another of Taylor Dickinson's poems appropriately titled "Four Walls." In this poem, she invokes the powerful walls of the Philistine temple to articulate how pressures to conform to gender expectations confine her spirit. Whereas "The Walls of Jericho" focuses on racial uplift, "Four Walls" uses the racialized image of Samson to explore complicated and ambivalent aspects of resistance to social conformity. The speaker in the poem mentions the "four strong, high walls" and how the "mighty pillars tremble." The speaker desires "Samson's strength" to "shove" the walls "away from where I stand" but also questions whether doing so would actually bring about the freedom she desires.[12]

The speaker feels "hemmed in" by high walls that limit her options along strictly regulated standards for proper gender expression. The strength of these "high walls" has shaped her conscience to a point where it is hard to imagine living free of their influence. In discussing the final line of the poem ("this conscious world with guarded men"), literary scholar Maureen Honey observed, "The speaker longs for the strength of Samson so she can break her bondage to 'this conscious world with guarded men' but fears that she has internalized their rules to a point where freedom would have no meaning."[13] For Professor Honey, the poem's final line emphasizes the gendered rules that restrict the speaker. These rules have shaped the only world that the poet knows. In fact, the poem's use of the Samson figure involves a strongly gendered image. Yet, the speaker's longing and fears are not only gendered but also racialized. As the last line of the poem indicates, the speaker's world is filled with "guarded men." In other words, it is filled with African American men whose behavior is carefully guarded, alert, and conscious of danger as they navigate a racist society.

The final stanza of "Four Walls" reflects an additional undercurrent in the Black Samson tradition. Some writers have interpreted the story of Samson as a warning against rash actions by those calling for more radical forms of resistance against racial injustice. As we discussed in chapter 5, this rhetoric peaked during the Civil Rights Era when established African American intellectuals like Ralph Ellison and St. Clair Drake criticized more militant activists for espousing destructive actions. They suggested that Samson's destruction of the Philistine temple illustrated imprudence rather than a thoughtful consideration of the consequences of their actions. Decades earlier, Taylor Dickinson anticipated this use of Black Samson when she thoughtfully considered what might happen if she quickly brought down the patriarchal walls that have shaped her world "if for a moment Samson's strength were given me." When read in the context of this tradition, Black Samson imagery allows Taylor Dickinson's poem to express both a deep desire for freedom and a real concern about a future without the rigid structures with which she is familiar.

Early twentieth-century poets such as Moody and Taylor Dickinson may seem to have little in common with African American women poets associated with the Black Arts movement. Yet some of the same themes found in Moody and Taylor Dickinson's work appear in the poetry of Nikki Giovanni, who, by the early 1970s, was known as the "Princess of Black Poetry."[14] Born Yolande Cornelia Giovanni, Jr. in Knoxville, Tennessee, she has received numerous awards and honorary doctorates and has served as a Distinguished University Professor at Virginia Tech. Like others involved in the Black Arts movement in the late 1960s, Giovanni's early poetry has a militant tone. Yet, she soon voiced concerns that such militancy understood the revolutionary nature of African American culture too narrowly.

In 1969, she published an essay titled "Black Poems, Poseurs and Power" in *Negro Digest*, an influential African American magazine later known as *Black World*. In the essay's opening paragraph, she argued that one could miss the revolutionary potential of love as expressed in popular music by African American artists if one simply equated revolution with militancy.

> I like all the militant poems that tell how we gonna kick the honkie's backside and purge our new system of all the honkie things like white women, TV, voting and all the ugly bad things that have been oppressing us so long. I mean, I wrote a poem asking, "Nigger can you kill?," 'cause to want to live under president-elect no-Dick Nixon is certainly to become a killer. Yet in listening to Smoky and the Miracles sing their Greatest Hits recently, I became aware again of the revolutionary quality of "You Can Depend On Me."... There is a tendency to look at the Black experience too narrowly.[15]

Throughout the 1970s, Giovanni's poetry began to explore this broader understanding of the Black experience. She sought out the revolutionary power of family and love in her 1972 collection of poetry titled *My House*.[16] The book's second poem, simply titled "Mothers," draws on Black Samson imagery to describe this understanding of revolution as found in the lived moments when one has the freedom to be oneself rather than trying to conform to a narrow idea of what a revolutionary should be.[17]

In "Mothers," Giovanni connects a revolutionary image with an intimate moment at home. The adult speaker in the poem returns home to visit her mother, and after a kiss, they have positive and negative interactions and retreat to reading separate books in a comfortable silence. Then, the speaker recalls a childhood memory of finding the mother in the kitchen sitting in the dark. The speaker remembers thinking of the mother as a beautiful woman. The poem describes this nocturnal encounter as the first time the speaker regarded the mother as a Samson-like revolutionary figure. The poem ends with the mother teaching the child a poem that night. As an adult, the speaker teaches the poem to the speaker's son, and that son recites the poem to his grandmother.

The mother's sitting in the dark may be only a vague allusion to the biblical hero's blindness, but the allusions become clearer several lines later with the description "her hair was three-quarters her height / which made me a strong believer in the samson myth / and very black." The mother's extraordinarily long hair reminds the speaker of the biblical character who, from birth, is prohibited from ever cutting the hair on his head (Judges 13:5; 16:17). The observation of the length and color of the mother's hair also describes the moment that the child identifies as racially and politically Black. The child associates the long hair with the biblical figure that she recognizes as a mythological Black hero. The child understands the mother as Black and beautiful. The first time that the speaker consciously sees the mother, the mother appears as a beautiful revolutionary. Her mother makes the speaker believe in the biblical story that generations of African Americans had associated with liberation and freedom. As a Black Samson figure, the mother connects the child with a larger cultural heritage. Giovanni expands our understanding of what she referred to in her 1969 essay as the "Black experience" by expanding our understanding of the Black Samson figure to include maternal love. In "Black Poems, Poseurs and Power," Giovanni became aware of the revolutionary quality of popular love songs by Smoky and the Miracles. In "Mothers," she found a Black Samson in the revolutionary act of a mother teaching her child a poem that the child will later teach to the speaker's own son.

By the mid-1970s, some people involved in the growing feminist movement argued that a more comprehensive understanding of women's inequality required a consideration of factors beyond strictly gender. In 1976, Elly Bulkin, Jan Clausen, Irena Klepfisz, and Rima Shore, four self-identified White lesbians living in Brooklyn, New York, founded *Conditions: a feminist magazine of writing by women with a particular emphasis on writing by lesbians*.[18] Although the founding editors of *Conditions* were White, the fifth and by far the most influential issue of the journal, *Conditions: Five—The Black Woman's Issue* was guest edited by Lorraine Bethel and Barbara Smith in 1979. Bethel and Smith were part of the Combahee River Collective, a group of Black feminists that formed in 1974. In April 1977 the Collective wrote "A Black Feminist Statement." The opening paragraph reads: "As Black women we see Black feminism as the logical political movement to combat the manifold and simultaneous oppressions that all women of color face."[19] Many of the poems, essays, and reviews published two years later in Bethel and Smith's *Conditions: Five* exhibit similar understandings of Black feminism.[20] The issue includes a short poem titled "Love Letter" by Carole Clemmons Gregory, who was among the eighteen African American women writers at the 1974 Jackson State conference. The poem was written in the first person as a letter from Delilah to Samson. In the poem, Delilah tells Samson that she has put some of his hair in a jar near a pear tree in what may be a conjuring spell. She lets him know that she has considered her actions and concludes that she still does not think that his God-given strength was to be used "to kill my people."[21]

Since the nineteenth century, racialized interpretations of the Samson story often equated Delilah and the Philistines with White America, although the Bible does not provide any ethnic or physical descriptions of Delilah.[22] Gregory turns this tendency to depict Delilah as a White woman on its head. In the poem, Delilah's speech suggests the vernacular style that Dunbar, Moody, and many other poets used to reflect certain African American oral forms of expression. Also, the fact that Gregory published this poem in *Conditions: Five—The Black Women's Issue* suggests that she uses Delilah's story to create a poignant image of the often-unacknowledged commitment of African American women to defend other African Americans. Gregory creatively imagined a biblical story well represented in African American literature to drive home this theme, which is found elsewhere in her poetry.[23] Typically, the biblical text and its interpreters focus on Samson and what he did or did not do to free his people from the Philistines. The story is rarely told from Delilah's perspective. While Judges 16:4 indicates that Samson "loved a woman in the valley of Sorek, whose name was Delilah," the Bible does not describe Delilah's feelings toward Samson. Although Delilah is often regarded as a cold-hearted mercenary because a group of Philistines offer to pay her 1,100 pieces of silver each if she can discover what will weaken Samson (Judges 16:5), we do not know how she felt about betraying Samson to the Philistines. The Philistines did not threaten her as they did Samson's wife (Judges 14:15), but we do not know if she really had a choice in complying with an offer that perhaps she could not refuse. It may have been a very painful choice on her part. Gregory imagines Delilah's decision as the heart-breaking sacrifice of a lover in order to defend her people. Framing the poem as an intimate love letter to Samson written from a Black Delilah allows Gregory to highlight the high price that African American women have paid on behalf of their people.[24]

Like Gregory's "Love Letter," Lucille Clifton's poem, "samson predicts from gaza the philadelphia fire" focuses on the cutting of Samson's hair to explore the price paid by African American women in defense of their communities. Along with Giovanni, Clifton was among the most celebrated poets associated with the Black Arts movement. Her poetry has received two Pulitzer Prize nominations and, in 2000, she received the National Book Award for Poetry. Her poem "samson predicts from gaza the philadelphia fire" was published in her 1993 collection of poetry, *The Book of Light*.[25] The volume contains poems that imagine characters from the Bible and Greek mythology reflecting on their lives in the first person.[26] Like Delilah's letter to Samson in Gregory's poem, this form of address intensifies the sense of intimacy between the two parties and the sense of raw pain and anger over the events that unfold in "samson predicts from gaza the philadelphia fire." Yet, while Delilah addresses Samson in "Love Letter," Samson addresses a woman named Ramona Africa in Clifton's poem. Gregory has Delilah tell Samson's story from her perspective; Clifton has Samson tell Ramona Africa's story from his perspective.

The dedication in Clifton's poem reads, "*for ramona africa, survivor.*" Ramona Africa is a member of MOVE, a controversial group that originated in Philadelphia in early 1972 under the leadership of John Africa, born Vincent Leaphart. Following what they understood as divinely inspired "natural law" as taught by John Africa, members of this majority Black group wore their hair naturally in dreadlocks, ate raw vegetables and fruits, rejected modern technologies and medicines, and took the surname Africa.[27] Beginning in 1972, MOVE members conducted numerous protests against many individuals and organizations, from the Philadelphia Zoo to civil rights icon Jesse Jackson. The protests lead to conflicts with law enforcement over the next several years, including a shootout on August 8, 1978, that resulted in the imprisonment of nine MOVE members convicted of voluntary manslaughter.[28] As journalist Linn Washington reported, "Arrests of MOVE members skyrocketed from thirty-three in 1974 to 142 in 1975, with few if any arrests accomplished without scuffles between MOVE and police."[29]

Washington was an eyewitness to the bombing of a row house on 6221 Osage Avenue owned by MOVE member Louise James Africa. In the early hours of May 13, 1985, police officers arrived at the row house to execute a number of arrest warrants for some of the members of MOVE who were living there. The tense day-long standoff included exchanges of gunfire and the police's use of tear gas and high-powered explosives, despite the fact that they knew children were in the house. Finally, at 5:27 p.m., a state police helicopter was used to drop a bomb on the row house. It ignited a fire that destroyed sixty-one homes and displaced over two hundred and fifty people. Eleven people who were in the MOVE residence, six adults, including John Africa, and five children, died. Only two people escaped the house with their lives, a child named Birdie Africa and an adult named Ramona Africa.

Clifton's *Book of Light* contains two poems on the MOVE bombing. The first poem, which appears immediately before "samson predicts from gaza the philadelphia fire," is simply titled "move." This poem vividly describes the moment of the bombing. Lest one misses the poem's historical reference, Clifton includes a preface that succinctly describes the events that inspired the poem. Clifton specifies the date, address, casualties, and the authorization of the bombing by Wilson Goode, the first African American mayor of Philadelphia.[30]

In "samson predicts from gaza the philadelphia fire," Clifton associates what Samson refers to in the King James Version as the "locks on my head" (Judges 16:13) with the way that members of MOVE wore their hair. This short but powerful poem is set in Gaza, where Samson was imprisoned following the removal of his hair and his eyes. From there, Samson—whose wife was burned to death by the Philistines (Judges 15:6)—warns Ramona Africa that they will come for the symbol of her strength.

> *for ramona africa, survivor*
> it will be your hair
> ramona africa
> they will come for you
> they will bring fire
> they will empty your eyes
> of everything you love
> your hair will writhe
> and hiss on your shoulder
> they will order you

> to give it up   if you do
> you will bring the temple down
> if you do not   they will[31]

The poem invokes images from climatic moments in Samson's life to describe the horrific events of May 13, 1985. The lines, "they will empty your eyes / of everything you love" allude to the blinding of Samson to convey the torture of losing all that Ramona Africa loved. With lines like "you will bring the temple down," the poem places Ramona Africa, a self-described revolutionary, within the long tradition of revolutionaries described as Black Samsons.[32] Yet, despite her unimaginable loss, this Black Samson is a survivor. The dedication *"for ramona africa, survivor"* connects the poem to a theme of African American women's survival that appears throughout *The Book of Lights*.[33] At the time that we write this, Ramona Africa is still living in Philadelphia and still fighting for the release of the surviving members of MOVE who remain incarcerated.

From the Harlem Renaissance to the Black Arts movement, the major artistic and literary movements that helped shape African American culture throughout the twentieth century involved women who found something in Samson's story that resonated with them deeply. One might think that the story of a hyper-masculine biblical hero would not provide much material for reflections upon the intersections of race and gender in America. Yet, from the playful audacity of Moody's claim that she could defeat Jack Johnson to the painful predictions from Gaza in Clifton's poem dedicated to Ramona Africa, a survivor, the twentieth century witnessed African American women claiming a place within the Black Samson tradition. Nikki Giovanni's poem "Mothers" considers the moment she discovered both a beautiful woman and a Black Samson in her mother. The final words of the poem declare "we must learn / to bear the pleasures / as we have borne the pains." Poetry by African American women has taught this lesson by returning to the rich, textured expressions of celebration and sorrow embodied in Black Samson.

7

Visual Representations of Black Samson

Tell me, I pray thee, wherein thy great strength lieth.

—Judges 16:6 (King James Version)

In early 1860, on the brink of the Civil War, a White illustrator from Philadelphia named Henry Louis Stephens published a cartoon with the caption "Sambo Agonistes" in the March 3 issue of *Vanity Fair* (figure 7.1).[1]

The cartoon portrays Samson as a racially stereotyped Sambo figure with thick lips, unkempt hair, and torn clothing trying unsuccessfully to topple two pillars that support an arch labeled "Constitution." The left pillar is labeled "1787," the year that the Constitution was drafted, and the right pillar is labeled "1860," the year the Sambo Agonistes cartoon was published. The cartoon's caption reads "Dey Don't Budge" as if this Black Samson is realizing that he cannot bring down the US Constitution. Although Longfellow and other abolitionists used Black Samson figures as a powerful warning of the dire threat that slavery posed for America's democracy, Stephens's caricature of Black Samson as a Sambo figure reassured his viewers that the debates over slavery were no real threat to the democracy.

Stephen's cartoon serves as our starting point for tracing the use of Black Samson figures in the visual arts from the mid-nineteenth century to the present. We follow the development of Samson imagery in political cartoons that address issues of racial injustice throughout the early twentieth century, particularly in African American newspapers. Then we consider representations of Samson as a Black man in film, paintings, comic books, graphic novels, and on television.

In the late 1860s, as the United States began the fraught process of Reconstruction, Thomas Nast, one of the most influential editorial cartoonists in America, drew a Black Samson figure in a cartoon to address another controversial question—suffrage for African American men. Nast is probably best known for creating the contemporary version of Santa Claus

Figure 7.1

and the elephant as the symbol of the Republican Party. His political cartoons also popularized images of Uncle Sam and Columbia as personifications of the United States and its government.[2] Nast was born in Germany but immigrated to the United States as a young child. Raised in New York City, he worked as an illustrator for the popular magazine *Harper's Weekly* for many years.[3] His cartoons for this magazine took on a number of the political controversies of his day and helped shape popular opinion regarding presidential campaigns during the late nineteenth century.

In 1868, he published cartoons that provided scathing critiques of the Democratic presidential nominee Horatio Seymour, a former governor of New York. With the support of southern Democrats, Seymour's campaign was heavily anti-Reconstruction and promoted the disenfranchisement of African Americans. On September 5, 1868, *Harper's Weekly* ran a cartoon by Nast titled "This Is a White Man's Government" (figure 7.2).

The cartoon depicts Seymour joining hands with a generic Irishman, who is depicted in an unflattering caricature, and Nathan Bedford Forrest, a

Figure 7.2

leading member of the Ku Klux Klan during its early years. The three men are standing on the head and back of a prostrated African American soldier in a Union army uniform. The Irishman is holding a raised club labeled "A Vote." Forrest has a raised dragger labeled "The Lost Cause." "The Lost Cause" is a term used by those who promoted a revisionist interpretation of the Civil War as a noble but doomed struggle by the Confederacy to defend the southern way of life rather than as a war primarily about slavery. Seymour is holding up a bundle of cash labeled "capital," suggesting the compromised integrity of this northern governor. The African American soldier is grasping for a ballot box, but the White men's feet ensure that it remains out of his reach.[4]

A month later, Nast continued his attack on Seymour and his alliance with southern Democrats over their promotion of African American disenfranchisement when he published a cartoon titled "The Modern Samson" in *Harper's Weekly* on October 3, 1868 (figure 7.3).[5]

The cartoon shows a White woman holding up the shorn locks of a muscular, bare-chested African American man. The man is lying next to her with his hand on his head. Together, they are representations of Delilah and Samson. The White woman's robe is labeled "Southern Democracy" and the shorn locks in her hand are labeled "Suffrage." To the right of the White Delilah figure, President Andrew Johnson, a Democrat from Tennessee,

Figure 7.3

holds a tablet with the words "Veto" written across the top. This is a reference to Johnson's veto of the First Reconstruction Act on March 2, 1867. To the left of the Delilah and Samson figures is a fire in which a Bible and other writings burn.

As with his "This Is a White Man's Government" cartoon, Nast once again includes Seymour, Forrest, and a caricature of a generic Irishman along with other figures such as the Confederate general Robert E. Lee in "The Modern Samson." Nast caricatures Seymour and his southern Democratic colleagues celebrating Samson's downfall as the Philistines did in the Bible (Judges 16:23–25). Seymour is in the center of a rowdy group of onlookers cheering on the White Delilah figure. He is wearing a Ku Klux Klan breastplate and holding up a large flag above his head labeled "Slavery," "Lost Cause Regained," "Fort Pillow," "Mob Law," and "Ku Klux Klan Democrats," along with references to recent draft and race riots. Lee is to Seymour's immediate left, holding a sword with his name on it. Forrest is to the left of Lee, with a gun raised above his head and a "Forrest Pillow" button on his chest. Forrest Pillow refers to the massacre of more than two hundred surrendering African American Union soldiers by Confederate soldiers under Forrest's command at Fort Pillow, Tennessee, on April 12, 1864. The generic Irishman is in the background to the far right of Seymour. Shortly after the publication of "The Modern Samson," Seymour would lose his bid for the presidency to the former Union general Ulysses S. Grant. It was reported that Grant credited his victory in 1868 in part to "the pencil of Thomas Nast."[6] By the late 1860s, the Black Samson figure had become such a polarizing image that its visual representation was considered powerful enough to help sway presidential elections.

Nast's "The Modern Samson" serves as an early example of the extension of Black Samson imagery beyond abolition into other social issues in the decades following the Civil War. While *Harper's Weekly* was probably the most influential publication to print a Black Samson political cartoon, a number of African American newspapers also printed cartoons that used Samson imagery to comment on race in America. In 1899, an unidentified artist published a cartoon in the *Indianapolis Freedman*, the first illustrated African American newspaper, titled "The Black Samson Asleep" (figure 7.4).[7]

Although the cartoon does not attribute the poem to Longfellow, the caption below the illustration quotes the final stanza of "The Warning" verbatim beginning with the line: "There is a poor, blind Samson in the land."[8] The cartoon depicts a giant Black man lying down on his side in front of the

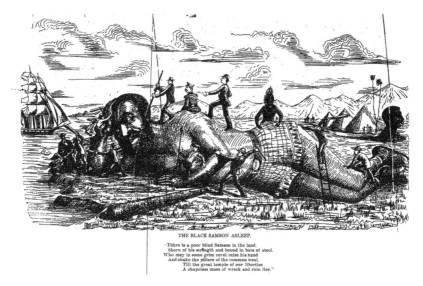

THE BLACK SAMSON ASLEEP.

"There is a poor blind Samson in the land,
Shorn of his strength and bound in bars of steel,
Who may in some grim revel raise his hand
And shake the pillars of the common weal,
Till the great temple of our liberties
A shapeless mass of wreck and ruin lies."

Figure 7.4

Egyptian pyramids while Lilliputian-size figures, the majority of whom are White, climb on him and strike him with tiny clubs. Like Gulliver on the island of Lilliput, the Black Samson figure in the illustration is awake and staring at a group of smaller White men crawling on him.

Other cartoons in African American newspapers involving Samson depict him in contexts that relate more explicitly to the stories about him from the Bible. On November 29, 1941, the *Pittsburgh Courier*, a leading African American newspaper during the first half of the twentieth century, published an editorial by an unidentified author titled "What Will This Samson Do?" (figure 7.5).[9]

Accompanying the article is an illustration by an African American artist named Wilbert Louie Holloway featuring a figure with the label "The Black Samson" written across his chest.[10] In this illustration, Black Samson is a massive and muscular figure dressed in a singlet with large chains on his ankles securing him to his seat. A dense crowd of jeering White men dressed in suits, coats, and ties surround him on all sides. One of the men in the foreground, representative of the crowd as a whole, is labeled "Modern Philistines." Samson is positioned between two pillars, with each of his hands gripping a pillar. The pillar of the left is labeled "Racial Prejudice" and the pillar on the right is labeled "Discrimination." The cartoon dramatically

WHAT WILL THIS SAMSON DO?
The Pittsburgh Courier (1911-1950); Nov 29, 1941; ProQuest Historical Newspapers: Pittsburgh Courier
pg. 6

WHAT WILL THIS SAMSON DO?   Illustrated By HOLLOWAY

Figure 7.5

illustrates the moment before Black Samson brings the temple down upon these modern Philistines.

The accompanying editorial explains how Black people throughout the world are in a similar position today. It compares "the ancient Samson sitting blinded between the pillars of the temple in Gaza and the modern black Samson sitting blinded and shackled in the temples of the modern world!"[11] The first half of the editorial observes that, despite Samson's physical gifts, he was very gullible and easily tricked into revealing his secrets. The

Philistines captured him, blinded him, and forced "Samson to CLOWN for them."[12] Yet, the editorial quotes the last lines of Judges 16:30 to stress the point that Samson took action during that defining moment in the Philistine temple: "And he bowed himself with all his might; and the house fell upon the lords, and upon all the people that were therein. So the dead which he slew at his death were more than they which he slew in his life." The editorial then turns to the "modern Samson who is as powerful as the ancient Samson, for the colored folks once ruled the world."[13] The editorial contends that this modern Samson is just as gullible because he possessed "the secrets of iron smelting, paper making, alphabets, architecture, religion, art, medicine and numbers, and yet today he is a SERVANT in the house his labor builded."[14] Although "this modern Samson represents at least HALF of the human race," he has been "blinded" by "doctrines of disunity which make him place superficial NATIONALISM over fundamental racialism."[15] The editorial continues by noting that this Samson's oppressors prioritize race over nationality. It explains, "Meantime, those whom he serves place racialism above nationalism, as shown by the almost unvarying attitude of ALL white nations toward him. Whether his oppressors are British, French, Portuguese, Spanish, Belgium, Dutch, or American, his status remains the SAME."[16]

The editorial holds out hope, however, that Black Samson's hair "is beginning to grow back and his strength, or the AWARENESS of that strength is returning."[17] Yet, Samson's oppressors try to keep him unaware of his collective strength by intensifying their efforts to promote nationalism over racial solidarity. The editorial suggests that Black Samson has reached a moment of truth in which he must decide whether to remain oppressed or follow the example of his ancient counterpart. It ends with a poignant question that returns to the earlier quotation from Judges 16:30. It asks, "Will he CONTINUE to sit there unaware of his strength, piling up treasure for OTHERS? Or will he some day 'bow himself with all his might' and bring down the temple upon the modern Philistines? . . . Very SOON, now, there should be action!"[18] Holloway's accompanying cartoon captures the urgency of this moment of truth before Black Samson takes action and topples the pillars labeled racial prejudice and discrimination.

In the August 17, 1946, edition of the *Baltimore Afro-American*, another major African American newspaper during the 1940s, Elmer Simms Campbell published a cartoon depicting the cutting of Samson's hair with a caption that reads "Uncle Samson and Delilah" (figure 7.6).[19] Campbell,

Editorial Cartoon 1 -- No Title
Afro-American (1893-1988); Aug 17, 1946; ProQuest Historical Newspapers: The Baltimore Afro-American
pg. 4

UNCLE SAMSON AND DELILAH

Figure 7.6

whose trademark signature "E. Simms Campbell" appears in the lower left corner of the cartoon, was among the most successful African American cartoonists of his day. Beginning in 1932, Campbell published cartoons in each issue of *Esquire* for several decades. He also published in *Cosmopolitan, Life, New Yorker, Playboy, Redbook,* and the *Saturday Evening Post.*[20] His cartoons were the first to cross the color line, but his race was kept a secret in the early years of his career.[21]

Campbell's "Uncle Samson and Delilah" cartoon combines a depiction of a White Uncle Sam with Samson imagery. A muscular bare-chested Uncle Samson is asleep on a couch dressed only in dark shorts with a star-spangled pattern. A White Delilah with a menacing grin stands above him with the words "White Supremacy" written across her dress. In her left hand, she holds a knife. In her right hand, she holds the shorn locks of Uncle Samson's hair. The hair is labeled "Catholics, Jews, Colored People." According to Judges 16:9, there were Philistines in Delilah's inner chamber "lying in wait" to capture Samson once he had lost his strength. In Campbell's cartoon, a figure representing these hidden Philistines is dressed in a Ku Klux Klan robe and hood and peers out from behind a pillar in the background. For Campbell, the Philistines are not just White; they represent members of the Ku Klux Klan. By combining Samson and Uncle Sam figures, Campbell depicts the United States as a nation that should include Catholics, Jews, and people of color. Yet, White Supremacy, represented by the Delilah figure, cuts off anyone other than White Protestants from what represents the United States.

Campbell drew Uncle Samson as a White man because he based his Samson on an earlier cartoon by Oliver Herford. Herford was a popular cartoonist who was born in England but immigrated to the United States with his family as a teenager. Herford's cartoon appeared in the November 9, 1922, issue of *Life* magazine (figure 7.7).[22]

Like Campbell's cartoon, Herford's cartoon also appears under the title, "Uncle Samson and Delilah" with a short editorial accompanying the cartoon. The editorial, which was written by Agnes Repplier, an essayist from Philadelphia, offered a critique of pacifism. She wrote, "The pacifists have made patriotism a discredited virtue. . . . There is a cardinal virtue named Justice. Pacifists and sentimentalists haven't caught on to her yet; but she can do surer work in preserving the peace of the world than international leagues and 'No More War' posters in the windows."[23] Herford illustrated Repplier's point with a cartoon of Uncle Samson asleep on his knees with his sword on the ground and his head in Delilah's lap. Delilah, who wears a headband labeled "Pacifism," is cutting Uncle Samson's hair with a pair of scissors labeled "Anthony Bill." This is a reference to the bill named after the suffragette and women's rights advocate Susan B. Anthony. It was ratified in 1920 as the Nineteenth Amendment, which prohibited the denial of the vote on the basis of one's sex. Although Herford's drawing is not the first "Uncle Samson and Delilah" cartoon to object to American pacifism in the early

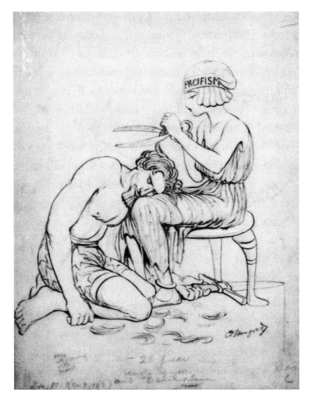

Figure 7.7

twentieth century, it is clearly the drawing that inspired Campbell's version of "Uncle Samson and Delilah."[24] In addition to the same title for their respective cartoons, Campbell's and Herford's Uncle Samsons bear a striking resemblance. They each have a similar goatee, are bare-chested, and sport dark shorts with a star-spangled pattern.

Campbell did not transform Herford's Uncle Samson into an African American. Instead, he transforms the political context of earlier "Uncle Samson and Delilah" cartoons. During the years leading up to and following World War I, Uncle Samson cartoons warned that American pacifism would result in the nation's downfall, represented by cutting Uncle Samson's locks. Campbell shifted the political frame of "Uncle Samson and Delilah" from foreign policy to domestic racism. For Campbell, it is not the politics of pacifism or isolationism that threaten the national welfare, but the racial terror and religious intolerance of White supremacy. While Campbell's Uncle Samson may not be a Black Samson figure, his cartoon presented Uncle Samson in a racialized context. He used Uncle Samson to comment on the dangers that White supremacy poses for the United States as a whole, which has been a central theme in Black Samson art and literature since Longfellow.

A few decades later, Black Samson would make the move from editorial cartoons to the silver screen when Warner Brothers released a feature film titled *Black Samson*, which opened on August 14, 1974.[25] The titular character, played by Rockne Tarkington, is a towering nightclub owner with a pet lion named Hoodoo, a reference to West African and West Central African spiritual practices that came to the United States through the transatlantic slave trade. This Samson defends his predominantly African American Los Angeles neighborhood from drug dealers trying to infiltrate the area. The film's theme song, with music by Allen Toussaint and vocals by Willie West, sets the tone for the film by asking: "What's his name? Black Samson. What's his game? He ain't got none. Trouble on both sides. Look out!" As the lyrics indicate, Samson faces "trouble on both sides" because he is caught between a clumsy gang of White drug dealers led by the hot tempered Johnny Nappa, played by William Smith, and an African American, cocaine sniffing, drug dealer named Arthur, played by Michael Payne, who runs a funeral home as a front for his operation.

The film traffics in many of the standard elements of the so-called blaxploitation films popular in the 1970s, including racial and gender stereotypes, urban violence, and martial arts.[26] It opened to very poor reviews. The *Los Angeles Times* referred to it as "a less than mediocre blaxploitation melodrama that reduces whites to corrupt sadistic scum and makes the black hero and heroine plaster-of-paris paragons of virtue." The review concluded, "CORE [Congress of Racial Equality] members in the preview audience wanted to ban the movie because it projects a derogatory image. It's not worth their efforts. The film's demerits speak too loudly for themselves."[27] Other equally critical reviews objected to the gendered violence throughout the film. The review in the *New York Times* stated, " 'Black Samson' is a cinematic masquerade. In the guise of presenting a story of courage against odds, it is, in truth, an ugly and brutal film, reveling in cruelty and the bloody abuse of women."[28] Similarly, the *Boston Globe* review warned that the script "strays down the beat-your-women, mafia-war, and cheap-gore path. Rockne Tarkington as Samson is as wooden as the storyline is flimsy, which is to say very."[29]

The film opens at Samson's crowded nightclub with a confrontation between him and Nappa. When one of Nappa's associates starts harassing one of the club's topless dancers, Samson beats him soundly with his giant staff and throws him out into the street. Nappa tries to pay Samson for his trouble, but Samson refuses to take his dirty money. Over the next few scenes, Samson establishes his credentials as a community hero as he provides for those down on their luck and challenges those using and distributing drugs. Samson confronts Arthur at his funeral home and says, "Word's out you got people on my street." Arthur denies it but warns Samson that "sooner or later, those White boys are gonna move in here. . . . I stay out as long as they stay out. When they make their move and the war comes down, well, I'm picking the pieces. Business is business." When Samson responds, "What about our people?" Arthur replies, "When Joseph Nappa brings his boys down into this neighborhood you are gonna be the only people on that street." Questions about whether the community will back Samson in his struggle to keep the streets clean build throughout the film.

Nappa's gang tries to bribe or intimidate Samson repeatedly. Nappa even pays off African American members of Samson's community to ambush Samson and Leslie, his lover, in an alley at night. Yet, each time, Samson beats off his hapless attackers with the aid of his giant staff. At one point, Nappa sends a lawyer with an offer of 15 percent of the gross if he allows them to sell drugs in his neighborhood. Samson and the lawyer go up to the roof of the nightclub to talk. On the rooftop, he tells the lawyer, "There's my people down there. All those souls scrambling around, hustling, trying to make a living, get a good time." After he hears the offer, he threatens to throw the lawyer from the roof, telling him, "I want you to go home and tell your clients this neighborhood ain't for sale." Finally, Nappa has his girlfriend Tina apply for a job as a topless dancer at Samson's nightclub to get inside information on Samson. Nappa tells Tina, "I wanna know what his weakness is. You understand?" His instructions to Tina recall the Philistines' orders to Delilah when they instruct her to "Entice him, and see wherein his great strength lieth, and by what means we may prevail against him" (Judges 16:5). Tina auditions for Samson and gets the job but does not secure any useful information about the film's hero. When Nappa suspects that Tina warned Samson of his plans, he attacks her and beats her savagely.

Meanwhile, Leslie is growing increasingly concerned for Samson's safety, but Samson promises, "The streets are clean. The people trust me." Leslie's frustration boils over when she screams, "The people? The people? Your brothers and sisters ain't gonna do no dying for you. . . . You're just one man! When you're dead, they're gonna move in and just take over anyhow."

Leslie echoes Arthur's earlier warning to Samson that he will be alone in the streets when Nappa's gang moves in. Despite Leslie's pleas for Samson to leave town, he responds, "This is the last chance for our people to stand up." Desperate to save Samson, Leslie goes to Arthur's funeral home to ask him to defend Samson, but Nappa's gang follows her. After Arthur refuses Leslie's request, Nappa's gang kidnaps Leslie as she leaves the funeral home, killing one of Arthur's men in the process. The same night, Nappa's gang firebombs Samson's nightclub.

After Nappa has Leslie tied up in a warehouse, he instructs his men to guard her. Nappa leaves the warehouse with Tina in the car, but he throws her out of the moving vehicle and chuckles, "Nigger-loving bitch." After Tina lies bloodied in the street, the next scene returns to the warehouse where Nappa's men cut Leslie's blouse open with a knife and then cut her breasts until blood covers her blouse. In other words, Nappa and his men brutalize the two leading women in the film in juxtaposed scenes. In contrast, Samson visits Tina in the hospital and, after learning the location of the warehouse from her, embarks on a daring mission to rescue Leslie. He single-handedly beats each of Nappa's men before escaping with Leslie in his car. Nappa's gang follows him in hot pursuit, and a high-speed car chase ensues. As they come closer to Samson's neighborhood, the members of the community begin preparations to carry out an undisclosed plan.

When Nappa and his men arrive in Samson's neighborhood and exit their vehicles, the entire community appears on the rooftops and fire escapes of the buildings on both sides of the street chanting "Samson! Samson!" The people are armed with discarded furniture and household appliances. Perched from their rooftops, members of the community bury Nappa's gang in an avalanche of broken tables, mattresses, refrigerators, bed frames, broomsticks, and cabinets. With garbage raining down upon the heads of Samson's opponents, the film's climatic scene reimagines the destruction of the Philistine temple as the community's defense against the White mobsters. Eventually, even Arthur joins the fight. When Samson appears, the people halt their attack. Nappa and Samson face off in a one-on-one battle while the people look on. When Samson finishes Napa with a devastating blow from his staff, the crowd erupts. Unlike his biblical counterpart, Black Samson does not fight alone or die along with his enemies under a pile of rubble. In the end, the people support Samson in his struggle against their oppressors.

The film's plot is not modeled after the biblical story of Samson. It makes only a few general nods to what we find in the Bible. The lion in the film recalls the lion that the biblical Samson battles in the vineyards of Timnah (Judges 14:5–9). Yet, rather than tearing the lion apart with his bare hands, Black Samson makes him his pet and names him Hoodoo. Tina plays the role of a quasi-Delilah, but she does not provide any useful information about him to his enemies. She is not Samson's love interest, and she does not cut his hair, which he wears in a short afro rather than seven long locks as the biblical Samson does (Judges 16:14). One might think that Black Samson's giant staff is meant to recall an image of a biblical prophet. Yet, according to a *Baltimore Afro-American* profile of Tarkington, the lead actor studied the Japanese martial art Kendo, which uses a heavy staff or pole, while stationed in Japan during his military service. Although the script indicated that Black Samson used karate, Tarkington persuaded the film's producers that his character should carry a staff and use Kendo instead.[30] Nevertheless, despite its differences with the biblical story, the film connects with commonplace themes and motifs in Black Samson art and literature, including militancy, self-determination, dignity, wisdom, strength, and resistance to injustice. When viewed in the context of earlier uses of Samson in African American literary traditions, the film allows its audience to imagine this American icon as surviving to continue the fight for his people.

Racial, economic, and political themes frequently associated with Black Samson figures also appear in the work of Jean-Michel Basquiat. Basquiat was a native New Yorker whose father emigrated from Haiti before Jean-Michel's birth. Having started as a graffiti artist, Basquiat took the art world by storm in the early 1980s. While the reception of his work by a lucrative and overwhelmingly White fine-art scene brought him wealth and fame, he was keenly aware of the commoditization and exploitation of his art and the racial overtones in reviews of it. He died in 1988, only a few years after he burst onto the scene and his art gained international recognition. He was twenty-seven years old. In 2017, one of his untitled paintings sold for $110,000,000.

Basquiat frequently combined texts and images in his paintings and created stark contrasts highlighting issues of racism, economic inequality, and other social injustices. Also, he incorporated elements from African American and Haitian traditions in his artwork. For example, his 1982 acrylic and oilstick on a 68 x 102-inch canvas painting *Obnoxious Liberals*, which can be viewed online, foregrounds three figures.[31] From right to left, the figures are a presumably American cowboy; Bawon Samdi, who is one of the spirits in Haitian Vodou; and a Black Samson. The central figure dressed in black is identifiable as Bawon Samdi, or possibly one of the similar Gede spirits in Haitian

Vodou, because he wears a top hat and has cotton in the nose and eyes of his skull-like face. Such items are part of the traditional representations of this spirit in Haitian Vodou. Bawon Samdi is known for his disruptive and defiant behavior, which may explain his role in Basquiat's painting. The unidentified figure on the right with the large cowboy hat and dollar signs on his torso would seem to represent the contemporary American art collectors who had profited from Basquiat's artistic labor. The Bawon Samdi figure, however, resists their exploitative efforts, as made clear from the words, "Not for Sale" scrawled across his chest. His right hand is raised with a clinched fist and his left hand holds up a sign that reads, "Obnoxious Liberals©."

Basquiat's use of Bawon Samdi to critique his conflicted experience in the contemporary art world dovetails well with his use of the Black Samson figure, which appears to the left of Bawon Samdi. In a 1993 essay on a Basquiat exhibition at the Whitney Museum in New York City, writer bell hooks explained, "The painting *Obnoxious Liberals* (1982) shows us a ruptured history by depicting a mutilated black Samson in chains."[32] In *Obnoxious Liberals*, a Black figure, with the word "Samson" written directly above his bald head, appears between two pillars, with each of his arms chained to one of them. In a possible allusion to Samson's forced labor in the Philistine prison house (Judges 16:21), the word "Gold" appears in the space between his legs, which seems to equate his labor with the defecation of gold for the art world's consumption. Basquiat's Black Samson is confined to poor living conditions. The word "Asbestos" appears three times just below the barred window above Samson's head. As the previous chapters demonstrate, the image of Samson threatening to bring the temple down is the biblical scene most often found in representations of Black Samson. Within traditions about Black Samson, the scene is not usually associated with passivity or a lack of agency on the part of oppressed or exploited parties. Rather, this image of resistance often communicates a threat to bring an oppressive establishment crashing down. Fueled by African American and Haitian traditions, Basquiat's creative depiction of a Black Samson figure alongside a Bawon Samdi figure conveys a bold critique of the racial exploitation that he encountered during his short but extraordinary artistic career.

Black Samson figures have continued to appear in the early twenty-first century. Similar to the movie *Black Samson*, some of the characters named Black Samson have little in common with the biblical hero, other than incredible strength. In 2003, Robert Kirkman introduced a character named Black Samson as a member of the Guardians of the Globe, a team of superheroes in the *Invincible* comic book series, published by Image Comics.[33] Kirkman, a White writer, is best known as the co-creator of *The Walking Dead* graphic novels that were adapted as a very popular television series of the same name for the American Movie Channel. Unlike his biblical counterpart, Kirkman's Black Samson character has an African American butler named Sanford, wears a power suit, and is eventually killed off while volunteering in a barbershop.[34] Other than this ironic nod to the haircut leading to Samson's downfall in the Bible, his storyline does not engage the biblical material in a substantive way. Nor do the comics that feature him show any evidence that that its writers are aware of traditions about Black Samson in earlier literature.

Other examples focus more directly on retelling the biblical story of Samson. In 2012, Justin Reed wrote and illustrated a self-published graphic novel titled *Samson: Blessed Savior of Israel*, which grew out of his undergraduate senior thesis at Stanford University (figure 7.8). Reed aimed to "illuminate some of the ambiguities of the biblical account without altering the meaning of the story in any significant ways."[35] Although Reed does not refer to his titular character as "Black Samson" explicitly, he renders Samson, as well as many of the other characters in the graphic novel, as Black.

Figure 7.8

Because the graphic novel began as a research project, Reed engages academic literature more so than the cultural traditions about Black Samson from outside academia.[36] Nevertheless, his retelling appeals to aspects of African American culture to help flesh out underdeveloped aspects of the biblical text. For example, after an enraged Samson leaves his wedding feast and storms off to kill thirty Philistines in Ashkelon before returning to his parents' home, Judges 14:20 states tersely, "Samson's wife was given to his companion." The Bible provides no additional details about this mysterious companion other than to repeat that Samson's wife was given to him in Judges 15:2 and 15:6. Reed develops this nameless companion into a childhood friend of Samson's named Jody. He explains that he chose the name Jody for this character because Jody "is somewhat of a mythical figure in twenty century African American culture . . . a man that has a reputation for knowing how to please your woman while you are away at work. The origins of this character go back to World War II and Vietnam War military cadences about a man named Jody who, while you are out at war, is at home with your wife."[37] While Reed does not engage traditions about Black Samson in other African American literature, he uses elements of African American culture to expand on and retell the biblical story.

One of the most polarizing representations of Black Samson in the twenty-first century to date came in 2013 when the History Channel aired a highly publicized, ten-episode miniseries simply titled *The Bible*.[38] Although the White producers were British (Mark Burnett) and Irish (Roma Downey), the miniseries was heavily promoted in the United States with all the epic flair of a Cecil B. DeMille film. The series was nominated for three Emmy awards, including Outstanding Sound Editing for a Miniseries, Movie, or a Special; Outstanding Miniseries or Movie; and Outstanding Sound Mixing for a Miniseries or a Movie. The third episode, titled "Homeland," directed by a White Canadian named Tony Mitchell, first aired on March 17, 2013. It covered Joshua's conquest of Canaan through the anointing of Saul as king of Israel, material found in the books of Joshua through 1 Samuel. On the night it first aired, 10.9 million people tuned in to watch, making it the most watched show on television that Sunday evening.[39] The segment devoted to Samson in this episode is roughly twenty-five minutes long.

The segment on Samson imagines the biblical hero as seeking to discover God's purpose for his life, although the biblical account does not focus on this issue. Early on in the segment, his mother recounts her encounter with the angel who foretold Samson's birth and mission. She tells Samson, "You must fight them [the Philistines]. It's what God wants you to do Samson. It's why God created you. . . . Your duty is to drive the Philistines away." Until the moment of his death, Samson is conflicted about the course of action that God wants him to take. When the Israelites confront Samson and seek to turn him over to the Philistines (Judges 15:11–13), he turns to his mother and asks, "Mother, is this what God wants?" Foreshadowing the loss of her son's eyesight, she replies, "Sometimes God leads us in ways we cannot see." After Samson escapes Philistine captivity, slaughtering many Philistines in the process, he prays, "Lord is this what you want from me? Guide me please."[40] Finally, when Samson is in the temple of Dagon before a crowd of Philistines, which includes Delilah in the television version, a Philistine leader taunts Samson. Echoing a statement by the biblical narrator in Judges 16:20, he tells Samson, "Your god has deserted you and taken your strength with him." Samson declares, "No. I can see him more clearly than ever. He wants me to destroy you all!" Moments later, Samson brings down the temple, killing himself, Delilah, and the crowd of Philistines. The segment ends with Samson's mother sobbing as she finds her son's body buried in the rubble.

A disclaimer at the beginning of each episode of *The Bible* miniseries states: "This program is an adaption of Bible stories. It endeavors to stay true to the spirit of the book. Some scenes contain violence. Viewer discretion is advised." The extremely violent segment on Samson contains notable differences with the biblical text, staying true to little more than "the spirit of the book." This abbreviated version contains no mention of Manoah, Samson's father (Judges 13:2). Among other missing details, there is no mention of Samson's battle with the lion (Judges 14:5–9) or his riddle to the Philistines (Judges 14:12–19), although his wedding is included. Samson's nocturnal rendezvous with a prostitute in Gaza (Judges 16:1–3), and the first three attempts of Delilah, played by the English actress Kierston Wareing, to discover the source of Samson's strength prior to the haircut are left out (Judges 16:6–14). Also, the episode makes noticeable changes to the biblical story. In the Bible, God provides the water for Samson to drink after Samson slaughters a thousand Philistines with a jawbone at Lehi (Judges 15:19). In the television version, Delilah provides him with a jug of water after his victory. Finally, there is a scene that does not appear in the Bible in which Samson frees captured Israelites from a Philistine prison. In the biblical text, Samson never fights directly on behalf of his people.

The Samson segment sparked controversy regarding its accuracy soon after it first aired but not because viewers questioned whether it stayed true to the spirit of the book as the disclaimer stated. Neither did the casting of actors of White European descent for the overwhelming majority of the main characters throughout the miniseries provoke much controversy regarding its historical accuracy. Nor was there much discussion of the casting of Terence Maynard, a lighter-skinned English actor of African descent, as the angelic commander of the Lord's army who appears to Joshua earlier in the "Homeland" episode (Joshua 5:13–15). The main controversy over the alleged accuracy of the episode focused on the casting of a dark-skinned British actor of African descent named Nonso Anozie to play the role of Samson.[41] On social media and other online platforms, many commentators remarked upon this choice. Blogger S. Michael Houdmann argued that Samson was Semitic and not African. Therefore, he concluded that "the true, historical Samson would not have been black."[42] Similarly, writer Mary Fairchild argued that Samson would not have been dark skinned but claimed that Samson's dreadlocks were accurate.[43] On her blog, biblical scholar Wil Gafney critiqued the miniseries for its choice to cast mostly White actors of European descent as well as its portrayal of Samson as "a big black man with brutish strength and a predilection for white women."[44] The mere inclusion of a Black Samson can generate controversy even when he appears in less overtly political retellings of the biblical story.

Since the mid-nineteen century, visual images of Black Samson have developed in editorial cartoons, film, paintings, comic books, graphic novels, and television alongside traditions about him in American literature and music. Similar to his literary representations, some artists from different racial backgrounds have created Black Samson figures that address various social and political controversies in the United States. From his nineteenth-century appearance in *Harper's Weekly* to his twenty-first-century appearance on the History Channel, visual representations of Black Samson in popular culture have continued to shape Black Samson into a polarizing American icon.

Epilogue

Black Samson, an American Icon

Ain't no Samson never come to no good end.

—Toni Morrison, 1970[1]

This book was written during an era of protest in America. We began research for this project in the fall of 2014, shortly after the protests in Ferguson, Missouri, over the police killing of Michael Brown on August 9, 2014, gained media coverage across the globe. We worked on our manuscript as White supremacists marched openly in the streets, as recorded acts of police brutality went unchecked, as race-baiting politicians gained a national platform, and as rollbacks of civil rights and voting rights continued. It is a period that caused Isabel Wilkerson, a Pulitzer Prize–winning journalist, to posit: "It is as if we have reentered the past and are living in a second nadir."[2] It is in such moments that Americans of earlier generations have invoked Samson. While Moses is often used as a symbol of overcoming racial barriers and of freedom and of liberation, Samson is more heavily associated with directly—and at times violently—confronting issues of race and racism. The American mythology around Samson's complicated life and tragic death addresses messier and less comfortable stories of race in America—stories as urgent today as at any point in American history.

We close with a comment about this book's cover art. The cover image is a sculpture from 1863 titled "Freedman" by a White artist named John Quincy Adams Ward. We did not select the image used for the artwork, and when we saw the cover design, we had some misgivings. We had hoped to have artwork that was based on the story of Samson and created by an African American artist. Yet, as we researched the sculpture, we found that the "freedman" figure was not waiting for others to grant him his freedom.[3] In contrast to popular depictions in abolitionist art and literature of African Americans waiting or pleading for a White savior, Ward's unnamed freedman is not a sentimentalized figure celebrating the moral courage of White abolitionists.[4] In a letter written a few months after the emancipation proclamation, Ward explains his intention for his freedman sculpture.

> I shall send tomorrow or the next day a plaster model of a figure which we call the "Freedman" for want of a better name, but I intend it to express not one set free by any proclamation so much as by his own love of freedom and a conscious power to brake [*sic*] things—the struggle is not over with him (as it never is in this life) yet I have tried to express a degree of hope in his undertaking.[5]

In this sense, Ward's sculpture fits within American Black Samson traditions. Although this was not our intention, the title of our book could serve as a caption for Ward's sculpture since, on the cover, this unnamed freedman becomes labeled as a Black Samson. In some way, our book's cover continues the tradition of identifying as "Black Samson" those who love freedom and are conscious of their power. What Ward wrote about the figure that he sculpted holds true for the subject of our book. Black Samson's struggle is not over, as it never is in this life. Yet, we have tried to express a degree of hope in Black Samson's undertaking by telling the story of this American icon.

Appendix

Most, if not all, of the people discussed in this book who reference the Bible utilize the King James Version of 1611. Thus, for the reader's convenience, this appendix contains the entire biblical story of Samson (Judges 13–16) and the only other biblical reference to Samson in the King James Version, where he is listed among the heroes of faith in Hebrews 11:32.[1]

Judges 13–16 according to the King James Version

Judges 13

1. And the children of Israel did evil again in the sight of the LORD; and the LORD delivered them into the hand of the Philistines forty years.
2. And there was a certain man of Zorah, of the family of the Danites, whose name *was* Manoah; and his wife *was* barren, and bare not.
3. And the angel of the LORD appeared unto the woman, and said unto her, Behold now, thou *art* barren, and bearest not: but thou shalt conceive, and bear a son.
4. Now therefore beware, I pray thee, and drink not wine nor strong drink, and eat not any unclean *thing*:
5. For, lo, thou shalt conceive, and bear a son; and no razor shall come on his head: for the child shall be a Nazarite unto God from the womb: and he shall begin to deliver Israel out of the hand of the Philistines.
6. Then the woman came and told her husband, saying, A man of God came unto me, and his countenance *was* like the countenance of an angel of God, very terrible: but I asked him not whence he *was*, neither told he me his name:
7. But he said unto me, Behold, thou shalt conceive, and bear a son; and now drink no wine nor strong drink, neither eat any unclean *thing*: for the child shall be a Nazarite to God from the womb to the day of his death.
8. Then Manoah intreated the LORD, and said, O my Lord, let the man of God which thou didst send come again unto us, and teach us what we shall do unto the child that shall be born.
9. And God hearkened to the voice of Manoah; and the angel of God came again unto the woman as she sat in the field: but Manoah her husband *was* not with her.
10. And the woman made haste, and ran, and shewed her husband, and said unto him, Behold, the man hath appeared unto me, that came unto me the *other* day.
11. And Manoah arose, and went after his wife, and came to the man, and said unto him, *Art* thou the man that spakest unto the woman? And he said, I *am*.
12. And Manoah said, Now let thy words come to pass. How shall we order the child, and *how* shall we do unto him?
13. And the angel of the LORD said unto Manoah, Of all that I said unto the woman let her beware.
14. She may not eat of any *thing* that cometh of the vine, neither let her drink wine or strong drink, nor eat any unclean *thing*: all that I commanded her let her observe.
15. And Manoah said unto the angel of the LORD, I pray thee, let us detain thee, until we shall have made ready a kid for thee.

16 And the angel of the LORD said unto Manoah, Though thou detain me, I will not eat of thy bread: and if thou wilt offer a burnt offering, thou must offer it unto the LORD. For Manoah knew not that he *was* an angel of the LORD.

17 And Manoah said unto the angel of the LORD, What *is* thy name, that when thy sayings come to pass we may do thee honour?

18 And the angel of the LORD said unto him, Why askest thou thus after my name, seeing it *is* secret?

19 So Manoah took a kid with a meat offering, and offered *it* upon a rock unto the LORD: and *the angel* did wondrously; and Manoah and his wife looked on.

20 For it came to pass, when the flame went up toward heaven from off the altar, that the angel of the LORD ascended in the flame of the altar. And Manoah and his wife looked on *it*, and fell on their faces to the ground.

21 But the angel of the LORD did no more appear to Manoah and to his wife. Then Manoah knew that he *was* an angel of the LORD.

22 And Manoah said unto his wife, We shall surely die, because we have seen God.

23 But his wife said unto him, If the LORD were pleased to kill us, he would not have received a burnt offering and a meat offering at our hands, neither would he have shewed us all these *things*, nor would as at this time have told us *such things* as these.

24 And the woman bare a son, and called his name Samson: and the child grew, and the LORD blessed him.

25 And the Spirit of the LORD began to move him at times in the camp of Dan between Zorah and Eshtaol.

Judges 14

1 And Samson went down to Timnath, and saw a woman in Timnath of the daughters of the Philistines.

2 And he came up, and told his father and his mother, and said, I have seen a woman in Timnath of the daughters of the Philistines: now therefore get her for me to wife.

3 Then his father and his mother said unto him, *Is there* never a woman among the daughters of thy brethren, or among all my people, that thou goest to take a wife of the uncircumcised Philistines? And Samson said unto his father, Get her for me; for she pleaseth me well.

4 But his father and his mother knew not that it *was* of the LORD, that he sought an occasion against the Philistines: for at that time the Philistines had dominion over Israel.

5 Then went Samson down, and his father and his mother, to Timnath, and came to the vineyards of Timnath: and, behold, a young lion roared against him.

6 And the Spirit of the LORD came mightily upon him, and he rent him as he would have rent a kid, and *he had* nothing in his hand: but he told not his father or his mother what he had done.

7 And he went down, and talked with the woman; and she pleased Samson well.

8 And after a time he returned to take her, and he turned aside to see the carcase of the lion: and, behold, *there was* a swarm of bees and honey in the carcase of the lion.

9 And he took thereof in his hands, and went on eating, and came to his father and mother, and he gave them, and they did eat: but he told not them that he had taken the honey out of the carcase of the lion.

¹⁰   So his father went down unto the woman: and Samson made there a feast; for so used the young men to do.

¹¹   And it came to pass, when they saw him, that they brought thirty companions to be with him.

¹²   And Samson said unto them, I will now put forth a riddle unto you: if ye can certainly declare it me within the seven days of the feast, and find *it* out, then I will give you thirty sheets and thirty change of garments:

¹³   But if ye cannot declare *it* me, then shall ye give me thirty sheets and thirty change of garments. And they said unto him, Put forth thy riddle, that we may hear it.

¹⁴   And he said unto them, Out of the eater came forth meat, and out of the strong came forth sweetness. And they could not in three days expound the riddle.

¹⁵   And it came to pass on the seventh day, that they said unto Samson's wife, Entice thy husband, that he may declare unto us the riddle, lest we burn thee and thy father's house with fire: have ye called us to take that we have? *is it* not *so*?

¹⁶   And Samson's wife wept before him, and said, Thou dost but hate me, and lovest me not: thou hast put forth a riddle unto the children of my people, and hast not told *it* me. And he said unto her, Behold, I have not told *it* my father nor my mother, and shall I tell *it* thee?

¹⁷   And she wept before him the seven days, while their feast lasted: and it came to pass on the seventh day, that he told her, because she lay sore upon him: and she told the riddle to the children of her people.

¹⁸   And the men of the city said unto him on the seventh day before the sun went down, What *is* sweeter than honey? and what *is* stronger than a lion? And he said unto them, If ye had not plowed with my heifer, ye had not found out my riddle.

¹⁹   And the Spirit of the LORD came upon him, and he went down to Ashkelon, and slew thirty men of them, and took their spoil, and gave change of garments unto them which expounded the riddle. And his anger was kindled, and he went up to his father's house.

²⁰   But Samson's wife was *given* to his companion, whom he had used as his friend.

Judges 15

¹   But it came to pass within a while after, in the time of wheat harvest, that Samson visited his wife with a kid; and he said, I will go in to my wife into the chamber. But her father would not suffer him to go in.

²   And her father said, I verily thought that thou hadst utterly hated her; therefore I gave her to thy companion: *is* not her younger sister fairer than she? take her, I pray thee, instead of her.

³   And Samson said concerning them, Now shall I be more blameless than the Philistines, though I do them a displeasure.

⁴   And Samson went and caught three hundred foxes, and took firebrands, and turned tail to tail, and put a firebrand in the midst between two tails.

⁵   And when he had set the brands on fire, he let *them* go into the standing corn of the Philistines, and burnt up both the shocks, and also the standing corn, with the vineyards *and* olives.

⁶   Then the Philistines said, Who hath done this? And they answered, Samson, the son in law of the Timnite, because he had taken his wife, and given her to his companion. And the Philistines came up, and burnt her and her father with fire.

7   And Samson said unto them, Though ye have done this, yet will I be avenged of you, and after that I will cease.

8   And he smote them hip and thigh with a great slaughter: and he went down and dwelt in the top of the rock Etam.

9   Then the Philistines went up, and pitched in Judah, and spread themselves in Lehi.

10 And the men of Judah said, Why are ye come up against us? And they answered, To bind Samson are we come up, to do to him as he hath done to us.

11 Then three thousand men of Judah went to the top of the rock Etam, and said to Samson, Knowest thou not that the Philistines *are* rulers over us? what *is* this *that* thou hast done unto us? And he said unto them, As they did unto me, so have I done unto them.

12 And they said unto him, We are come down to bind thee, that we may deliver thee into the hand of the Philistines. And Samson said unto them, Swear unto me, that ye will not fall upon me yourselves.

13 And they spake unto him, saying, No; but we will bind thee fast, and deliver thee into their hand: but surely we will not kill thee. And they bound him with two new cords, and brought him up from the rock.

14 *And* when he came unto Lehi, the Philistines shouted against him: and the Spirit of the LORD came mightily upon him, and the cords that *were* upon his arms became as flax that was burnt with fire, and his bands loosed from off his hands.

15 And he found a new jawbone of an ass, and put forth his hand, and took it, and slew a thousand men therewith.

16 And Samson said, With the jawbone of an ass, heaps upon heaps, with the jaw of an ass have I slain a thousand men.

17 And it came to pass, when he had made an end of speaking, that he cast away the jawbone out of his hand, and called that place Ramathlehi.

18 And he was sore athirst, and called on the LORD, and said, Thou hast given this great deliverance into the hand of thy servant: and now shall I die for thirst, and fall into the hand of the uncircumcised?

19 But God clave an hollow place that *was* in the jaw, and there came water thereout; and when he had drunk, his spirit came again, and he revived: wherefore he called the name thereof Enhakkore, which *is* in Lehi unto this day.

20 And he judged Israel in the days of the Philistines twenty years.

Judges 16

1   Then went Samson to Gaza, and saw there an harlot, and went in unto her.

2   *And it was told* the Gazites, saying, Samson is come hither. And they compassed *him* in, and laid wait for him all night in the gate of the city, and were quiet all the night, saying, In the morning, when it is day, we shall kill him.

3   And Samson lay till midnight, and arose at midnight, and took the doors of the gate of the city, and the two posts, and went away with them, bar and all, and put *them* upon his shoulders, and carried them up to the top of an hill that *is* before Hebron.

4   And it came to pass afterward, that he loved a woman in the valley of Sorek, whose name *was* Delilah.

5   And the lords of the Philistines came up unto her, and said unto her, Entice him, and see wherein his great strength *lieth*, and by what *means* we may prevail against

him, that we may bind him to afflict him: and we will give thee every one of us eleven hundred *pieces* of silver.

6   And Delilah said to Samson, Tell me, I pray thee, wherein thy great strength *lieth*, and wherewith thou mightest be bound to afflict thee.

7   And Samson said unto her, If they bind me with seven green withs that were never dried, then shall I be weak, and be as another man.

8   Then the lords of the Philistines brought up to her seven green withs which had not been dried, and she bound him with them.

9   Now *there were* men lying in wait, abiding with her in the chamber. And she said unto him, The Philistines *be* upon thee, Samson. And he brake the withs, as a thread of tow is broken when it toucheth the fire. So his strength was not known.

10   And Delilah said unto Samson, Behold, thou hast mocked me, and told me lies: now tell me, I pray thee, wherewith thou mightest be bound.

11   And he said unto her, If they bind me fast with new ropes that never were occupied, then shall I be weak, and be as another man.

12   Delilah therefore took new ropes, and bound him therewith, and said unto him, The Philistines *be* upon thee, Samson. And *there were* liers in wait abiding in the chamber. And he brake them from off his arms like a thread.

13   And Delilah said unto Samson, Hitherto thou hast mocked me, and told me lies: tell me wherewith thou mightest be bound. And he said unto her, If thou weavest the seven locks of my head with the web.

14   And she fastened *it* with the pin, and said unto him, The Philistines *be* upon thee, Samson. And he awaked out of his sleep, and went away with the pin of the beam, and with the web.

15   And she said unto him, How canst thou say, I love thee, when thine heart *is* not with me? thou hast mocked me these three times, and hast not told me wherein thy great strength *lieth*.

16   And it came to pass, when she pressed him daily with her words, and urged him, *so* that his soul was vexed unto death;

17   That he told her all his heart, and said unto her, There hath not come a razor upon mine head; for I *have been* a Nazarite unto God from my mother's womb: if I be shaven, then my strength will go from me, and I shall become weak, and be like any *other* man.

18   And when Delilah saw that he had told her all his heart, she sent and called for the lords of the Philistines, saying, Come up this once, for he hath shewed me all his heart. Then the lords of the Philistines came up unto her, and brought money in their hand.

19   And she made him sleep upon her knees; and she called for a man, and she caused him to shave off the seven locks of his head; and she began to afflict him, and his strength went from him.

20   And she said, The Philistines *be* upon thee, Samson. And he awoke out of his sleep, and said, I will go out as at other times before, and shake myself. And he wist not that the LORD was departed from him.

21   But the Philistines took him, and put out his eyes, and brought him down to Gaza, and bound him with fetters of brass; and he did grind in the prison house.

22   Howbeit the hair of his head began to grow again after he was shaven.

23   Then the lords of the Philistines gathered them together for to offer a great sacrifice unto Dagon their god, and to rejoice: for they said, Our god hath delivered Samson our enemy into our hand.

24   And when the people saw him, they praised their god: for they said, Our god hath delivered into our hands our enemy, and the destroyer of our country, which slew many of us.

25   And it came to pass, when their hearts were merry, that they said, Call for Samson, that he may make us sport. And they called for Samson out of the prison house; and he made them sport: and they set him between the pillars.

26   And Samson said unto the lad that held him by the hand, Suffer me that I may feel the pillars whereupon the house standeth, that I may lean upon them.

27   Now the house was full of men and women; and all the lords of the Philistines *were* there; and *there were* upon the roof about three thousand men and women, that beheld while Samson made sport.

28   And Samson called unto the LORD, and said, O Lord GOD, remember me, I pray thee, and strengthen me, I pray thee, only this once, O God, that I may be at once avenged of the Philistines for my two eyes.

29   And Samson took hold of the two middle pillars upon which the house stood, and on which it was borne up, of the one with his right hand, and of the other with his left.

30   And Samson said, Let me die with the Philistines. And he bowed himself with *all his* might; and the house fell upon the lords, and upon all the people that *were* therein. So the dead which he slew at his death were more than *they* which he slew in his life.

31   Then his brethren and all the house of his father came down, and took him, and brought *him* up, and buried him between Zorah and Eshtaol in the buryingplace of Manoah his father. And he judged Israel twenty years.

Hebrew 11:32–34 according to the King James Version

32   And what shall I more say? for the time would fail me to tell of Gedeon, and of Barak, and of Samson, and of Jephthae; of David also, and Samuel, and of the prophets:

33   Who through faith subdued kingdoms, wrought righteousness, obtained promises, stopped the mouths of lions,

34   Quenched the violence of fire, escaped the edge of the sword, out of weakness were made strong, waxed valiant in fight, turned to flight the armies of the aliens.

Notes

Introduction

1. Marcus Garvey, "The Future as I See It," in *The Philosophy and Opinions of Marcus Garvey or, Africa for the Africans* (compiled by Amy Jacques Garvey; Dover, MA: The Majority Press, 1986), 77.

2. Recent examples of scholarship on Samson in reception history include Erik Eynikel and Tobias Nicklas, *Samson: Hero or Fool?: The Many Faces of Samson*, Themes in Biblical Narrative: Jewish and Christian Traditions, 17 (Leiden: Brill, 2014); David Gunn, *Judges*, Blackwell Bible Commentaries (Oxford: Blackwell, 2005); Caroline Vander Stichele and Hugh S. Pyper, eds., *Text, Image, and Otherness in Children's Bibles: What's in the Picture?* (Atlanta: Society of Biblical Literature, 2012). These scholars, who are representative of those working in reception history, focus on White European and American representations of Samson.

3. Samson is not a popular figure in African American biblical scholarship. Consult, among the many other examples, Randall C. Bailey, ed., *Yet with a Steady Beat: Contemporary U.S. Afrocentric Biblical Interpretation* (Atlanta: Society of Biblical Literature, 2003); Allen Dwight Callahan, *The Talking Book: African Americans and the Bible* (New Haven: Yale University Press, 2006); Cain Hope Felder, ed., *Stony the Road We Trod: African-American Biblical Interpretation* (Minneapolis: Fortress Press, 1991); Emerson B. Powery and Rodney S. Sadler, Jr., *The Genesis of Liberation: Biblical Interpretation in the Antebellum Narratives of the Enslaved* (Louisville: Westminster John Knox Press, 2016); Vincent L. Wimbush, ed., *African Americans and the Bible: Sacred Texts and Social Textures* (New York: Continuum, 2000).

4. To be clear, this book does not provide a history of African American religions. For a recent study of the history of African American religions, consult Sylvester A. Johnson, *African American Religions, 1500–2000: Colonialism, Democracy, and Freedom* (New York: Cambridge University Press, 2015); for a study focusing on the early twentieth century, consult Judith Weisenfeld, *New World A-Coming: Black Religion and Racial Identity during the Great Migration* (New York: New York University Press, 2017). On the influence of religion in twentieth-century African American literature, consult Josef Sorett, *Spirit in the Dark: A Religious History of Racial Aesthetics* (New York: Oxford University Press, 2016).

5. This is not to say that uses of the Black Samson figure were limited to the United States. For example, on racialized interpretations of Samson primarily from Jamaica, consult Ariella Y. Werden-Greenfeild, "Warriors and Prophets of Livity: Samson and Moses as Moral Exemplars in Rastafari" (PhD dissertation, Temple University, 2016). On the use of Black Samson imagery in Black labor publications in South Africa in

the 1920s, consult the cartoon and the brief discussion in Victoria J. Collins, "Anxious Records: Race, Imperial Belonging, and the Black Literary Imagination, 1900–1946" (PhD dissertation, Columbia University, 2013), 198–99. By comparison, consult chapter 4 of this book for a discussion of Black Samson imagery in debates over race and labor in the United States during the same time period.

6. The appendix provides a complete list of biblical texts mentioning Samson. Unless otherwise specified, the biblical quotations throughout this book use the King James Version because nearly all of the writers that we discuss use that version.

7. This book focuses on racialized representations of Samson in American literature and art. It does not address questions about whether the Samson from the Bible ever existed or whether representations of the biblical character in literature and art accurately reflect any commonplace physical features among ancient Israelites. Thus, this book does not entertain questions regarding Samson's possible physical features if he had been an actual person.

8. That most of Samson's life involved ethnic conflicts with the Philistines does not explain why his story was interpreted along racial lines. After all, the Bible provides far more extensive and detailed accounts of David's battles with the Philistines in the books of Samuel and Chronicles.

9. Reprinted in William Hand Browne, *Archives of Maryland: Proceedings of the Council of Maryland, 1732–1753* (Baltimore: Maryland Historical Society, 1908), 137.

10. Reprinted in Terry W. Lipscomb, ed., *Journal of the Commons House of Assembly of South Carolina, November 21, 1752–September 6, 1754* (Columbia: University of South Carolina Press, 1983), 333.

11. Reprinted in George H. Reese, ed., *Journal of the Council of the State of Virginia, Vol. IV (December 1, 1786–November 10, 1788)* (Richmond: Virginia State Library, 1967), 210.

12. Absalom Jones and Richard Allen, *A Narrative of the Proceedings of the Black People, during the Late Awful Calamity in Philadelphia, in the Year 1793: And a Refutation of Some Censures, Thrown upon Them in Some Late Publications* (Philadelphia: William W. Woodward, at Franklin's Head, 1794), 11.

13. This is not to say that slaveholders were the only ones to give such names to enslaved persons of African descent. For example, enslaved parents also gave their children biblical names.

14. On this topic, consult Nyasha Junior, *Reimaging Hagar: Blackness and Bible* (New York: Oxford University Press, 2019).

15. Brace told his story to Benjamin Prentiss, a White lawyer. When Brace met Prentiss, Brace was living in Vermont, the first state to make slavery illegal, but years earlier, he was captured from West Africa, shipped to Barbados, and eventually taken to Connecticut where he was enslaved by the Stiles family in Woodbury, Connecticut.

16. Kari J. Winter, ed., *The Blind African Slave, or, Memoirs of Boyrereau Brinch, Nicknamed Jeffrey Brace* (Madison: University of Wisconsin Press, 2004), 159. Originally published as *The Blind African Slave, or, Memoirs of Boyrereau Brinch, Nicknamed Jeffrey Brace* (transcribed with commentary by Benjamin F. Prentiss; St. Albans, VT: Harry Whitney, 1810).

17. Although Samson is often remembered as a martyr, a desire for revenge fuels many of Samson's attacks against the Philistines more than a concern for the freedom of his fellow Israelites. In Judges 15:7–8, he swears revenge against the Philistines after they kill his wife and her household: "And Samson said unto them, Though ye have done this, yet will I be avenged of you, and after that I will cease. And he smote them hip and thigh with a great slaughter." When Samson's fellow Israelites question the wisdom of his actions, he indicates that vengeance was his primary motivation: "Three thousand men of Judah went to the top of the rock Etam, and said to Samson, Knowest thou not that the Philistines are rulers over us? what is this that thou hast done unto us? And he said unto them, As they did unto me, so have I done unto them" (Judges 15:11). Finally, in Judges 16:28, as Samson leans on the pillars in the Philistine temple of Dagon in his final moments of life, he cries out to be avenged of the Philistines for his eyes.

18. Although scholars have debated the scope and details of the plan, allegedly Vesey planned to kill slaveholders, liberate enslaved persons in Charleston, and escape to Haiti. For a detailed treatment of Vesey's life, death, and its aftermath, consult Douglas R. Egerton, *He Shall Go Out Free: The Lives of Denmark Vesey,* revised and updated edition (Lanham, MD: Rowman and Littlefield, 2004).

19. These texts include Exodus 21:16 ("And he that stealeth a man, and selleth him, or if he be found in his hand, he shall surely be put to death") among other texts (e.g., Exodus 1; Joshua 6:21; Isaiah 19; Zechariah 14:1–3). For a discussion of biblical references in the trial of Denmark Vesey, consult Jeremy Schipper, *Denmark Vesey's Bible* (Princeton: Princeton University Press, forthcoming); Jeremy Schipper, "'Misconstruction of the Sacred Page': On Denmark Vesey's Biblical Interpretations," *Journal of Biblical Literature* 138 (2019): 23–38; Jeremy Schipper, "'On Such Texts Comment Is Unnecessary': Biblical Interpretation in the Trial of Denmark Vesey," *Journal of the American Academy of Religion* 85 (2017): 1032–49.

20. For the full text of this letter, consult Douglas R. Egerton and Robert L. Paquette, eds., *The Denmark Vesey Affair: A Documentary History* (Gainesville: University of Florida Press, 2017), 376–81.

21. Phillis Wheatley was a formerly enslaved woman who became a celebrated author. Wheatley's 1773 volume *Poems on Various Subjects, Religious and Moral* was the first book of poetry published by an African American. In 1834, fifty years after Wheatley's death in 1784, Margaretta Matilda Odell edited a collection of Wheatley's poetry that includes a brief biography of Wheatley and an introduction. Margaretta Matilda Odell, ed., *Memoir and Poems, a Native African and a Slave* (Boston: George W. Light, 1834). By 1838, Odell's book was already in its third edition. The 1838 edition includes *Poems by a Slave*, written by George Moses Horton, another formerly enslaved person.

22. Odell, *Memoir and Poems of Phillis Wheatley*, vi–vii.

23. Samson was not always associated with resistance in early nineteenth-century literature about slavery. In 1838, James Williams published an autobiographical account of his life as an enslaved man on a plantation in Alabama, where he witnessed the degrading behavior of enslaved persons forced to entertain their slaveholders. Williams

compares this behavior to Samson's entertainment of the Philistines when "they called for Samson out of the prison house; and he made them sport" (Judges 16:25). James wrote, "On almost every plantation at the South you may find one or more individuals whose look and air show that they have preserved their self-respect as *men*;—that with them the power of the tyrant ends with the coercion of the body—that the soul is free, and the inner man retaining the original uprightness of the image of God. You may know them by the stern sobriety of their countenances, and the contempt with which they regard the jests and pastimes of their miserable and degraded companions, who, like Samson, make sport for the keepers of their prison-house." James Williams, *Narrative of James Williams, an American Slave, Who Was for Several Years a Driver on a Cotton Plantation in Alabama* (Boston: American Anti-Slavery Society, 1838), 53–54 (emphasis in the original). In this passage, Williams does not associate Samson with the rare individual whose spirit cannot be broken by slavery. Instead, he links Samson with enslaved people who cannot or do not resist the degradation of slavery.

24. As some were skeptical about whether enslaved or formerly enslaved African Americans could produce narratives or poetry, their publications often included letters of endorsement meant to authenticate the work's legitimacy. Consult the brief discussion in Henry Louis Gates, Jr. and Nellie Y. McKay, eds., *The Norton Anthology of African American Literature*, 2nd ed. (New York: W. W. Norton, 2004), 214.

25. Austin Steward, *Twenty-Two Years a Slave, and Forty Years a Freeman; Embracing a Correspondence of Several Years, While President of Wilberforce Colony, London, Canada West* (Rochester: William Alling, 1857), vi.

26. In the 1850s and 1860s, tours of the southern states by White journalists living in the North or Midwest were not uncommon. For representative examples, consult Horace Cowler Atwater, *Incidents of a Southern Tour: Or The South, as Seen with Northern Eyes* (Boston: J. P. Magee, 1857); John Richard Dennett, "The South As It Is: 1865–1866," serialized in *The Nation* 1–2 (July 1865 to April 1866); Whitelaw Reid, *After the War: A Southern Tour (May 1, 1865 to May 1, 1866)* (London: Samson Low, Son, and Marston, 1866).

27. James Redpath, *Roving Editor: Or, Talks with Slaves in Southern States* (New York: A. B. Burdick, 1859), 245–54.

28. Redpath, *Roving Editor*, 254. The poem's description of enslaved persons in the South as "Black Samson, dumb and bound" also occurs in an April 27, 1861, editorial from the African American newspaper, *Weekly Anglo African*. The editorial calls for free African Americans in the North to support the cause of enslaved people of African descent in the South. The unidentified author writes, "The free colored Americans cannot be indifferent to the progress of this struggle. . . . Not alone are the free colored Americans involved in the contest, but their action in the Free States will be representative. They speak for the voiceless. They stand for dumb and bound Black Samson." "Have We a War Policy?" *Weekly Anglo African* (April 27, 1861): n.p.

29. John Townsend Trowbridge, *The South: A Tour of Its Battlefields and Ruined Cities, a Journey through the Desolated States, and Talks with the People: Being a Description of*

the Present State of the Country—Its Agriculture—Railroads—Business and Finances (Hartford, CT: L. Stebbins, 1866), 183.

30. Albion W. Tourgée, *Bricks without Straw: A Novel* (New York: Fords, Howard and Hulbert, 1880), 31, 55, 312. *Plessy v. Ferguson* was an 1896 Supreme Court case in which Homer Plessy, who was mixed race, challenged a law that required him to sit in segregated seating while on the train. The Court upheld racial segregation in public places under the policy of supposedly "separate but equal" accommodations. Eventually, the ruling was overturned in the 1954 Supreme Court decision in *Brown v. Board of Education*, which involved the lack of equality in segregated public schools.

31. Timothy Thomas Fortune, *Black and White: Land, Labor, and Politics in the South* (New York: Fords, Howard, and Hulbert, 1884), 133.

32. William Henry Crogman, "The Negro Problem," in William Henry Crogman, *Talks for the Times* (South Atlanta, GA: Franklin, 1896), 241–69.

33. Crogman, "The Negro Problem," 262. In 1988, Clark University (formerly Clark College) and Atlanta University merged to form Clark Atlanta University, a private, historically Black university. The school should not be confused with the Clark University currently in Worcester, Massachusetts.

34. Library of Congress, Thirteenth Amendment to the US Constitution, https://www. loc.gov/rr/program/bib/ourdocs/13thamendment.html#American. While the Thirteenth Amendment is commonly understood as prohibiting slavery, it does so "except as a punishment for crime whereof the party shall have been duly convicted." Consult the documentary film *13th*, directed by Ava DuVernay, which addresses issues related to mass incarceration in the United States. Internet Movie Database, *13th*, http://www.imdb.com/title/tt5895028/.

35. Crogman, "The Negro Problem," 262.

36. For example, consult Rev. W. H. Hickman, "Black Samson and the American Republic," *Manual of the Methodist Episcopal Church* 8 (1888): 76.

37. "Dr. Thirkeild Delivered a Lecture on the 'Black Samson,'" *Savannah Tribune* 14.34 (June 3, 1899): 2. Thirkeild also gave an address titled "The Black Samson: His Freedom and His Future" (cited in the program for the Cincinnati Camp Meeting Association in 1900 in "Editorial Notes," *Western Christian Advocate* 67 [October 24, 1900]: 1346). Thirkeild also delivered a sermon titled "The Black Sampson" on July 12, 1902 (cited in the program for the Cincinnati Camp Meeting Association in *Western Christian Advocate* 68 [July 2, 1902]: 31).

38. "A 20th Century Negro: Will the Negro of that Century be an Improvement as Compared with a Negro of this Day and Generation? Let's Hope So," *Plain Dealer* 1.33 (August 18, 1899): 1. The saying "a lion in the way" is a partial quotation of Proverbs 26:13 ("The slothful man saith, There is a lion in the way; a lion is in the streets"). It refers to an excuse for inaction because of an imagined or greatly exaggerated danger. The author may also be influenced by Henry Wadsworth Longellow's poem "The Warning," which describes how Samson tore apart "the lion in his path." We discuss Longfellow's poem in chapter 1. The article invokes images from two episodes in the biblical story of Samson. The first takes place when he tears apart a lion, the "king of

the forest," with his bare hands (Judges 14:8–9). The second episode happens when he uses the jawbone of an ass to kill one thousand Philistines (Judges 15:15).

39. "Black Sampson—Fall of the Chair Factory Ruins," *The Baltimore Sun* (May 15, 1874): 1.

40. Henry Downes Miles, *Pugilistica: The History of British Boxing Containing Lives of the Most Celebrated Pugilists; Full Reports of Their Battles from Contemporary Newspapers, with Authentic Portraits, Personal Anecdotes, and Sketches of the Principal Patrons of the Prize Ring, Forming a Complete History of the Ring from Fig and Broughton, 1719– 40, to the Last Championship Battle between King and Heenan, in December 1863*, 3 vols. (London: Weldon, 1880), 1:285. The spelling "Dalilahs" follows the original. In Roman mythology, Bacchus and Venus are deities associated with winemaking and love, respectively. Molineaux was born into slavery in Virginia in 1784 but fought primarily in England and Ireland after gaining his freedom. He unsuccessfully challenged the champion Tom Cribb for the English title in 1810 and then again in 1811.

41. "Marvels of Strength: 'Jimmy' Golden Is Called the 'Black Samson,'" *Boston Daily Globe* (July 4, 1908): 8.

42. Johnson won the heavyweight title on December 26, 1908, by defeating the White champion Tommy Burns in Sydney, Australia. On July 4, 1910, in Reno, Nevada, Johnson defended his title against Jeffries, who had retired undefeated six years earlier, in what was promoted as "The Fight of the Century." When Jeffries came out of retirement for the title fight, some hailed him as the "Great White Hope" who would defeat Johnson and reclaim the title for the White race. Yet, by the fifteenth round, Jeffries's corner threw in the towel. Johnson had resoundingly defeated his White opponent. Across the nation, the film of the fight was banned from theaters and widespread violence against African Americans ensued. Consult Geoffrey C. Ward, *Unforgiveable Blackness: The Rise and Fall of Jack Johnson* (New York: Knopf, 2004). Also, consult *Unforgiveable Blackness: The Rise and Fall of Jack Johnson*, directed by Ken Burns (Public Broadcasting Service, 2005), https://www.pbs.org/kenburns/unforgivable-blackness/.

43. Reprinted in "Views of the Afro-American Press on the Johnson-Jeffries Fight," *Baltimore Afro-American* (July 16, 1910): 4.

44. Among other examples, consult "John Arthur Johnson Still Holds the Championship Belt of the World," *Broad Ax* (July 9, 1910): 1; Dr. M. A. Majors, "Jack Johnson Is Crucified for His Race," *Chicago Defender* (July 5, 1913): 1. In a 1917 poem, the White American poet Vachel Lindsay linked Johnson with Samson. He wrote, "The bold Jack Johnson Israelite,—Samson—The Judge, The Nazarite." Vachel Lindsay, "How Samson Bore Away the Gates of Gaza (A Negro Sermon)," in Vachel Lindsay, *The Chinese Nightingale and Other Poems* (New York: Macmillan, 1917), 124. In addition to Johnson's physical prowess, the press and the public also compared Johnson to Samson due to what some regarded as an excessive lifestyle. Known for his outspoken courage and pride, he raced fast cars, bought expensive clothes, and married three different White women, which was considered especially taboo at the time (consult Majors, "Jack Johnson Is Crucified for His Race," 1). An article in the *Philadelphia Tribune* stated that Johnson "was the architect of his own making and

his own undoing. No braver man ever faced [a] host of enemies than he did in Reno and Havana. . . . But he dragged himself down by all his excesses, and like the Israelite Samson, helped to drag his people down with him" ("Jack Johnson Still Nagged by White Hopes," *Philadelphia Tribune* [August 7, 1915]: 4). This article compares Johnson with Samson but contends that he has harmed his own people rather than just the Philistines (Judges 15:11).

45. "Black Sampson," *Broad Ax* (October 15, 1921): 2.

Chapter 1

1. Juliet M. Bradford, "Trinity of Slavery Poets," *The Colored American Magazine* (July 1, 1909): 27.
2. Quoted in W. T. Sherwin, *Memoirs of the Life of Thomas Paine, with Observations on His Writings, Critical and Explanatory. To Which Is Added, an Appendix, Containing Several of Mr. Paine's Unpublished Pieces* (London: R. Carlile, 1819), 260–61. Paine's poem shares suspicious similarities with Phillis Wheatley's poem "To His Excellency, George Washington" (1775), which Paine published in the *Pennsylvania Magazine*. Wheatley's poem depicts the arrival of a goddess named Columbia, which was a term used for America since at least 1738. Consult "The State of Affairs in Lilliput," *The Gentlemen's Magazine* 8 (June 1738): 285.
3. Quoted in Joseph B. Varnum, Jr., "The Seat of Government of the United States," *The Merchant's Magazine* 18.2 (February 1848): 145.
4. Odell, *Memoir and Poems of Phillis Wheatley*, vi. Similarly, Wheatley comments on the obvious contradiction of slaveholders who advocate for independence from England. In a letter to Reverend Samson Occum published in 1774, she writes of her desire "to convince them of the strange Absurdity of their Conduct whose Words and Actions are so diametrically, opposite. How well the Cry for Liberty, and the reverse Disposition for the exercise of oppressive Power over others agree,—I humbly think it does not require the Penetration of a Philosopher to determine" (Phillis Wheatley, "Letter to Samson Occum," *The Connecticut Gazette*, March 11, 1774).
5. Abraham Lincoln, "Address before the Young Men's Lyceum of Springfield, Illinois," in *The Collected Works of Abraham Lincoln*, 9 vols. (ed. Roy P. Basler; New York: Abraham Lincoln Association, 1953), 1:113.
6. Lincoln, "Address before the Young Men's Lyceum," 109.
7. Lincoln, "Address before the Young Men's Lyceum," 115.
8. Lincoln, "Address before the Young Men's Lyceum," 115.
9. Henry Wadsworth Longfellow, *Poems on Slavery* (Cambridge: J. Owen, 1842), 30–31. Longfellow's poem contains several of the same images as Odell's introduction to Wheatley's poetry. The similarities between Odell's and Longfellow's work may not be a coincidence. Beginning in 1837, soon after he joined Harvard's faculty, Longfellow lived in the house that served as George Washington's headquarters in Cambridge, Massachusetts. On February 28, 1776, Washington responded to Wheatley's poem, "To His Excellency, George Washington," with an invitation to visit him at this

Cambridge residence. In 1851, a journalist named Benson John Lossing wrote that Wheatley took Washington up on this invitation. He explained, "She passed half an hour with the commander-in-chief" (Benson John Lossing, *Pictorial Field-book of the Revolution; or, Illustrations, by Pencil and Pen, of the History, Biography, Scenery, Relics, and Traditions of the War for Independence* [New York: Harper and Brothers, 1851], 556). Lossing seems to have learned of this alleged meeting during his visit to Washington's residence, which Longfellow occupied at the time. It is possible that Longfellow knew of Wheatley's poetry and Odell's *Memoir and Poetry*.

10. For example, Longfellow's poem "The Quadroon Girl" from the same collection describes the moral conflict that a poor farmer experiences when he sells his mixed-race daughter into slavery. The unsuspecting daughter's smile is described as "holy, meek, and faint, / As lights in some cathedral aisle, / The features of a saint" (Longfellow, *Poems on Slavery*, 29). In "The Slave in the Dismal Swamp," Longfellow portrays an escaped and hunted enslaved man hiding in the swamp.

> A poor old slave, infirm and lame;
>   Great scars deformed his face;
> On his forehead he bore the brand of shame,
> And the rags, that hid his mangled frame,
>   Were the livery of disgrace ...
> On him alone was the doom of pain,
>   From the morning of his birth;
> On him alone the curse of Cain
> Fell, like a flail on the garnered grain,
>   And struck him to the earth! (Longfellow, *Poems on Slavery*, 19, 20).

11. Harriet Beecher Stowe, *Uncle Tom's Cabin; or, Life among the Lowly* (Boston: John P. Jewett, 1852).

12. The letter, dated January 9, 1843, is cited in Christoph Irmscher, *Public Poet, Private Man: Henry Wadsworth Longfellow at 200* (Amherst: University of Massachusetts Press, 2009), 112.

13. Irmscher, *Public Poet, Private Man*, 112.

14. John Kennedy, *The Natural History of Man; or Popular Chapters on Ethnography* (London: J. Cassell, 1851), 143.

15. Wilson Armistead, *The Garland of Freedom; a Collection of Poems, Chiefly Anti-Slavery* (London: W. and F. G. Cash/William Tweedie, 1853), 125.

16. Frederick Douglass, "What to the Slave Is the Fourth of July?: An Address Delivered in Rochester, New York on 5 July 1852," *The Frederick Douglass Papers, Series One: Speeches, Debates, and Interviews*, vol. 2: *1847–54* (ed. John W. Blassingame; New Haven: Yale University Press, 1982), 368 (emphasis added). In the same speech, Douglass quotes directly from Longfellow's poem, "The Psalm of Life" that appears in Henry Wadsworth Longfellow, *Voices of the Night* (Cambridge: John Owen, 1839), 6.

17. "The Moral of Statistics," *The New Englander* 13 (May 1855): 206.

18. Darius Lyman, *Leaven for Doughfaces; or, Threescore and Ten Parables. By a Former Resident of the South* (Cincinnati, OH: Bangs, 1856), 75.

19. Atwater, *Incidents of a Southern Tour*, viii.

20. Quoted in Loring Moody, *The Destruction of Republicanism the Object of the Rebellion: The Testimony of Southern Witnesses* (Boston: Emancipation League, 1863), 14. Toomb's speech may have influenced the rhetoric of other secessionists. After South Carolina voted to leave the Union in December 1860, a man identified as Mr. Calhoun declared, "We have pulled the temple down that has been built for three-quarters of a century. We must now clear the rubbish away and reconstruct another." Consult David Stephen Heidler, *Pulling the Temple Down: The Fire-eaters and the Destruction of the Union* (Mechanicsburg, PA: Stackpole Books, 1994).

21. Untitled editorial reprinted as "Mrs. Harriet Beecher Stowe," *The Principia* 2.45 (September 21, 1861): 770.

22. Although it is uncertain whether Stowe alludes to Longfellow's poem directly, Stowe references Samson in a similar context in her earlier novel, *Dred: A Tale of the Great Dismal Swamp*, 2 vols. (Boston: Phillips, Sampson, 1856). In the novel, Dred, the fictitious titular character, is the precocious son of the historical figure Denmark Vesey. Like his father, Dred preaches retribution against slaveholders in Stowe's novel. Stowe wrote, "He thrilled with fierce joy as he read how Samson, with his two strong arms, pulled down the pillars of the festive temple, and whelmed his triumphant persecutors in one grave with himself" (1:256). Later in the novel, an enslaved mixed-race man named Harry runs a plantation for years and clashes with the cruel slaveholder Thomas Gordon. After years in this position, Harry warns Gordon's lawyer, "Twenty years of faithful service have gone for nothing! . . . I shall fight it out to the last! I've nothing to hope, and nothing to lose. Let him [Gordon] look out! They made sport of Samson,—they put out his eyes,—but he pulled down the temple over their heads, after all! Look out!" (2:144).

23. Frederick Douglass, "The Reason for Our Troubles: Speech on the War Delivered in the National Hall, Philadelphia, January 14, 1862," in *The Life and Writings of Frederick Douglass*, vol. 3: *The Civil War 1861–1865* (ed. Philip S. Foner; New York: International, 1952), 198.

24. The Cookman Institute merged with the Daytona Normal and Industrial Institute and became the Daytona-Cookman Collegiate Institute in 1925. It was the forerunner of Bethune-Cookman University. Consult Bethune-Cookman University: http://www.cookman.edu/about_bcu/history/.

25. S. B. Darnell, "Education an Indispensable Agency in the Redemption of the Negro Race," in *Christian Educators in Council. Sixty Addresses by American Educators; with Historical Notes upon the National Education Assembly, Held at Ocean Grove, N.J. August 9–12, 1883. Also, Illiteracy and Education Tables from Census of 1880* (ed. Joseph Crane Hartzell; New York: Phillips and Hunt, 1883), 65.

26. Darnell, "Education an Indispensable Agency," 65.

27. John Braden, "Educational Work among the Freedman by the Methodist Episcopal Church," in *Christian Educators in Council*, 180.

28. Braden, "Educational Work among the Freedman," 180. Other African American clergy invoked "The Warning" even if they did not quote the poem directly. For example, in a sermon delivered on October 21, 1889, Reverend Johnson, an African American minster at Second Baptist Church in Washington, DC, stated that the

African American "is the blood and bones of the nation, and if undisturbed will do no harm; but if stirred up may grasp the pillars of our civilization and like Samson of old, in his death pull down the temple of liberty" ("Southern Outrages: Baptist Ministers Discuss Them in the Pulpits," *Plaindealer* [October 25, 1889]: 2).

29. The Josie D. Heard African Methodist Episcopal Church is named after her. It is currently located at 4321 Tower Street in Philadelphia.

30. For example, a stanza from her poem, "They are Coming" celebrates African Americans' march toward progress:

> They are coming, they are coming—
> Listen! You will hear the humming
> Of the thousands that are falling into line:
> There are Doctors, Lawyers, Preachers;
> There are Sculptors, Poets, Teachers—
> Men and women, who with honor yet shall shine (Josephine D. [Henderson] Heard, *Morning Glories* [Philadelphia: Publisher unidentified, 1890], 91).

31. Heard, *Morning Glories*, 88–89.

32. In Phillis Wheatley's poem, England, personified as Britannia, is "blind" to Columbia's plight. In part, the poem reads:

> The Goddess comes, she moves divinely fair,
> Olive and laurel binds Her golden hair . . .
> Fix'd are the eyes of nations on the scales,
> For in their hopes Columbia's arm prevails.
> Anon Britannia droops the pensive head,
> While round increase the rising hills of dead.
> Ah! Cruel blindness to Columbia's state!
> Lament thy thirst of boundless power too late.

33. Heard's quotation of Hosea 8:7 ("For they have sown the wind, and they shall reap the whirlwind") lends a divine endorsement to the punishment that awaits Black Samson's oppressors. Longfellow alludes to Hosea 8:7 in a similar manner. On December 2, 1859, the day that John Brown was executed, he wrote in his diary, "This will be a great day in our history, the date of a new Revolution quite as much needed as the old one. Even now as I write, they are leading old John Brown to execution in Virginia, for attempting to rescue slaves! This is sowing the wind to reap the whirlwind, which will come soon" (Samuel Longfellow, ed., *Life of Henry Wadsworth Longfellow: With Extracts from His Journals and Correspondence*, 2 vols. [Boston: Ticknor, 1886], 2:347). We discuss John Brown in detail in chapter 3.

34. Francis Ellen Watkins Harper, *Iola Leroy, or Shadows Uplifted* (Philadelphia: Garrigues, 1892). *Iola Leroy* was once thought to be the first novel published by an African American. Currently, the earliest known novel published by an African American is either *Our Nig, or Sketches from the Life of a Free Black* published anonymously by Harriett E. Wilson in Boston in 1859 or *The Bondswoman's Narrative* written by Hannah Bonds under the pseudonym Hannah Crafts sometime between 1853 and 1861. Consult Hannah Crafts, *The Bondwoman's Narrative* (ed. Henry Louis Gates, Jr.; New York: Time-Warner Books, 2002).

35. Harper, *Iola Leroy, or Shadows Uplifted*, 69–70.

36. Harper, *Iola Leroy, or Shadows Uplifted*, 75.

37. One also finds sentimental depictions of slavery in Harper's poetry. For a representative example, consult Frances Harper, "The Dying Fugitive," *The Anglo African Magazine,* 1 (May 1859): 253–54.

38. Wells-Barnett wrote an editorial published on May 21, 1892, in her Memphis-based newspaper *Free Speech*. Regarding false rape accusations, she explained, "Nobody in this section of the country believes the old thread-bare lie that Negro men rape white women. If Southern white men are not careful, they will overreach themselves and public sentiment will have a reaction; a conclusion will then be reached which will be very damaging to the moral reputation of their women." Cited in Ida B. Wells, *Southern Horrors: Lynch Law in All Its Phases* (New York: New York Age Print, 1892), 3.

39. Wells, *Southern Horrors*, 1, 4.

40. Thomas Nelson Page, *The Negro: The Southerner's Problem* (New York: C. Scribner's Sons, 1904), 111.

41. Page, *The Negro*, 111, 112–13. Allegedly, the gunman who carried out the shooting on June 17, 2015, that killed nine African Americans at the Emanuel African Methodist Episcopal Church in Charleston, South Carolina, had a similar rationale.

42. "The Black Samson," *The Colored American Magazine* 12.4 (April 1, 1907): 251. *The Colored American* may have also printed the poem in response to the racially motivated riots in Atlanta beginning on September 22, 1906. The massacre began after unfounded newspaper reports of alleged sexual assaults of White women by four African American men sparked widespread violence against African Americans. The violence continued until September 24 and resulted in the deaths of at least twenty-five African Americans, although some estimate that the death toll was closer to one hundred. Several African American newspapers printed poetry about what became known as the Atlanta race riot of 1906. For example, George Washington Forbes, a civil rights advocate and editor of African American newspapers in Boston, wrote "Requiem Dirge for Atlanta's Slain." One stanza uses Samson imagery:

    > *Haughtily* speak they of the murdered dead /
    > Not deeming them worth more than passing mention; /
    > Yet Sampson's Temple on his captor's head / '
    > Mid mocking thundered down an inattention.

    George Washington Forbes, "Requiem Dirge for Atlanta's Slain." Reprinted in Jesse Max Barber, "The Atlanta Tragedy," *The Voice of the Negro* (November 1906): 479 (emphasis in the original).

43. "Report of UNIA Meeting," in *The Marcus Garvey and Universal Negro Improvement Association Papers*, vol. 2: *27 August 1919–31 August 1920* (ed. Robert Abraham Hill; Berkeley: University of California Press, 1983), 311.

44. "Report of the UNIA Delegation to Liberia," in *The Marcus Garvey and Universal Negro Improvement Association Papers*, vol. 10: *Africa for the Africans, 1923–1945* (ed. Robert Abraham Hill; Berkeley: University of California Press, 2006), 253.

Chapter 2

1. Madison C. Peters, *The Distribution of Patriotism in the United States* (New York: The Patriotic League, 1918), 65.
2. George Lippard, *Legends of Mexico* (Philadelphia: T. B. Peterson, 1847), 26–27.
3. George Lippard, *Blanche of Brandywine: Or, September the Eighth to Eleventh, 1777. A Romance of the American Revolution. The Scenes Are Laid on the Battleground of Brandywine* (Philadelphia: G. B. Zieber, 1846); George Lippard, *Washington and His Generals, or, Legends of the Revolution by George Lippard; with a Biographical Sketch of the Author, by C. Chauncey Burr* (Philadelphia: T. B. Peterson, 1847). Throughout these legends, Lippard spells Samson as "Sampson." We follow his spelling when referring to Lippard's character.
4. Respectively, Lippard, *Blanche of Brandywine*, 37; Lippard, *Washington and His Generals*, 355.
5. Lippard, *Washington and His Generals*, 361–62.
6. Longfellow, *Poems on Slavery*, 30, 31.
7. This image of Black Sampson appears in other nineteenth-century writings. For example, an 1884 collection of folk songs contains a poem about a formerly enslaved man identified as "Old Rueb." The poem advises the reader, "If a service you should need / Find this great Black Sampson true." Harry J. Richardson, *A Selection of Dialect Poems; Written on the Rail, and Dedicated to the "Army of the Gripsack"* (Boston: Travelers, 1884), 90.
8. Lippard, *Washington and His Generals*, 115. At another point in the story, Hirpley Hawson calls Sampson, "Charcoal" and "Darkness" (Lippard, *Washington and His Generals*, 133).
9. Jenna M. Gibbs observes that, in addition to Sampson, Lippard uses stereotyped speech patterns for other poor laborers of various ethnic groups throughout the story. Consult Jenna M. Gibbs, *Performing the Temple of Liberty: Slavery, Theater, and Popular Culture in London and Philadelphia, 1760–1850* (Baltimore: Johns Hopkins University Press, 2014), 238.
10. Lippard, *Blanche of Brandywine*, 37.
11. Lippard, *Blanche of Brandywine*, 37.
12. The description of African American men as "demons" is a common racist stereotype. When describing Michael Brown in the moments before he shot Brown to death on August 9, 2014, East St. Louis police officer Darren Wilson said in his grand jury testimony that Brown had "the most aggressive face. That's the only way I can describe it, it looks like a demon, that's how angry he looked." Consult the testimony and other documents at Damien Cave, "Officer Darren Wilson's Grand Jury Testimony in Ferguson, Mo., Shooting," *New York Times*, November 25, 2014, https://www.nytimes.com/interactive/2014/11/25/us/darren-wilson-testimony-ferguson-shooting.html.
13. Lippard, *Blanche of Brandywine*, 223, 224.
14. Lippard, *Washington and His Generals*, 361.
15. Gibbs, *Performing the Temple of Liberty*, 241.

16. Augustine Joseph Hickey Duganne, *The Tenant-House: Or, Embers from Poverty's Hearthstone* (New York: R. M. De Witt, 1857). For a detailed analysis of race and class in Duganne's and Lippard's fiction, consult Timothy Wade Helwig, "Race, Nativism, and the Making of Class in Antebellum City Mysteries" (PhD dissertation, University of Maryland, 2006).

17. On this topic, consult Helwig, "Race, Nativism, and the Making of Class," 140–45.

18. Duganne, *The Tenant-House*, 52.

19. Granby refers to Samson as his "old friend" elsewhere in the novel (Duganne, *The Tenant-House*, 132, 226, 424).

20. Duganne, *The Tenant-House*, 23–24.

21. Duganne, *The Tenant-House*, 393, 445, 9, respectively.

22. Samuel Fletcher, *Black Samson: A Narrative of Old Kentucky* (Munro's Ten Cent Novels; New York: George Munro, 1867), 9. All our citations of this novel come from the 1909 edition published by the Arthur Westbrook Company in Cleveland, Ohio.

23. Fletcher, *Black Samson: A Narrative of Old Kentucky*, 36.

24. Fletcher, *Black Samson: A Narrative of Old Kentucky*, 71.

25. Fletcher, *Black Samson: A Narrative of Old Kentucky*, 96. Like Lippard and Duganne, Fletcher uses several racial stereotypes throughout the novel. Samson and other African American characters are repeatedly referred to as "darkey." For examples, consult Fletcher, *Black Samson: A Narrative of Old Kentucky*, 10, 20, 36, 97, 98. Like Lippard, Fletcher uses the stereotype of African American men as demons when explaining the reaction of the Native Americans to Samson. "They said he was not a man, but a great black demon in human form . . . the fire flashed from his eyes and blazed out of his mouth and nostrils." Fletcher, *Black Samson: A Narrative of Old Kentucky*, 39; cf. 40, 68, 69, 71, 75, 88.

26. Fletcher, *Black Samson: A Narrative of Old Kentucky*, 99.

27. Charles M. Skinner, *Myths and Legends of Our Own Land*, 2 vols. (Philadelphia: J.P. Lippincott, 1896).

28. Skinner, *Myths and Legends*, 1:166–68.

29. Skinner, *Myths and Legends*, 1:168.

30. The term "figure of Time" is a reference to a personification of death or a Grim Reaper–like figure. In his 1842 short story "The Pit and the Pendulum," Edgar Allan Poe uses the term in a similar fashion. "It was the painted figure of Time as he is commonly represented, save that, in lieu of a scythe, he held what, at a casual glance, I supposed to be the pictured image of a huge pendulum, such as we see in antique clocks." Edgar Allan Poe, "The Pit and the Pendulum," in *The Gift: A Christmas and New Year's Present, 1843* (ed. Eliza Leslie; Philadelphia: Carey and Hart, 1842), 142.

31. Paul Laurence Dunbar, "Black Samson of Brandywine," in Paul Laurence Dunbar, *Lyrics of Love and Laughter* (New York: Dodd, Mead, and Company, 1903), 120–23.

32. For an example of this nickname, note the subtitle of his poetry collection published posthumously by his widow and her colleagues: Alice Moore Dunbar-Nelson, William Sanders Scarborough, and Reverdy Cassius Ransom, eds., *Paul Laurence Dunbar: Poet Laureate of the Negro Race* (Philadelphia: A. M. E. Church Review, 1914). Two years after the publication of "Black Samson of Brandywine," an article in

Colored American Magazine compared Dunbar favorably to the nineteenth-century romantic poet William Cullen Bryant: "'Black Samson of Brandywine' will live as long as [Bryant's] 'African Chief.' Read Bryant's and Dunbar's 'Lincoln'—the black poet does not suffer by comparison. . . . Each is a master in his respective sphere. As a writer of blank verse Bryant has no equal in America; and as a lyrical poet with a large vein of rich humor Dunbar is without peer in the Western Continent" (Joseph G. Bryant, "Negro Poetry," *The Colored American Magazine* [May 1905]: 257).

33. Dunbar, "Black Samson of Brandywine," 120–23.

34. For a critique of the patriotism of Dunbar's Black Samson, consult Jean Wagner, *Black Poets of the United States: Paul Laurence Dunbar to Langston Hughes* (trans. Kenneth Douglas; Urbana: University of Illinois Press, 1973), 94–95. Wagner writes, "For some tastes it lays too much stress on the loyalty of the Black hero. . . . He could fight for the freedom of his country, while his black brothers were still enslaved" (Wagner, *Black Poets of the United States*, 98).

35. Debates over the full humanity and citizenship of African Americans have existed since the beginnings of the nation. In determining the population of a state for the purposes of taxation and legislative representation, enslaved persons were counted as three-fifths of a freeperson according to Article one, Section two, Paragraph three of the US Constitution. For the full text, consult the US National Archives, "The Constitution of the United States," https://www.archives.gov/founding-docs/constitution.

36. Dunbar expresses similar sentiments elsewhere in his poetry. For example, in an 1895 poem about the Civil War titled "The Colored Soldiers," he praises African Americans for their military service. Paul Laurence Dunbar, "The Colored Soldiers," in Paul Laurence Dunbar, *Majors and Minors* (Toledo, OH: Hadley and Hadley, 1895), 38. Similarly, Julia Hicks Shanks published a poem in which she wrote: "Whenever I see the sunlight / Upon the white strips shine / I think of brave Black Samson / On the field of Brandywine" (Julia Hicks Shanks, "Whenever I See Old Glory: Flag Day 1933," *The Baltimore Afro-American* [June 17, 1933]: 24). Two weeks later, she published another poem that also mentions Black Samson. She wrote: "Where was the Negro on that day in '76 / . . . Perhaps Black Samson worked amid the wheat / Swinging his scythe about each ripened head" (Julia Hicks Shanks, "Where Was the Negro on the Fourth of July?" *The Baltimore Afro-American* [July 1, 1933]: 7).

37. Consult *The Crisis: A Record of the Darker Races* 13 (September 1917): 255.

38. Alice Dunbar Nelson, "Negro Literature for Negro Pupils," *The Southern Workman* 51.2 (February 1922): 62. "Paul Revere's Ride" is the title of a poem by Longfellow published in 1861. Henry Wadsworth Longfellow, "Paul Revere's Ride," *The Atlantic Monthly* 7.39 (January 1861): 27–29.

39. "No Colored Members in Delaware D.A.R: White Sons of Revolution Never Heard of Negro Heroes of 1776," *Baltimore Afro-American* (October 4, 1930): 3; "D. A. R. Representative Gets Lesson in History," *Philadelphia Tribune* (October 9, 1930): 8.

40. For example, Black Samson is listed alongside various combinations of these names in "The Buffaloes: A First-Class Colored Regiment by One of Its Battalion Staff Officers Lieutenant O. E. McKaine: With an Introduction by Its Commander, Colonel James

A. Moss," *The Outlook* (May 22, 1918): 145; "Our Solider Boys Are Busy," *Cleveland Gazette* (June 22, 1918): 1; "A Page from History," *Our Colored Missions* 26.7 (July 1, 1930): 109; "Reading," *Baltimore Afro-American* (June 4, 1932): 5; "Dr. E. J. Scott Addresses Vets at Legion Confab: Howard University Official Pleads for New Deal," *Chicago Defender* (October 7, 1933): 4; "My Mamma Done Told Me," *Philadelphia Tribune* (April 11, 1942): 1, 3; George M. Coleman, "Black Heroes Helped Gain New Nation: The Negro Fought for Independence of U.S.," *Atlanta Daily World* (July 4, 1962): 1, 4; "School Decision Freedom Quest's Most Significant Step, Dr. Mays Tells Emancipation Observance: Morehouse President Traces Struggle of the Negro Race," *Atlanta Daily World* (February 13, 1963): 1; James Egert Allen, "Black History Past and Present: Corps of Rugged Men," *New York Amsterdam News* (January 9, 1971): 15.

41. Crispus Attucks, often thought of as the first martyr of the Revolutionary War, was killed by British troops in the Boston massacre on March 5, 1770. William Carney was a formerly enslaved man who fought in the Civil War and won the Medal of Honor for his actions in the attack on Fort Wagner in Charleston, South Carolina, during the Civil War. Salem Poor, who bought his freedom from his slaveholder James Poor, is credited with fatally shooting the British officer James Abercrombie during the Battle of Bunker Hill on June 23, 1775. Peter Salem, who was freed by his slaveholder Lawson Buckminster to serve in a militia, fought in the 1775 battles at Concord and Bunker Hill. Consult chapter 1 for a discussion of Phyllis Wheatley. Similarly, Melvin Tolson lists Black Samson alongside historical figures in his poem "Rendezvous with America":

> And I saw
> Black Samson mowing down Hessians with a scythe at Brandy-wine,
> Marian Anderson bewitching continents with the talisman of art,
> Fred Douglass hurling from tombstones the philippies of freedom,
> Private Brooks dying at the feet of MacArthur in Bataan.

Melvin B. Tolson, "Rendezvous with America," in Melvin B. Tolson, *Rendezvous with America* (New York: Dodd, Mead, 1944), 7–8. In addition to his career as a poet, Tolson taught English and coached the debate team at Wiley College, a historically Black school in Marshall, Texas. The actor Denzel Washington portrayed him in *The Great Debaters*, the 2007 Metro-Goldwyn-Mayer film about Wiley's debate team.

42. Peters, *The Distribution of Patriotism in the United States*.

43. Peters, *The Distribution of Patriotism in the United States*, 65.

44. Peters, *The Distribution of Patriotism in the United States*, 65.

45. "What Shall We Do with the Negro?" *Christian Observer* (December 23, 1903): 1.

Chapter 3

1. Fales Henry Newhall, *The Conflict in America: A Funeral Discourse Occasioned by the Death of John Brown of Ossawattomie, Who Entered into Rest, from the Gallows, at*

Charlestown, Virginia, Dec. 2, 1859, Preached at the Warren St. M.E. Church, Roxbury, Dec. 4 (Boston: J. M. Hewes, 1859), 21.

2. Harpers Ferry became part of West Virginia when the state separated from Virginia in 1861 and was admitted into the Union on June 20, 1863.

3. Consult the introduction for other examples.

4. We provide a detailed discussion of "The Warning" in chapter 1.

5. William J. Snelling, "Song, Supposed to Be Sung by Slaves in Insurrection," *The Liberator* 29 (November 4, 1859): 176. The *Liberator* published a number of poems praising Captain John Brown during his imprisonment and, after his death, memorizing him. For a discussion of these poems, consult Joe Lockard, "'Earth Feels the Time of Prophet-Song': John Brown and Public Poetry," in *The Afterlife of John Brown* (ed. Andrew Taylor and Eldrid Herrington; New York: Palgrave Macmillan, 2005), 69–87.

6. Snelling, "Song, Supposed to Be Sung by Slaves in Insurrection," 176.

7. Reprinted in Franklin Benjamin Sanborn, "John Brown and His Friends," *Atlantic Monthly* 30 (July 1872): 54; Franklin Benjamin Sanborn, *Recollections of Seventy Years* (Boston: R. G. Badger, 1909), 150–51.

8. Quoted in James Redpath, *The Public Life of Captain John Brown, with an Autobiography of His Childhood and Youth* (London: Thickbroom and Stapleton, 1860), 254.

9. Franklin Benjamin Sanborn, ed., *The Life and Letters of John Brown: Liberator of Kansas, and Martyr of Virginia* (Boston: Roberts Brothers, 1885), 604 (emphasis in the original).

10. Sanborn, *The Life and Letters of John Brown*, 575.

11. Frederick Douglass, "Captain John Brown Not Insane," *Douglass' Monthly* (November 1859): 1 (capitalization in the original).

12. Douglass, "Captain John Brown Not Insane," 1.

13. Douglass, "Captain John Brown Not Insane," 1.

14. Newhall, *The Conflict in America*, 21.

15. Newhall, *The Conflict in America*, 22. Newhall doubles the "s" and the "t" in his spelling of Osawatomie and spells the Philistine city of Ashkelon as "Ascalon."

16. For another example of an extended comparison of the two men, consult William Weston Patton, *The Execution of John Brown: A Discourse, Delivered at Chicago, December 4th, 1859, in the First Congregational Church* (Chicago: Church, Goodman and Cushing, 1859), 4.

17. A. D. A. B., "The Execution of John Brown," *The Liberator* 29 (December 9, 1859): 196.

18. A few of the many examples include W. E. B. Dubois, *John Brown* (Philadelphia: G. W. Jacobs, 1909); Hermann von Holst, *John Brown* (ed. Frank Preston Stearns; trans. Phillippe Marcou; Boston: DeWolfe, Fiske, 1888); Redpath, *The Public Life of Captain John Brown*; Franklin Benjamin Sanborn, *Memoirs of John Brown, Written for Rev. Samuel Orcutt's History of Torrington, Ct., by F. B. Sanborn, with Memorial Verses by William Ellery Channing* (Concord: J. Munsell, 1878). John Brown was also featured in novels with anti-slavery themes, such as the early African American novelist Pauline Elizabeth Hopkins's novel *Winona*, which was serialized in *Colored American*

Magazine in 1902. Pauline Elizabeth Hopkins, "Winona: A Tale of Negro Life in the South and Southwest," *Colored American Magazine* 5.1–6 (March to October 1902).

19. Holst, *John Brown*, 120.

20. Examples include Dubois, *John Brown*, 234; Sanborn, *Memoirs of John Brown*, 90, 100; Sanborn, *The Life and Letters of John Brown*, 578; Oswald Garrison Villard, *John Brown, 1800–1859: A Biography Fifty Years After* (Boston: Houghton Mifflin, 1910), 323. Dubois cites Sanborn's *The Life and Letters of John Brown* as his source for this quotation. Villard also cites Sanborn, *Recollections of Seventy Years* as his source for this quotation.

21. Redpath, *The Public Life of Captain John Brown*, 10.

22. Redpath, *The Public Life of Captain John Brown*, 9–10.

23. Redpath, *The Public Life of Captain John Brown*, 208 (emphasis in the original).

24. Like Redpath's inclusion of the poem "A Curse on Virginia" in his earlier book *Roving Editor*, which we discuss in the introduction, Redpath uses anti-slavery poetry by another writer to support his point.

25. Redpath, *The Public Life of Captain John Brown*, 228.

26. In his December 4, 1859, sermon, which we discussed earlier in this chapter, Fales Henry Newhall uses a similar rhetorical technique when he compares Brown to Samson but associates blindness with Brown's enemies when he declares, "In the blindness of their fear and passion they did not see that when they placed him on the scaffold, they had set him between the very pillars of their idol's temple" (Newhall, *The Conflict in America*, 22).

27. Robert Penn Warren, *John Brown: The Making of a Martyr* (New York: Payson and Clarke Limited, 1929), 430.

28. J. W. Schulte Nordholt, *The People That Walk in Darkness* (trans. M. B. van Wijngaarden; London: Burke, 1960), 122. The title of this book comes from Isaiah 9:2: "The people that walked in darkness have seen a great light: they that dwell in the land of the shadow of death, upon them hath the light shined." In the early 1960s, portions of this book were serialized in the *Chicago Defender*, a prominent African American newspaper. The portion of the book that contains this quote appears as J. W. Schulte Nordholt, "The People That Walk in Darkness: Sea of Blood and Tears," *Chicago Defender* (December 10, 1962): 11.

29. *In Memoriam: Frederick Douglass* (Philadelphia: John C. Yorsto, 1897), 33.

30. On May 30, 1881, Douglass delivered an address at Harpers Ferry, which had become part of West Virginia by that time, in which he contrasted Brown's death on behalf of enslaved persons with his own life lived on their behalf. According to Douglass, Brown's "zeal in the cause of my race was far greater than mine—it was as the burning sun to my taper light—mine was bounded by time, his stretched away to the boundless shores of eternity. I could live for the slave, but he could die for him. The crown of martyrdom is high, far beyond the reach of ordinary mortals, and yet happily no special greatness or superior moral excellence is necessary to discern and in some measure appreciate a truly great soul." Fredrick Douglass, *John Brown: An Address by Fredrick Douglass at the Fourteenth Anniversary of Storer College, Harper Ferry, West Virginia, May 30, 1881* (Dover, NH: Morning Star Job Printing House, 1881), 9.

31. William Lloyd Garrison, the co-founder and editor of the *Liberator* and a former mentor of Douglass, also compares Douglass to Samson. Yet, he uses his comparison to question rather than praise Douglass's work. In 1853, Garrison accused Douglass of having an inappropriate relationship with Julia Griffiths, a White English woman who worked with Douglass as an editor in Rochester, New York. At one point, Garrison quotes Douglass, who praises Julia Griffiths for "*opening my eyes*(!) to many things connected to my anti-slavery relations, to which I had before been partially blind." After this quotation, Garrison concludes his article by observing, "In what condition his vision now is—and whether in slumbering in the lap of a prejudiced, sectarian Delilah, he has not at last enabled the pro-slavery Philistines to ascertain the secret of his strength, cut off his locks, and rejoice over his downfall—we leave to our reader and the uncompromising friends of the Anti-slavery cause to judge." William Lloyd Garrison, "The Mask Entirely Removed," *The Liberator* 23 (December 16, 1853): 196 (emphasis in the original).

32. The full text of this speech may be found in *The Booker T. Washington Papers*, vol. 3 (ed. Louis R. Harlan; Urbana: University of Illinois Press, 1974), 583–587. Washington's views are often contrasted with those of W. E. B. Dubois, who offered a scathing critique of Washington's speech that he referred to as the "Atlanta Compromise." He considered Washington's proposal to be an example of accommodation and argued that African Americans should instead continue to fight for their civil rights. Consult W. E. B. Dubois, "Of Mr. Booker T. Washington and Others," in W. E. B. Dubois, *Souls of Black Folk: Essays and Sketches* (Chicago: A. C. McClurg, 1903), 41–59.

33. Quoted in "Meet to Honor Leader: With a Spirit to Pay Homage to One Whom They Loved Young and Old Pay Respectful Tribute," *The Chicago Defender* (November 27, 1915): 3.

34. "Meet to Honor Leader," 3.

35. Consult Douglas R. Egerton, *Gabriel's Rebellion: The Virginia Slave Conspiracies of 1800 and 1802* (Chapel Hill: University of North Carolina Press, 1993), 179–181.

36. Cited in Egerton, *Gabriel's Rebellion*, 179 (emphasis added).

37. Cited in Egerton, *Gabriel's Rebellion*, 180. As examples of nineteenth-century scholarship that mention Gabriel without any association with Samson, Egerton cites Joshua Coffin, *An Account of Some of the Principle Slave Insurrections* (New York: American Anti-Slavery Society, 1860), 24–28; Thomas W. Higginson, *Travellers and Outlaws: Episodes in American History* (Boston: Lee and Shepard, 1889), 190; Robert R. Howison, *A History of Virginia*, 2 vols. (Philadelphia: Carey and Hart, 1846), 2:390.

38. Egerton, *Gabriel's Rebellion*, 180.

39. Marion Harland, *Judith: A Chronicle of Old Virginia* (New York: Scribner, 1883), 24. Cited in Egerton, *Gabriel's Rebellion*, 179–80. The quotation "wherein his great strength lay" comes from Judges 16:5 where the Philistines commission Delilah to discover the source of Samson's strength.

40. Arna Bontemps, *Gabriel's Revolt: Virginia 1800* (New York: Macmillan, 1936).

41. Arnold Rampersad, "Introduction to the 1992 Edition," in Arna Bontemps, *Gabriel's Revolt: Virginia 1800* (Boston: Beacon, 1992), xvi.

42. Joseph C. Carroll, *Slave Insurrections in the United States, 1800–1865* (Reprint; New York: Negro Universities Press, 1973), 49. Cited in Egerton, *Gabriel's Rebellion*, 180. Egerton lists several other examples of this claim in scholarly sources and concludes "the Samson story has appeared in virtually every reference to the conspiracy" (Egerton, *Gabriel's Rebellion*, 180).

43. Egerton, *Gabriel's Rebellion*, 180. It is unclear whether Carroll was influenced by nineteenth-century depictions of other leaders of insurrections, like John Brown, as Samson figures or by the Black Samson motif in general, since it was familiar to many African American intellectuals by the 1930s, or by some other source. We discuss the use of Samson imagery by African American intellectuals in the 1920s and 1930s in chapter 4.

44. Cornel West, *Prophesy Deliverance!: An Afro-American Revolutionary Christianity* (Philadelphia: Westminster, 1982), 102. West does not cite a source for this assertion.

45. Dwight N. Hopkins, *Down, Up, and Over: Slave Religion and Black Theology* (Minneapolis, MN: Fortress, 2000), 133.

46. "Black Is Beautiful! by DAL: How Aware Are You?: Gabriel Prosser (1776–1800)," *Philadelphia Tribune* (September 28 1968): 19.

47. Cited in Egerton, *Gabriel's Rebellion*, 21.

48. The biblical story does not indicate Samson's height. The only physical features that it discusses are his hairstyle (Judges 13:5; 16:13–14, 17, 19, 22) and his eyesight (Judges 16:21, 28).

49. Willie Dixon, Jr., "Resistance-Resistance-Resistance: Let Your Motto be Resistance!" *Chicago Metro News* (October 18, 1986): 6.

50. Thomas R. Gray, *The Confessions of Nat Turner: The Leader of the Late Insurrection in Southampton, Va., as Fully and Voluntarily Made to Thomas R. Gray, in the Prison where he was Confined, and Acknowledged by Him to be Such, when Read before the Court of Southampton: with the Certificate, under Seal of the Court convened at Jerusalem, Nov. 5, 1831, for his Trial* (Richmond: T. R. Gray, 1832).

51. For a reassessment of the debates over the accuracy of Gray's book, consult Patrick H. Breen, *The Land Shall Be Deluged in Blood: A New History of the Nat Turner Revolt* (New York: Oxford University Press, 2016).

52. Gray's book also influenced prominent abolitionists such as Henry Wadsworth Longfellow and Harriet Beecher Stowe. Longfellow owned a copy of Gray's *The Confessions of Nat Turner*. His copy still exists and is currently housed in Stanford University's collections. (This was confirmed by Professor Shelley Fisher Fishkin of Stanford University in an email on June 2, 2015.) Stowe's novel *Dred: A Tale of the Great Dismal Swamp* includes Gray's work under the title "Nat Turner's Confessions," as the first appendix at the end of the novel (Stowe, *Dred*, 2:338–46). Also, while none of the poems in Longfellow's *Poems on Slavery* mention Nat Turner directly, one of the poems is titled, "The Slave in the Dismal Swamp." In the months between the revolt and Turner's capture, various newspapers connected him with the Great Dismal Swamp. For example, in an article dated August 24, 1831, the *Norfolk Herald* reported that "a band of insurgent slaves (some of whom believed to be runaways from the neighboring swamps), had turned out on Sunday night last, and murdered several

whole families, amounting to 40 or 50 individuals. . . . [They are] probably making their way for the Dismal Swamp, in which they will be able to remain for a short time in security" (Reprinted as "Insurrection of the Blacks" *Niles' Weekly Register* 40 [August 27, 1831]: 455).

53. Daniel Panger, *Ol' Prophet Nat* (Winston-Salem: John F. Blair, 1967) and William Styron, *The Confessions of Nat Turner* (New York: Random House, 1967).

54. For example, consult John Henrik Clarke, ed., *William Styron's Nat Turner: Ten Black Writer's Respond* (Boston: Beacon, 1968). For a response by Styron, consult William Styron, "Nat Turner Revisited," *American Heritage* (October 1992): 65–73. At the time of the novel's release, James Baldwin was one of the few African American intellectuals to defend it. As he explained in an interview toward the end of his life, "[Styron] had to try to put himself in the skin of Nat Turner. . . . The book meant something to me because it was a white Southern writer's attempt to deal with something that was tormenting him and frightening him. I respect him very much for that. . . . I said before that America's effort to avoid the presence of black people constricts American literature" (Julius Lester, "James Baldwin—Reflections of a Maverick," *The New York Times Book Review* [May 27, 1984]. Reprinted in *James Baldwin: The Last Interview and Other Conversations* [New York: Melville House, 2014], 49).

55. Styron, *The Confessions of Nat Turner*, 13. One of Styron's minor characters is an enslaved African American named Samson (Styron, *The Confessions of Nat Turner*, 285). Yet, as we discuss in the introduction, the name of this character may simply reflect a common biblical name given to enslaved persons rather than an allusion to the biblical story involving Samson.

56. For example, consult Celeste-Marie Bernier, *Characters of Blood: Black Heroism in the Transatlantic Imagination* (Charlottesville: University of Virginia Press, 2012), 131–33.

57. Panger, *Ol' Prophet Nat*, 131–32.

Chapter 4

1. W. E. B. Dubois, "The Problem of Problems," *The Intercollegiate Socialist* (December–January 1917–18): 7.

2. As discussed in chapter 2, George Lippard's folklore from the 1840s used a Black Sampson figure in its idealized picture of racial solidarity among workers. Yet, in 1855, Fredrick Douglass offered an economic explanation for the lack of solidarity among poor White laborers and the enslaved in states where slavery was legal at the time. He argued that, because the slaveholder robs the enslaved of all earnings, using slave labor is cheaper than paying a White laborer a fair wage under what Douglass referred to as "the slave system." Thus, the poor White laborer "is flung into competition with a class of laborers who work without wages . . . the slaveholders blind them [the poor, White laborers] to this competition, by keeping alive their prejudice against slaves, *as men*—not against men *as slaves*." Douglass argued that this competition results in White laborers' enmity against the enslaved rather than solidarity with

them. Fredrick Douglass, *My Bondage and My Freedom* (New York: Miller, Orton and Mulligan, 1855), 309–10 (emphasis in the original).

3. Isabel Wilkerson, *The Warmth of Other Suns: The Epic Story of America's Great Migration* (New York: Vintage, 2010), 9.

4. "Report of the Special Committee Authorized by Congress to Investigate the East St. Louis Riots: 65th Congress, 2nd Session, House of Representatives, Document 1231," in *Congressional Edition*: Volume 7444 (Washington, DC: US Government Printing Office, 1918), 4.

5. Ida B. Wells-Barnett, *The East St. Louis Massacre: The Greatest Outrage of the Century* (Chicago: Negro Fellowship Herald, 1917), 23.

6. Wells-Barnett, *The East St. Louis Massacre*, 23.

7. Jessie Redmon Fauset, "A Negro on East St. Louis," *The Survey* 38 (August 18, 1917): 448.

8. Fauset, "A Negro on East St. Louis," 448. According to Dubois, in the East St. Louis massacre "one hundred twenty-five Negroes were killed by their fellow white laborers; their homes looted and destroyed; and hundreds of others maimed." W. E. B. Dubois, *Dusk of Dawn: An Essay toward an Autobiography of a Race Concept* (ed. Henry Louis Gates; New York: Oxford University Press, 2007), 126.

9. Fauset, "A Negro on East St. Louis," 448.

10. Fauset, "A Negro on East St. Louis," 448.

11. Fauset, "A Negro on East St. Louis," 448.

12. Fauset, "A Negro on East St. Louis," 448.

13. Fauset, "A Negro on East St. Louis," 448.

14. Claude McKay, "Socialism and the Negro," in *The Passion of Claude McKay: Selected Poetry and Prose, 1912–1948* (ed. Wayne F. Cooper; New York: Schocken, 1973), 51, 53; originally published in *Workers' Dreadnought* (January 31, 1920): 1–2.

15. Claude McKay, "The Racial Question: The Racial Question in the United States," *International Press Correspondence* 2 (November 21, 1922): 817.

16. The poem includes lines such as, "The crimson rides the universal wind. . . . The toilers, tired of yielding and false giving, Bend to the mightily task, with solacing groans, Of making the earth fit for human living. . . . Where the scarlet pennants blaze like tongues of fire, There-where high passion swells--is my heart's desire." Claude McKay, "Travail," in Claude McKay, *The Complete Poems* (ed. William J. Maxwell; Urbana-Champaign: University of Illinois Press, 2008), 139. Originally published in *Workers' Dreadnought* (January 10, 1920): 1601.

17. Claude McKay, "Samson," *Workers' Dreadnought* (January 10, 1920): 1602.

18. "What Is a Communist?" *New York Amsterdam News* (November 4, 1925): 12.

19. Jean Toomer, "Reflections on the Race Riots," *New York Call* (August 2, 1919): 8.

20. Toomer, "Reflections on the Race Riots," 8.

21. Jean Toomer, *Cane* (New York: Boni and Liveright, 1923), 105.

22. For a detailed discussion of the enclosure imagery as a critique of the values of the African American professional class, consult Sandra Hollin Flowers, "Solving the Critical Conundrum of Jean Toomer's 'Box Seat,'" *Studies in Short Fiction* 25.3 (1988): 301–5.

23. The Lincoln Theatre opened in 1921. It is currently located at 1215 U Street in Washington, DC.

24. Toomer, *Cane*, 126.

25. Toomer, *Cane*, 126.

26. Toomer, *Cane*, 127.

27. Flowers, "Solving the Critical Conundrum of Jean Toomer's 'Box Seat,'" 305.

28. Toomer, *Cane*, 126.

29. Langston Hughes, "Union," *New Masses* 7.4 (September 1931): 12. One can access the full poem online.

30. Langston Hughes, "On the Road," *Esquire* (January 1935): 92, 154.

31. Hughes, "On the Road," 92.

32. Hughes, "On the Road," 92.

33. Hughes, "On the Road," 92.

34. Hughes, "On the Road," 92.

35. Hughes, "On the Road," 92.

36. Hughes, "On the Road," 92.

37. Hughes, "On the Road," 92.

38. Hughes, "On the Road," 154.

39. Hughes, "On the Road," 154.

40. Richard Wright, "Fire and Cloud," *Story* 12 (March 1938): 9–41.

41. The spiritual "Gawd's a-Gwineter Move All de Troubles Away" includes the verse, "a-Read about Samson from his birth, De stronges' man ever walked on earth. a-Read way back in de ancient time, He slew ten thousan' Philistine. a-Samson he went a-walkin' a bout, a-Samson's strength-a was never found out, Twell his wife sat down upon his knee, An'-a Tell me wharyo' strength-a lies, ef you please. a-Samson's wife she done talk so fair, a-Samson tol' her 'Cut off-a ma hair, Ef you shave ma head jes' as clean as yo' han', Ma strength-a will become-a like a natcherl man!'" Consult Natalie Curtis Berlin, *Hampton Series Negro Folk Songs* (New York: G. Schirmer, 1918), 32–44. Likewise, the spiritual, "My Soul Is a Witness to My Lord" (known by various titles including "That's Another Witness for My Lord") includes the verse "Delila' talked so good and fair He told her his strength lie in his hair, 'Shave my head just as clean as your hands, And my strength 'll be like a nachual mans." Consult Howard Washington Odum, "Religious Folk-Songs of the Southern Negroes" (PhD dissertation, Clark University, 1909). Reprinted from the *American Journal of Religious Psychology and Education* 3 (July 1909): 265–365.

42. In the late 1920s, other artists recorded versions of this song under titles such as "If I Had My Way I'd Tear the Building Down" by Reverend T. E. Weems (1927) and "If I Had My Way" by Reverend T. T. Rose (1927). More recently, the song appears in the critically acclaimed novel *The Price of a Child* by Lorene Cary. The novel is loosely based on the life of Jane Johnson, a woman who escaped from her slaveholder John Hill Wheeler on July 18, 1855, while traveling with him, his family, and her children in Pennsylvania, which was a free state. When Wheeler charged William Still, an African American abolitionist who aided Johnson in her escape, with assault, Johnson testified on Still's behalf, contributing to his acquittal. In a scene that narrates

the thoughts of the character inspired by Johnson as she approaches the stand to give her testimony, Cary writes: "Somewhere in the corner of her mind, she heard the tune:

> *If I could*
> *If I could*
> *If I could*
> *I'd tear this building down*

It came up in her own voice from far away."
Lorene Cary, *The Price of a Child* (New York: Vintage, 1995), 196. This character thinks of this song again during a climactic moment later in the novel (Cary, *The Price of a Child*, 290–91).

43. Johnson's version of this traditional song was included in the compilation album *The Complete Blind Willie Johnson*. Blind Willie Johnson, "If I Had My Way I'd Tear the Building Down," *The Complete Blind Willie Johnson*, recorded 1927–1930, New York City: Columbia Records/Legacy Recordings, C2K 52835, 1993, compact disc.

44. Wright, "Fire and Cloud," 33.

45. Wright, "Fire and Cloud," 40.

46. Charles Austin Miles's "The Cloud and Fire" was published by the Hall-Mack Company. The full chorus of Miles's version reads: "So the sign of the fire by night, And the sign of the cloud by day, hov'ring o'er, just before, As they journey on their way, Shall a guide and a leader be, Till the wilderness be past, For the Lord our God in His own good time, Shall lead us to the light at last."

47. In the 1930s, the use of Samson imagery to address race and labor was not limited to those who wanted to make communist or socialist ideas more palatable to African Americans. For example, in the March 31, 1938, issue of the prominent African American newspaper the *Philadelphia Tribune*, an article titled "Samson Gets His Hair Back" alleged that John Kelly and Matthew McCloskey, who were powerful leaders in Philadelphia's Democratic Party, broke their campaign promises to African Americans. The article's unidentified author charged that they had promised more jobs to African Americans, presumably through President Roosevelt's Works Progress Administration, in order to secure the African American vote. Drawing on a well-established comparison between Samson and African Americans, the author noted that after the Philistines enslaved him: "Samson's hair grew long. He became strong again. One day he had a boy lead him to the pillars which sustained the temple. With one hand on one pillar and one hand on the other Samson gave one big push and the temple came tumbling down, killing Samson's tormentors. The strength of the Negro power is the ballot. The Kelly-McCloskey machine used it to erect a great and powerful political temple in Philadelphia. After the temple was secure, they thought they could discard the colored vote. . . . Colored votes built the Democratic machine in Philadelphia. And what they built they can destroy" ("Samson Gets His Hair Back," *Philadelphia Tribune* [March 31, 1938]: 4).

48. Claude McKay, "Negro Author Sees Disaster If the Communist Party Gains Control of Negro Workers," *New Leader* (September 10, 1938): 5.

49. Richard Wright, "I Tried to Be a Communist," *Atlantic Monthly* 159 (August 1944): 61–70.

50. For example, Ellison published book reviews such as "Stormy Weather," *New Masses* (September 24, 1940): 20–21, and "Recent Negro Fiction," *New Masses* (August 5, 1941): 22–26.

51. This letter, dated August 5, 1945, is cited in Carol Polsgrove, *Divided Minds: Intellectuals and the Civil Rights Movement* (New York: W. W. Norton, 2001), 69. For a detailed discussion of Wright's and Ellison's relationship with communism, consult Polsgrove, *Divided Minds*, 65–99.

52. Ralph Ellison, *Invisible Man* (New York: Vintage International, 1995), 197. Originally published as Ralph Ellison, *Invisible Man* (New York: Random House, 1952). All quotations come from the 1995 edition.

53. Ellison, *Invisible Man*, 224.

54. Ellison, *Invisible Man*, 228 (emphasis in the original).

55. Ellison, *Invisible Man*, 230.

56. Ellison, *Invisible Man*, 243.

57. Ellison, *Invisible Man*, 396–97.

58. Ellison, *Invisible Man*, 502.

59. Ellison, *Invisible Man*, 505.

60. Ellison, *Invisible Man*, 508.

61. Ellison, *Invisible Man*, 16.

62. The *Partisan Review* was a journal that was affiliated with the Communist Party USA in the 1930s but had turned against it by the 1950s. Ralph Ellison, "Change the Joke and Slip the Yoke," *Partisan Review* 25.2 (Spring 1958): 220. Ellison's expression "mask of meekness" refers to Dunbar's idea about African Americans in his poem "We Wear the Mask." Consult Paul Laurence Dunbar, "We Wear the Mask," in Paul Laurence Dunbar, *Majors and Minors* (Toledo, OH: Hadley and Hadley, 1895), 21.

63. The term "Eyeless in Gaza" does not come from the biblical text, but from lines 40–41 in John Milton's epic poem, *Samson Agonistes*. "Ask for this great Deliverer now, and find him / Eyeless in Gaza at the Mill with slaves." Also, the term is the title of a 1936 novel by the English author Aldous Huxley.

64. Ellison, *Invisible Man*, 508, 509.

Chapter 5

1. L. W. Collins, "No Master Great Enough to Make Slavery Sweet, Says Reader," *Los Angeles Tribune* (June 26, 1959): 11. Although its name is shared with other shorter lived publications, the *Los Angeles Tribune* in which this article appeared was a newspaper founded by the African American journalist Hallie Almena Lomax. Published from 1941 to 1960, the newspaper served a primarily African American readership.

2. With the permission of Ellison's widow, John F. Callahan edited some of Ellison's drafts into the 1999 novel *Juneteenth* (New York: Vintage International, 1999). Eleven years later, Callahan and Adam Bradley compiled Ellison's multiple unpublished

drafts along with eight excerpts previously published by Ellison into a much larger book *Three Days Before the Shooting . . .* (ed. John F. Callahan and Adam Bradley; New York: Modern Library, 2010).

3. Ralph Ellison, "The Roof, the Steeple and the People," *Quarterly Review of Literature* 10 (1960): 121–22. This quotation appears nearly verbatim in a draft of book II of the novel published posthumously. Consult Ellison, *Three Days Before the Shooting . . .* , 287.

4. Ellison, "The Roof, the Steeple and the People," 122; cf. Ellison, *Three Days Before the Shooting . . .* , 288.

5. Ellison, "The Roof, the Steeple and the People," 123–24; cf. Ellison, *Three Days Before the Shooting . . .* , 289. The spelling "dont" is in the original.

6. Ellison, *Three Days Before the Shooting . . .* , 317. The line, "We were eyeless like Samson in Gaza?" alludes to John Milton's epic poem *Samson Agonistes*. Consult chapter 4, note 63.

7. Quoted in "Yorty Assails Boast of Black Muslim Chief: Death of 130 in French Air Disaster Hailed in Tape Recording of Negro's Talk," *Los Angeles Times* (June 7, 1962): A1. Sam Yorty was the mayor of Los Angeles from 1961 until 1973. While Malcolm used the idiom "an eye for an eye and a tooth for a tooth" to describe what Muslims believe (Qur'an 5:45), variations on the idiom also appear in legal material from the Bible (Exodus 21:23–25; Leviticus 24:19–20; Deuteronomy 19:21).

8. Later, in a twenty-week lecture series when dedicating Temple number 2 in Chicago in the summer of 1972, Elijah Muhammad used the story of Samson and Delilah as a cautionary tale when condemning racial integration. On June 4, he said that White women "will make you think that we just now realized that we have to live as one people, and you yet blind, will say 'yes, yes, that's right.' . . . She is a universal Delilah. That's in your Bible. See how Delilah deceived Samson, the strongest man. You are the strongest man" (Elijah Muhammad, *The Theology of Time: The Secret of Time* [Phoenix: Secretarious, 2002], 25, 26). He returned to this biblical story on June 11 stating that Delilah's tactics provided an example, or parable, for White people of how to destroy Black people through interracial relationships. He explained: "You must remember the parable of Delilah was for her people and not for Samson because Samson was a strong man that her people didn't like and she only wanted to find out his strength. . . . We are the Samson of the time, but we can destroy ourselves by giving over to the enemy all of our secrets" (Muhammad, *The Theology of Time*, 39). On July 2, he stated, "You are modern Samsons. Please brothers, do not let Delilah's sister, a deceiver, trick you like that. They are falsely making love with you. They don't love you. They only want you to go to the fire like they are in for. Read that and study it good. This means a modern Samson and a modern Delilah" (Muhammad, *The Theology of Time*, 101). The image of the White Christian Delilah stripping the Black Muslim Samson of his strength appears as early as an influential 1910 article by the White British author Bertram Lenox Simpson, writing under the name B. L. Putnam Weale. Under the heading "The Negro Samson and the White Delilah," Putnam Weale wrote that the Christianizing of the Negro involves "weaning him from the militant bent of mind which he assumes under Islam. . . . If the Negro, in measure as he is civilized, goes to Islamism, he must become a greater peril; if he is Christianized, his destructive strength is stripped from him as was

Samson's strength when his locks were cut. The part the white man is politically called upon to play in Africa is the part of Delilah, and no other" (B. L. Putnam Weale, "The Conflict of Color IV: The World's Black Problem," *The World's Work* 19 (November 1909–April 1910): 12331–32). Putnam Weale's work evoked a strong response from the prominent West Indian American secular humanist Hebert H. Harrison, who promoted "atheistic agnosticism" over organized religion. In 1917, Harrison wrote, "Mr. Putnam Weale makes no pretense of believing in the Christian myth himself; but he wants it taught to the Negroes . . . and, with less fear than an angel, frankly advises the white Lords of Empire not so much to civilize as to christianize Africa, so that Delilah's work may be well done. Here in America her work has been well done" (Herbert H. Harrison, *The Negro and the Nation* [New York: Cosmo-Advocate, 1917], 45). Also, consult the discussion in chapter 1 of Ida B. Wells-Barnett's earlier use of the "White Delilah" image in the anti-lynching campaign.

9. Louis Lomax, *When the Word Is Given: A Report on Elijah Muhammad, Malcolm, and the Black Muslim World* (Cleveland: World, 1963), 204.

10. Lomax, *When the Word Is Given*, 205.

11. Lomax, *When the Word Is Given*, 205–6.

12. Lomax, *When the Word Is Given*, 207.

13. Lomax, *When the Word Is Given*, 207. Malcolm X made his departure from the Nation of Islam public in March 1964 and formed the Organization of Afro-American Unity (OAAU), a Pan-Africanist group, that July. In an interview with the photographer and writer Gordon Parks conducted on February 19, 1965, Malcolm X did not mention his comments about Flight 007 specifically but expressed remorse over his time and actions in the Nation of Islam. He explained: "That was a bad scene, brother. The sickness and madness of those days—I'm glad to be free of them. It's a time for martyrs now. And if I'm to be one, it will be in the cause of brotherhood. . . . I did many things as a Muslim that I'm sorry for now. I was a zombie then—like all Muslims—I was hypnotized, pointed in a certain direction and told to march. Well, I guess a man's entitled to make a fool of himself if he's ready to pay the cost. It cost me twelve years." (Gordon Parks, "Violent End of a Man Called Malcolm X," *Life* 58.9 [March 5, 1965]: 28, 29). In this quotation, Malcolm X uses "Muslim" when referring to a member of the Nation of Islam rather than Muslims in general. Two days after the interview, on February 21, 1965, Malcolm X was assassinated as he prepared to speak at an OAAU event at the Audubon Theatre in Manhattan. He was thirty-nine years old. Two years earlier, Parks had spent a significant amount of time with Malcolm X while writing an earlier article on the Nation of Islam. Gordon Parks, "What Their Cry Means to Me: A Negro's Own Evaluation," *Life* 54.22 (May 31, 1963): 31–32, 78–79.

14. "Racial Violence Assailed by Dr. Luther King," *Los Angeles Times* (June 16, 1962): 11. Harry Belafonte was a popular singer and a supporter of King and the Civil Rights movement.

15. Martin Luther King, Jr., *Strength to Love* (New York: Harper and Row, 1963). King developed the version of "Love in Action" published in this volume from outlines from April 1960. It appears he also used these outlines for his sermons, "Love in

Action," which he preached on April 3, 1960, at Ebenezer Baptist Church in Atlanta and "Levels of Love," which he preached on September 16, 1962, at Ebenezer Baptist Church. A version of the outline is published as "Love in Action I," in *The Papers of Martin Luther King, Jr.*, vol. 6: *Advocate of the Social Gospel, September 1948–March 1963* (ed. Clayborne Carson, senior editor; Susan Carson, Susan Englander, Troy Jackson, and Gerald L. Smith; Berkeley: University of California Press, 2007), 405–7. The sermon "Levels of Love" is published in *Papers of Martin Luther King, Jr.*, 6:437–45. All quotations of "Love in Action" comes from "Draft of Chapter IV 'Love in Action,'" in *Papers of Martin Luther King, Jr.*, 6:486–95. This version contains minor differences from the version published in *Strength to Love*.

16. King, "Draft of Chapter IV 'Love in Action,'" 489.
17. King, "Draft of Chapter IV 'Love in Action,'" 488.
18. Consult the introduction for a discussion of this theme in the biblical story.
19. King, "Draft of Chapter IV 'Love in Action,'" 489. The biblical quotation that King uses comes from the versions of the law in Exodus 21:23–24 and Deuteronomy 19:21 rather than Leviticus 24:19–20. A portion of this quotation appears in an outline for the sermon "Love in Action," dated April 3, 1960. Consult King, "Draft of Chapter IV 'Love in Action,'" 406, n. 7.
20. More recently, some scholars have used Samson imagery in offering a more positive view of King's approach. In a 2000 interview with Hisham Aidi, Michael Eric Dyson stated, "I think Martin Luther King Jr. was a courageous and brave man who in the ultimate sense was more militant because, like Samson, he went into the temple and pulled it down from the inside. And though one might argue that the edifice fell partly on him and destroyed him, the reality is that King was more effective because he got inside the edifice of American democracy, the edifice of white supremacy, inside the edifice of American moral hypocrisy, and revealed to America the basis of its own fundamental contradictions between its speech and its practices." Reprinted in Michael Eric Dyson, *Open Mike: Reflections on Philosophy, Race, Sex, Culture, and Religion* (New York: Basic Books, 2003), 329.
21. Martin Luther King, Jr., *Where Do We Go from Here: Chaos or Community?* (Boston: Beacon, 1967), 23–66.
22. King, *Where Do We Go from Here*, 11. The survey King cites comes from the August 22, 1966, issue of *Newsweek*.
23. King, *Where Do We Go from Here*, 44–63.
24. www.thekingcenter.org/archive/document/modern-day-samson (accessed February 16, 2018).
25. As we discussed in chapter 3, when the angel announces Samson's birth, he does not tell Samson's mother that her son will complete the task of freeing his people from Philistine oppression. He only claims that "he shall begin to deliver Israel out of the hand of the Philistines" (Judges 13:5).
26. Albert B. Cleage, Jr., *The Black Messiah* (New York: Sheed and Ward, 1968), 116, 128–29.
27. Cleage, *The Black Messiah*, 127, 128.

28. Grace H. McPherson, "Letter to the Editor," *Life* 63.7 (August 18, 1967): 19 (emphasis in the original).

29. "Dr. Fry Insists Racial Crisis May Get Worse and Not Better," *Atlanta Daily World* (January 28, 1968): 2.

30. "Dr. Fry Insists Racial Crisis May Get Worse and Not Better," 2.

31. LeRoi Jones and Larry Neal, eds., *Black Fire: An Anthology of Afro-American Writing* (New York: William Morrow, 1968). In the wake of Malcolm X's assassination, Jones moved to Harlem in March 1965 and, along with Neal and others, helped found the Black Arts Repertory Theater School. The theater school produced plays, concerts, and poetry readings by its members.

32. For a more detailed discussion of the Black Arts movement, consult John H. Bracey, Jr., Sonia Sanchez, and James Smethurst, eds., *SOS—Calling All Black People: A Black Arts Movement Reader* (Amherst: University of Massachusetts Press, 2014); Lisa Gail Collins and Margo Natalie Crawford, eds., *New Thoughts on the Black Arts Movement* (New Brunswick: Rutgers University Press, 2006).

33. Larry Neal, "The Black Arts Movement," *The Drama Review* 12.4 (1968): 29.

34. Stokely Carmichael, "Toward Black Liberation," in *Black Fire*, 119–32. Originally published in *The Massachusetts Review* 7.4 (Autumn 1966): 639–51.

35. Carmichael, "Toward Black Liberation," 119–20.

36. Welton Smith, "Malcolm," in *Black Fire*, 288.

37. Pulitzer Prize–winner August Wilson also alludes to this song in his play *Ma Rainey's Black Bottom*, which was first performed in 1984 and published in 1985 (August Wilson, *Ma Rainey's Black Bottom: A Play in Two Acts* [New York: New American Library, 1985]). The play is set in 1927, the same year that Blind Willie Johnson recorded his version of the song. Toward the end of the first act, an argument breaks out between members of the band, who will play on a record of blues singer Ma Rainey, after Toledo, the piano player, makes fun of Levee, the trumpet player, about Levee's deference toward the White record producer. A perturbed Levee defends his actions by claiming that he learned how to deal with White people from his father who smiled and did business with the White men who raped his wife while he was secretly planning to kill them. According to Levee, he killed about half of them before they captured and lynched him. Levee concludes, "So you all just back up and leave Levee alone about the white man. I can smile and say yessir to whoever I please. I got time coming to me. You all just leave Levee alone about the white man" (Wilson, *Ma Rainey's Black Bottom*, 70). After Levee's speech, the first act ends with Slow Dang, the bassist, singing, "If I had my way If I had my way If I had my way I would tear this old building down" (Wilson, *Ma Rainey's Black Bottom*, 71). Like Samson, Levee's father dies while attempting to kill a large number of his oppressors. At the end of the play, Levee stabs Toledo with a knife in a momentary act of rage that ruins Levee's dream of starting his own band.

38. Huey P. Newton, *Revolutionary Suicide* (New York: Penguin Books, 1973) 120, 128.

39. Newton, *Revolutionary Suicide*, 122. The ten-point plan was originally published in the *Black Panther* 1.2 (May 15, 1967), 3.

40. Newton, *Revolutionary Suicide*, 122–25.

41. Newton, *Revolutionary Suicide*, 36. Over sixty years earlier, the unnamed protagonist in James Weldon Johnson's classic novel *An Autobiography of an Ex-Colored Man* expresses a similar admiration for Samson and David. He states, "For a long time King David, with Samson as a close second, stood at the head of my list of heroes" (James Weldon Johnson, *An Autobiography of an Ex-Colored Man* [Boston: Sherman, French, 1912], 22). To be clear, as this book is a work of fiction, Johnson, who was the first African American executive secretary of the NAACP, is not necessary claiming that David and Samson are his actual heroes.

42. Although Newton claims that Samson had "an ability to solve riddles put to him," the biblical text depicts him as the one who poses a riddle to the Philistines for them to solve rather the one who solves a riddle (Judges 14:12–19). Nonetheless, this does not take away from Newton's larger point that Samson used his intellect to engage his opponents.

43. "Conn. Fascist Pigs Vamp on Panthers," *The Black Panther* 2.18 (August 23, 1969): 7. "Vamping" was a term used in the 1960s and 1970s for police harassment and assaults often aimed at people involved in political protests or other forms of activism.

44. "Conn. Fascist Pigs Vamp on Panthers," 7.

45. H. Rap Brown, *Die Nigger Die: A Political Autobiography* (New York: Dial, 1969), 134.

46. Michael Lackey, ed., *The Haverford Discussions: A Black Integrationist Manifesto for Racial Justice* (Charlottesville: University of Virginia, 2013), 42–43. The book contains the transcripts of the meetings in May 1969.

47. Prior to the publication of *The Haverford Discussions* in 2013, the only publication to result from these discussions was Betty Jenkins, *Black Separatism: A Bibliography* (Westport, CT: Greenwood, 1976).

48. For a brief history of the Haverford group, consult Lackey, *The Haverford Discussions*, xi–xlv.

49. James Baldwin, *The Fire Next Time* (New York: Dial, 1963), 119–20. The song highlights the fact that, after the flood, God does not promise to never again destroy everything that breathes. Rather, God only promises to never again destroy them by means of a flood. Genesis 9:11 reads, "And I will establish my covenant with you; neither shall all flesh be cut off any more by the waters of a flood; neither shall there any more be a flood to destroy the earth." This verse leaves open the possibility that God may destroy everything that breathes by other means, such as fire.

50. The title alludes to Job 18:17, which serves as the epigraph for this chapter.

51. James Baldwin, *No Name in the Street* (New York: Dial, 1972), vi. Earlier, Baldwin quoted the song in a talk that he gave at the West Indian Student Centre in London. During the talk, Baldwin stated, "[In church, the African American] is able to act out, to sing out, to dance out, his pride, and his terrors, and his desire for revenge. All those sermons are blood thirsty and they're not talking about devils and Samson, Delilah, any of those things. They're talking about the master. In a song which says, it supposed to be about Samson, and, and the master thought it was about Samson, only now he's going to think it's about something else. The man says, the slave says, 'If I had my way, if I had my way, I'd tear this building down.' That sounds like a very happy, innocent church song. It's lethal!" James Baldwin, *Baldwin's Nigger*, documentary,

directed by Horace Ové (London: Infilm, 1969). As discussed in detail in chapter 4, the song to which Baldwin refers had its roots in African American spirituals and has been recorded under various titles beginning in the 1920s.

52. Baldwin, *No Name in the Street*, 196.

53. Baldwin, *No Name in the Street*, 196.

Chapter 6

1. The earliest reference to Harlem Renaissance poet Blanche Taylor Dickinson, who we will discuss later in this chapter, appears in a 1907 book titled *The Progression of the Race in the United States and Canada: Treating of the Great Advancement of the Colored Race*. The book aims to illustrate the advancement of the race by documenting the stories of thousands of "business men and women" of African descent, including doctors, farmers, mechanics, and lawyers among others. The reference to Blanche Taylor Dickinson occurs in the entry on her father Thomas Taylor. This entry reports that the Taylors "have one child, a little girl named Blanche, who is an intelligent child and who says, Tell the world we are rising" (Daniel Dana Buck, *The Progression of the Race in the United States and Canada: Treating of the Great Advancement of the Colored Race* [Chicago: Atwell, 1907], 370).

2. Luci Horton, "The Legacy of Phillis Wheatley: Women Poets Honor American's First Black Woman of Letters at Mississippi Festival," *Ebony* 29.5 (March 1974): 94–96, 98–100, 102.

3. For a detailed discussion of this issue, consult Nyasha Junior, *An Introduction to Womanist Biblical Interpretation* (Louisville: Westminster John Knox, 2015).

4. Christina Moody, *A Tiny Spark* (Washington, DC: Murray Brothers Press, 1910). In 1917, Moody wrote a second book under her married name Christina Moody Briggs titled *Story of the East St. Louis Riot*. Consult chapter 4 for a discussion of the East Saint Louis riot.

5. Moody, "To My Dear Reader," in Moody, *A Tiny Spark*, 7.

6. In her poem "The Soldier's Letter," a dying soldier assures his mother that the African American soldiers fought bravely during the Battle of San Juan Hill. The Battle of San Juan was a crucial battle fought on July 1, 1898, near Santiago, Cuba, during the Spanish-American War. Moody's poems, "The American Flag" and "The Negro's Flag and Country" claim full American citizenship for African Americans by emphasizing that African American soldiers fought and died for their country.

7. Christina Moody, "Samson No. 2," in Moody, *A Tiny Spark*, 43.

8. Moody, "Samson No. 2," 43.

9. Countee Cullen, ed., *Caroling Dusk: An Anthology of Verse by Negro Poets* (New York: Harper and Row, 1927), 105–11.

10. In a letter to W. E. B. Dubois, dated March 15, 1926, Taylor Dickinson wrote, "I want to be a Georgia Douglass Johnson or a Fausett." Blanche Taylor Dickinson, Letter from Blanche Taylor Dickinson to W. E. B. Dubois, March 15, 1926. W. E. B. Dubois Papers (MS 312). Special Collections and University Archives, University

of Massachusetts Amherst Libraries. Georgia Douglas Johnson, whose name Taylor Dickinson misspelled as Georgia Douglass Johnson, was a poet and playwright who published poetry in the *Crisis* in the early 1920s. Jessie Redmon Fauset, whose name Taylor Dickinson misspells as Fausett, was the literary editor for the *Crisis*. Consult chapter 4 for further discussion of Fauset.

11. Taylor Dickinson, "The Walls of Jericho," in Cullen, *Caroling Dusk*, 106.

12. Taylor Dickinson, "Four Walls," in Cullen, *Caroling Dusk*, 110–11.

13. Maureen Honey, "Introduction," in *Shadowed Dreams: Women's Poetry of the Harlem Renaissance*, 2nd ed. (ed. Maureen Honey; New Brunswick: Rutgers University Press, 2006), xliii.

14. Ida Lewis, "Forward," in Nikki Giovanni, *My House: Poems by Nikki Giovanni* (New York: William Morrow, 1972), ix.

15. Nikki Giovanni, "Black Poems, Poseurs and Power," *Negro Digest* 18.8 (June 1969): 30. The line "Nigger can you kill?," comes from her poem "The True Import of Present Dialogue, Black vs. Negro (For Peppe, Who will Ultimately Judge our Efforts)," in Nikki Giovanni, *Black Feeling, Black Talk* (New York: Distributed by Nikki Giovanni, 1968), 11–12.

16. Nikki Giovanni, "My House," in Giovanni, *My House*, 67, 68.

17. Giovanni, "Mothers," in Giovanni, *My House*, 6–7.

18. The magazine was published until 1990. For a brief historical overview of *Conditions* magazine, consult Julie R. Enszer, "'Fighting to Create and Maintain Our Own Black Women's Culture': *Conditions* Magazine 1977–1990," *American Periodicals: A Journal of History & Criticism* 25.2 (2015): 160–76.

19. Combahee River Collective, "A Black Feminist Statement," in *All the Women Are White, All the Blacks Are Men, but Some of Are Us Are Brave: Black Women's Studies* (ed. Gloria T. Hull, Patricia Bell Scott, and Barbara Smith; Old Westbury, NY: Feminist Press, 1982), 13. The collective's name was inspired by a military operation on June 1–2, 1863, along the Combahee River in South Carolina during the Civil War. Under the leadership of Harriett Tubman, the operation freed seven hundred and fifty enslaved persons.

20. In the early 1980s, the number of editors of *Conditions* increased when a new editorial collective that included women connected to the Combahee River Collective was formed (Enszer, "Fighting to Create and Maintain Our Own Black Women's Culture," 167–72).

21. Carole Clemmons Gregory, "Love Letter," *Conditions: Five—The Black Woman's Issue* 2.2 (Autumn 1979): 64. Often, pear trees are associated with sex, love, and fertility. For example, in Zora Neale Hurston's classic 1937 novel *Their Eyes Were Watching God*, Janie, the protagonist, connects a blooming pear tree with her developing ideas about sexual desire, love, and marriage throughout the novel. Also, hair and nail clippings are used within conjure or root work to cast spells that could bring misfortune. Consult Yvonne P. Chireau, *Black Magic: Religion and the Conjuring Tradition* (Berkeley: University of California Press, 2003).

22. While Judges 13:2 identifies Samson as a member of the Israelite tribe of Dan, the Bible never identifies Delilah's ethnicity despite the popular belief that Delilah is a

Philistine. The biblical text only states that Samson fell in love with her in the valley of Sorek (Judges 16:4). As this valley is on the border of Israelite and Philistine territories, one could easily encounter either Philistine or Israelite women in this area. The fact that Delilah works with the Philistines does not necessarily confirm that she is a Philistine. The biblical scholar Susan Ackerman compares Delilah to Jael, another woman who brings down a powerful man earlier in the book of Judges. In Judges 4, Jael helps the Israelites defeat an enemy even though she is not an Israelite herself. Consult Susan Ackerman, "What If Judges Had Been Written by a Philistine?," *Biblical Interpretation* 8 (2000): 33–41.

23. Elsewhere, Gregory's poetry expresses frustration over the lack of recognition that African American women receive for their contributions to the struggle for racial equality and freedom. For example, consult Gregory, "Revelation," in *Conditions: Five*, 61–63; Carole Clemmons Gregory, "A Freedom Song for the Black Woman," in *Black Sister: Poetry by Black American Women, 1746–1980* (ed. Erlene Stetson; Bloomington: Indiana University Press, 1981), 188–90. Gregory's poem "Revelation" appears immediately before "Love Letter" in *Conditions: Five*.

24. In a 1982 article in *Ms.* magazine, Letty Cottin Pogrebin implied that "Love Letter" is anti-Semitic. She writes, "In Carole Clemmons Gregory's poem, 'Love Letter,' a black Delilah suggests that the Jewish Samson would use his God-given strength to kill black people" (Letty Cottin Pogrebin, "Anti-Semitism in the Women's Movement," *Ms.* [June 1982]: 71). While Gregory may imagine Delilah as a Black woman, she does not indicate how she imagines Samson's race, ethnicity, or religion in the poem. One should not assume that he represents a Jewish figure by default. Moreover, the comparison of Delilah to an African American woman who defends her people against terrorism by a White Christian community occurs in earlier African American literature. For example, written under the pseudonym Jack Thorne, David Bryant Fulton's 1900 novel *Hanover* was based on the massacre of the African American community in Wilmington, North Carolina, on November 10, 1898. In the novel, a non-Jewish White man named Ben Hartright reveals the plan to massacre the local African American community to his mixed-race lover named Molly Pierrepont. In response Molly declares, "Samson has revealed his secret to his Delilah, and it's Delilah's duty to warn her people of the dangers that await them." David Bryant Fulton [Jack Thorne], *Hanover, or the Persecution of Lowly: A Story of the Wilmington Massacre* (New York: M.C.L. Hill, 1900), 38. The idea that the poem depicts "the Jewish Samson" shows no awareness of the rich and varied uses of Samson within African American religious and literary traditions.

25. Consult Lucille Clifton, *Book of Light* (Portownsend, WA: Copper Canyon Press, 1993), 37. The book's title is a word play on the author's first name, Lucille. Clifton concludes her poem "daughters," with a biblical-like genealogy that reads, "i am / lucille, which stands for light / daughter of thelma, daughter / of georgia, daughter of / dazzling you" ("daughters," in Clifton, *Book of Light*, 13).

26. In addition to Samson, the biblical characters include Sarah, Naomi, and Cain. Consult Clifton, "sarah's promise," "naomi watches as ruth sleeps," and "cain," in Clifton, *Book of Light*, 56, 57, 58, respectively. The characters from Greek mythology

include Atlas and Leda. Consult Clifton, "atlas," "leda 1," "leda 2," and "leda 3," in Clifton, *Book of Light*, 55, 59, 60, 61, respectively.

27. Linn Washington, "MOVE: A Double Standard of Justice?," *Yale Journal of Law and Liberation* 1 (1989): 69. Washington provides a detailed and well-documented overview of MOVE's checkered legal history.

28. The officers involved in the brutal beating of MOVE member Delbert Africa during the same incident, which was caught by television cameras, were acquitted by the judge before a jury could render a verdict. "Philadelphia Judge Stanley L. Kubacki issued a directed verdict of acquittal—unrequested by either the defense or the prosecution—moments before the case was to be decided by a specially impaneled out of town jury" (Washington, "MOVE: A Double Standard of Justice?," 72).

29. Washington, "MOVE: A Double Standard of Justice?," 71.

30. Clifton, "move," in Clifton, *Book of Light*, 35.

31. Lucille Clifton, "samson predicts from gaza the philadelphia fire," in Clifton, *Book of Light*, 37. (Emphasis in the original.)

32. In January 2016, this book's co-author Nyasha Junior moderated a panel during a conference in Philadelphia titled "Reclaiming Our Future: The Black Radical Tradition in Our Time," which included Ramona Africa. When Junior asked Africa how she would like to be introduced, Africa simply said, "Tell them I'm a revolutionary."

33. For example, Clifton's poem titled "she lived" concludes "she walked away / from the hole in the ground / deciding to live. and she lived" (Clifton, "she lived," in Clifton, *Book of Light*, 20). Clifton's "won't you celebrate with me," arguably the most famous poem in the book, includes the lines, "born in Babylon / both non-white and woman . . . come celebrate / with me that everyday / something has tried to kill me / and has failed" (Clifton, "won't you celebrate with me," in Clifton, *Book of Light*, 25).

Chapter 7

1. Henry Louis Stephens, "Sambo Agonistes," *Vanity Fair* 1.10 (1860): 153.

2. Nast did not create these personifications of the United States. As discussed in chapter 1, the image of Columbia as a symbol of the American colonies dates to the eighteenth century.

3. For detailed discussions of Nast's life and reprints of many of his cartoons, consult Fiona Deans Halloran, *Thomas Nast: The Father of Modern Political Cartoons* (Chapel Hill: University of North Carolina Press, 2012); Morton Keller, *The Art and Politics of Thomas Nast* (New York: Oxford University Press, 1968); Albert Bigelow Paine, *Thomas Nast: His Period and His Pictures* (New York: Macmillan, 1904); J. Chal Vinson, *Thomas Nast: Political Cartoonist* (Athens: University of Georgia Press, 1967).

4. For a detailed discussion of "This Is a White Man's Government," consult Halloran, *Thomas Nast*, 107–12; Vinson, *Thomas Nast*, 13.

5. Thomas Nast, "The Modern Samson," *Harper's Weekly* 12.614 (October 3, 1868): 632.

6. Quoted in Paine, *Thomas Nast*, 129.

7. "The Black Samson Asleep," *Freeman* (October 5, 1889): 4.

8. Consult chapter 1 for a discussion of Longfellow's "The Warning" and references to the poem in African American literature from the late nineteenth century.

9. "What Will This Samson Do?" *Pittsburgh Courier* (November 19, 1941): 6.

10. Holloway, who was born in Indiana, is probably best known for his long-running comic strip *Sunny Boy Sam*, drawn for the *Pittsburgh Courier* beginning in 1928. In addition to his comic strip, he regularly published editorial cartoons that addressed political issues of the day. For brief discussions of Holloway's career, consult Tim Jackson, *Pioneering Cartoonists of Color* (Jackson: University Press of Mississippi, 2016), 28, 47–48, 50, 144; John Stevens, "Reflections in a Dark Mirror: Comic Strips in Black Newspapers," *Journal of Popular Culture* 10.1 (1976): 239–44; Allan Holtz, "Ink-Slinger Profiles: Wilbert Holloway," Strippers Guide, February 13, 2012, http://bit.ly/HoltzHolloway.

11. "What Will This Samson Do?," 6.

12. "What Will This Samson Do?," 6 (capitalization in the original).

13. "What Will This Samson Do?," 6.

14. "What Will This Samson Do?," 6 (capitalization and spelling in the original).

15. "What Will This Samson Do?," 6 (capitalization in the original).

16. "What Will This Samson Do?," 6 (capitalization in the original).

17. "What Will This Samson Do?," 6 (capitalization in the original).

18. "What Will This Samson Do?," 6 (capitalization in the original).

19. Elmer Simms Campbell, "Uncle Samson and Delilah," *Baltimore Afro-American* (August 17, 1946): 4. For a detailed discussion of Campbell's career, consult Robert C. Harvey, "Withdrawing the Color Line: The First Famous African American Cartoonist," in Robert C. Harvey, *Insider Histories of Cartooning: Rediscovering Forgotten Famous Comics and Their Creators* (Jackson: University Press of Mississippi, 2014), 86–97. Harvey does not, however, discuss Campbell's work in the *Baltimore Afro-American*.

20. Harvey, "Withdrawing the Color Line," 92.

21. Harvey, "Withdrawing the Color Line," 97.

22. Oliver Herford, "Uncle Samson and Delilah," *Life* 80 (November 9, 1922): 3.

23. Agnes Repplier, "Uncle Samson and Delilah," *Life* 80 (November 9, 1922): 3.

24. The *Chicago Tribune* published an earlier cartoon also titled "Uncle Samson and Delilah" by John T. McCutcheon, a Pulitzer Prize–winning cartoonist who spent most of his long career at the *Tribune*. It was reprinted in the *Literary Digest* 40.8 (August 25, 1917): 10. As in Herford's cartoon, McCutcheon's Delilah wears a headband labeled "Pacifism," although her scissors are labeled "Premature Peace Propaganda." A bare-chested Uncle Samson with hair labeled "Loyalty, Strength, Determination, Morale" and a belt buckle labeled "US" is walking as Delilah tells him to "Hold Still, Dearie." Although the title and anti-pacifist themes are similar to Herford's cartoon, McCutcheon's Uncle Samson does not physically resemble either Herford's or Campbell's Uncle Samson.

25. *Black Samson*, directed by Charles Bail (Hollywood: Warner Brothers, 1974). Consult Internet Movie Database, https://www.imdb.com.

26. For a detailed discussion of blaxploitation films, consult Novotny Lawrence and Gerald R. Butters, Jr., eds., *Beyond Blaxploitation* (Detroit: Wayne State University Press, 2016). This volume does not, however, discuss the film *Black Samson*.

27. Linda Gross, "'Back Samson': Walks Softly, Carries Staff," *Los Angeles Times* (September 11, 1974): G14.

28. Lawrence Van Gelder, "'Black Samson' from Film Netherworld," *New York Times* (August 15, 1974): 25.

29. Pat McGilligan, "'Black Samson' at Saxon," *Boston Globe* (August 22, 1974): 61.

30. "'Black Samson' Fights Mob with Ancient Art Kindo," *Baltimore Afro-American* (September 7, 1974): 11; "Black Samson to Open in Black Areas," *Chicago Metro News* (August 17, 1974): D5.

31. Jean-Michel Basquiat, *Obnoxious Liberals* (1982), L. Broad Collection, Los Angeles, California. For online access to the painting, consult The Broad: https://www.thebroad.org.

32. bell hooks, "Altars of Sacrifice: Re-membering Basquiat," *Art in America* 81.6 (June 1993): 72. bell hooks is the pen name of Gloria Jean Watkins, a writer, activist, and educator whose work often addresses the intersections of race, class, and gender.

33. Black Samson first appears in *Invincible* 6 (October 2003): 9, https://imagecomics.com/comics/series/invincible.

34. *Invincible* 112 (June 2014): 5.

35. Justin Reed, *Samson: Blessed Savior of Israel, The Remastered Edition* (New York: Published by Justin Reed, 2012), 12.

36. For Reed's detailed bibliography of contemporary scholarly literature on Samson, consult Reed, *Samson: Blessed Savior of Israel*, 242–45. Shortly after the completion of his graphic novel, Reed entered the doctoral program in biblical studies at Princeton Theological Seminary in New Jersey. Currently, he teaches biblical studies at Louisville Presbyterian Theological Seminary in Kentucky.

37. Reed, *Samson: Blessed Savior of Israel,* 232.

38. *The Bible*, Lightworkers Media, 2013. Consult Internet Movie Database, http://www.imdb.com/title/tt2245988/.

39. Dominic Patten, "History's 'The Bible' & 'Vikings' Rise in Week 3," Deadline.com (March 19, 2013), http://bit.ly/PattenWeek3.

40. In the biblical story, Samson does not pray for guidance after defeating the Philistines. Instead, he calls out to God, "Thou hast given this great deliverance into the hand of thy servant: and now shall I die for thirst, and fall into the hand of the uncircumcised?" (Judges 15:18).

41. Anozi's full name is Chukwunonso Nwachukwu "Nonso" Anozie. Consult Internet Movie Database, https://www.imdb.com.

42. S. Michael Houdmann, "Is The History Channel's 'The Bible' Mini-series Bbiblically Accurate," Blogos, http://bit.ly/HoudmannBlogos.

43. Mary Fairchild, "Was Samson of the Bible a Black Man?" Thought Co., March 17, 2017 (updated), http://bit.ly/FairchildSamson.

44. Wil Gafney, "Black Samson and White Women on the History Channel," March 11, 2013, http://bit.ly/GafneySamson.

Epilogue

1. Toni Morrison, *The Bluest Eye* (New York: Plume, 1993), 133. Originally published as Toni Morrison, *The Bluest Eye* (New York: Holt, Rinehart and Winston, 1970). In this particular scene, a character named Cholly asks his great aunt Jimmy why he was not named after his father Samson Fuller. Aunt Jimmy explains that not only was his father not around when Cholly was born but also that fate does not treat people named Samson kindly.

2. Isabel Wilkerson, "Where Do We Go from Here?" *Essence* 45.10 (January 2015): 88; cf. N. D. B. Connolly, "This, Our Second Nadir," *Boston Review*, Forum 1: Race, Capitalism, Justice (January 2017): 95–104. The title of Wilkerson's article comes from the title of Martin Luther King, Jr.'s final book, which we discussed in chapter 5. This use of the term "nadir" was coined by Rayford Logan, a Harvard-trained historian who taught at Howard University, in his book *The Negro in American Life and Thought: The Nadir, 1877–1901* (New York: Dial, 1954). The nadir is the lowest point in the social standing of African Americans, often used in reference to the post-Reconstruction Era through the early twentieth century.

3. Although it is not visible on this book's cover, in some casts of the sculpture Ward's freedman has a manacle hanging from his left wrist with an inscription commemorating the 54th Regiment Massachusetts Volunteer Infantry, an African American regiment in the Union army involved in the battle of Fort Wagner on July 18, 1863. The inscription contributes to the idea of the freedman fighting for rather than waiting for his freedom.

4. Kirk Savage, "Molding Emancipation: John Quincy Adams Ward's 'The Freedman' and the Meaning of the Civil War," *Art Institute of Chicago Museum Studies* 27.1 (2001): 35.

5. John Quincy Adams Ward to J. R. Lambdin, April 2, 1863, in Albert Rosenthal Papers, Archives of American Art, roll D34, frame 1302. Quoted in Savage, "Molding Emancipation," 35.

Appendix

1. Following the standard Hebrew text, the King James Version translates 1 Samuel 12:11 as "And the LORD sent Jerubbaal, and Bedan, and Jephthah, and *Samuel*, and delivered you out of the hand of your enemies on every side, and ye dwelled safe" (emphasis added). Since Samuel is speaking, a reference to himself among the heroes from the book of Judges may result from an error that occurred somewhere in the long transmission of the text. Thus, some translations, such as the New Revised Standard Version, follow a Greek version of the verse and change 1 Samuel 12:11 to read, "And the LORD sent Jerubbaal and Barak, and Jephthah, and *Samson*, and rescued you out of the hand of your enemies on every side; and you lived in safety" (emphasis added).

Bibliography

A. D. A. B. "The Execution of John Brown." *The Liberator* 29 (December 9, 1859): 196.

Ackerman, Susan. "What If Judges Had Been Written by a Philistine?" *Biblical Interpretation* 8 (2000): 33–41.

Allen, James Egert. "Black History Past and Present: Corps of Rugged Men." *New York Amsterdam News* (January 9, 1971): 15.

Armistead, Wilson. *The Garland of Freedom; A Collection of Poems, Chiefly Anti-Slavery*. London: W. and F. G. Cash/William Tweedie, 1853.

Atwater, Horace Cowler. *Incidents of a Southern Tour: Or the South, as Seen with Northern Eyes*. Boston: J. P. Magee, 1857.

Bailey, Randall C., ed. *Yet with a Steady Beat: Contemporary U.S. Afrocentric Biblical Interpretation*. Atlanta: Society of Biblical Literature, 2003.

Baldwin, James. *The Fire Next Time*. New York: Dial, 1963.

Baldwin, James. "Baldwin's Nigger." Documentary, directed by Horace Ové. London: Infilm, 1969.

Baldwin, James. *No Name in the Street*. New York: Dial, 1972.

Basquiat, Jean-Michel. "Obnoxious Liberals." L. Broad Collection, Los Angeles, California. 1982.

Berlin, Natalie Curtis. *Hampton Series Negro Folk Songs*. New York: G. Schirmer, 1918.

Bernier, Celeste-Marie. *Characters of Blood: Black Heroism in the Transatlantic Imagination*. Charlottesville: University of Virginia Press, 2012.

Bontemps, Arna. *Gabriel's Revolt: Virginia 1800*. New York: Macmillan, 1936.

Bracey, John H., Jr., Sonia Sanchez, and James Smethurst, eds. *SOS—Calling All Black People: A Black Arts Movement Reader*. Amherst: University of Massachusetts Press, 2014.

Braden, John. "Educational Work among the Freedman by the Methodist Episcopal Church." Pages 178–83 in *Christian Educators in Council. Sixty Addresses by American Educators; with Historical Notes upon the National Education Assembly, Held at Ocean Grove, N.J. August 9–12, 1883. Also, Illiteracy and Education Tables from Census of 1880*. Edited by Joseph Crane Hartzell. New York: Phillips and Hunt, 1884.

Bradford, Juliet M. "Trinity of Slavery Poets." *The Colored American Magazine* (July 1, 1909): 26–29.

Breen, Patrick H. *The Land Shall Be Deluged in Blood: A New History of the Nat Turner Revolt*. New York: Oxford University Press, 2016.

Briggs, Christina Moody. *Story of the East St. Louis Riot*. Publisher unidentified, 1917.

Brinch, Boyrereau. *The Blind African Slave, or, Memoirs of Boyrereau Brinch, Nicknamed Jeffrey Brace*. Transcribed with commentary by Benjamin F. Prentiss. St. Albans, VT: Harry Whitney, 1810.

Brown, H. Rap. *Die Nigger Die: A Political Autobiography*. New York: Dial, 1969.

Browne, William Hand. *Archives of Maryland: Proceedings of the Council of Maryland, 1732–1753*. Baltimore: Maryland Historical Society, 1908.

Bryant, Joseph G. "Negro Poetry." *The Colored American Magazine* (May 1905): 254–57.

Buck, Daniel Dana. *The Progression of the Race in the United States and Canada: Treating of the Great Advancement of the Colored Race.* Chicago: Atwell Printing and Binding, 1907.

Callahan, Allen Dwight. *The Talking Book: African Americans and the Bible.* New Haven: Yale University Press, 2006.

Campbell, Elmer Simms. "Uncle Samson and Delilah." *Baltimore Afro-American* (August 17, 1946): 4.

Carmichael, Stokely. "Toward Black Liberation." Pages 119–32 in *Black Fire: An Anthology of Afro-American Writing.* Edited by LeRoi Jones and Larry Neal. New York: William Morrow, 1968. Originally published in *The Massachusetts Review* 7.4 (Autumn 1966): 639–51.

Carroll, Joseph C. *Slave Insurrections in the United States, 1800–1865.* Reprint. New York: Negro Universities Press, 1973.

Cary, Lorene. *The Price of a Child.* New York: Vintage, 1995.

Chireau, Yvonne P. *Black Magic: Religion and the Conjuring Tradition.* Berkeley: University of California Press, 2003.

Clarke, John Henrik, ed. *William Styron's Nat Turner: Ten Black Writer's Respond.* Boston: Beacon, 1968.

Cleage, Albert B., Jr. *The Black Messiah.* New York: Sheed and Ward, 1968.

Clifton, Lucille. *Book of Light.* Portownsend, WA: Copper Canyon Press, 1993.

Coffin, Joshua. *An Account of Some of the Principle Slave Insurrections.* New York: American Anti-Slavery Society, 1860.

Coleman, George M. "Black Heroes Helped Gain New Nation: The Negro Fought for Independence of U.S." *Atlanta Daily World* (July 4, 1962): 1, 4.

Collins, L. W. "No Master Great Enough to Make Slavery Sweet, Says Reader." *Los Angeles Tribune* (June 26, 1959): 11.

Collins, Lisa Gail, and Margo Natalie Crawford, eds. *New Thoughts on the Black Arts Movement.* New Brunswick: Rutgers University Press, 2006.

Collins, Victoria J. "Anxious Records: Race, Imperial Belonging, and the Black Literary Imagination, 1900–1946." PhD dissertation. Columbia University, 2013.

Combahee River Collective. "A Black Feminist Statement." Pages 13–22 in *All the Women Are White, All the Blacks Are Men, but Some of Are Us Are Brave: Black Women's Studies.* Edited by Gloria T. Hull, Patricia Bell Scott, and Barbara Smith. Old Westbury, NY: Feminist Press, 1982.

Connolly, N. D. B. "This, Our Second Nadir." *Boston Review,* Forum 1: Race, Capitalism, Justice (January 2017): 95–104.

Crafts, Hannah. *The Bondwoman's Narrative.* Edited by Henry Louis Gates, Jr. New York: Time-Warner Books, 2002.

Crogman, William Henry. "The Negro Problem." Pages 241–69 in William Henry Crogman, *Talks for the Times.* South Atlanta, GA: Franklin, 1896.

Cullen, Countee, ed. *Caroling Dusk: An Anthology of Verse by Negro Poets.* New York: Harper and Row, 1927.

Darnell, S. B. "Education an Indispensable Agency in the Redemption of the Negro Race." Pages 62–65 in *Christian Educators in Council. Sixty Addresses by American Educators; with Historical Notes upon the National Education Assembly, Held at Ocean Grove, N.J. August 9–12, 1883. Also, Illiteracy and Education Tables from Census of 1880.* Edited by Joseph Crane Hartzell. New York: Phillips and Hunt, 1883.

Demond, Rev. A. L. "The Negro Element in American Life." *Colored American* (April 1, 1902): 357–66.

Dennett, John Richard. "The South As It Is: 1865–1866." Serialized in *The Nation* 1–2 (July 1865 to April 1866).

Dickinson, Blanche Taylor. *Letter from Blanche Taylor Dickinson to W. E. B. Dubois, March 15, 1926.* W. E. B. Dubois Papers (MS 312). Special Collections and University Archives, University of Massachusetts Amherst Libraries.

Dickinson, Blanche Taylor. "Four Walls." Pages 110–11 in *Caroling Dusk: An Anthology of Verse by Negro Poets*. Edited by Countee Cullen. New York: Harper and Row, 1927.

Dickinson, Blanche Taylor. "The Walls of Jericho." Pages 106–7 in *Caroling Dusk: An Anthology of Verse by Negro Poets*. Edited by Countee Cullen. New York: Harper and Row, 1927.

Dixon, Willie, Jr. "Resistance-Resistance-Resistance: Let Your Motto be Resistance!" *Chicago Metro News* (October 18, 1986): 6.

Douglass, Frederick. *My Bondage and My Freedom*. New York: Miller, Orton and Mulligan, 1855.

Douglass, Frederick. "Captain John Brown Not Insane." *Douglass' Monthly* (November 1859): 1.

Douglass, Frederick. *John Brown: An Address by Fredrick Douglass at the Fourteenth Anniversary of Storer College, Harper Ferry, West Virginia, May 30, 1881*. Dover, NH: Morning Star Job Printing House, 1881.

Douglass, Frederick. "The Reason for Our Troubles: Speech on the War Delivered in the National Hall, Philadelphia, January 14, 1862." Pages 196–208 in *The Life and Writings of Frederick Douglass*. Vol. 3: *The Civil War 1861–1865*. Edited by Philip S. Foner. New York: International, 1952.

Douglass, Frederick. "What to the Slave Is the Fourth of July?: An Address Delivered in Rochester, New York on 5 July 1852." Pages 359–88 in *The Frederick Douglass Papers, Series One: Speeches, Debates, and Interviews*. Vol. 2: *1847–54*. Edited by John W. Blassingame. New Haven: Yale University Press, 1982.

Du Bois, W. E. B. *Souls of Black Folk: Essays and Sketches*. Chicago: A. C. McClurg, 1903.

Du Bois, W. E. B. *John Brown*. Philadelphia: G. W. Jacobs, 1909.

Du Bois, W. E. B. "The Problem of Problems." *The Intercollegiate Socialist* (December–January 1917–18): 5–9.

Du Bois, W. E. B. *Dusk of Dawn: An Essay toward an Autobiography of a Race Concept*. Edited by Henry Louis Gates, Jr. New York: Oxford University Press, 2007.

Duganne, Augustine Joseph Hickey. *The Tenant-House: Or, Embers from Poverty's Hearthstone*. New York: R. M. De Witt, 1857.

Dunbar, Paul Laurence. "The Colored Soldiers." Pages 38–40 in Paul Laurence Dunbar, *Majors and Minors*. Toledo, OH: Hadley and Hadley, 1895.

Dunbar, Paul Laurence. "We Wear the Mask." Page 21 in Paul Laurence Dunbar, *Majors and Minors*. Toledo, OH: Hadley and Hadley, 1895.

Dunbar, Paul Laurence. "Black Samson of Brandywine." Pages 120–23 in Paul Laurence Dunbar, *Lyrics of Love and Laughter*. New York: Dodd, Mead, 1903. Reprinted in *The Crisis: A Record of the Darker Races* 13 (September 1917): 255.

Dunbar Nelson, Alice. "Negro Literature for Negro Pupils." *The Southern Workman* 51.2 (February 1922): 59–63.

Dunbar Nelson, Alice Moore, William Sanders Scarborough, and Reverdy Cassius Ransom, eds. *Paul Laurence Dunbar: Poet Laureate of the Negro Race.* Philadelphia: A. M. E. Church Review, 1914.

Dyson, Michael Eric. *Open Mike: Reflections on Philosophy, Race, Sex, Culture, and Religion.* New York: Basic Books, 2003.

Egerton, Douglas R. *Gabriel's Rebellion: The Virginia Slave Conspiracies of 1800 and 1802.* Chapel Hill: University of North Carolina Press, 1993.

Egerton, Douglas R. *He Shall Go Out Free: The Lives of Denmark Vesey.* Revised and updated edition. Lanham: Rowman and Littlefield, 2004.

Egerton, Douglas R., and Robert L. Paquette, eds., *The Denmark Vesey Affair: A Documentary History.* Gainesville: University of Florida Press, 2017.

Ellison, Ralph. "Stormy Weather." *New Masses* (September 24, 1940): 20–21.

Ellison, Ralph. "Recent Negro Fiction." *New Masses* (August 5, 1941): 22–26.

Ellison, Ralph. "Change the Joke and Slip the Yoke." *Partisan Review* 25.2 (Spring 1958): 212–22.

Ellison, Ralph. "The Roof, the Steeple and the People." *Quarterly Review of Literature* 10 (1960): 115–28.

Ellison, Ralph. *Invisible Man.* New York: Vintage International, 1995. Originally published as *Invisible Man.* New York: Random House, 1952.

Ellison, Ralph. *Juneteeth.* New York: Vintage International, 1999.

Ellison, Ralph. *Three Days Before the Shooting . . .* Edited by John F. Callahan and Adam Bradley. New York: Modern Library, 2010.

Enszer, Julie R. "'Fighting to Create and Maintain Our Own Black Women's Culture': Conditions *Magazine 1977–1990.*" *American Periodicals: A Journal of History & Criticism* 25.2 (2015): 160–76.

Eynikel, Erik, and Tobias Nicklas, eds. *Samson: Hero or Fool?: The Many Faces of Samson.* Themes in Biblical Narrative: Jewish and Christian Traditions 17. Leiden: Brill, 2014.

Fairchild, Mary. "Was Samson of the Bible a Black Man?" *Thought Co.,* May 20, 2018 (updated). http://bit.ly/FairchildSamson.

Fauset, Jessie Redmon. "A Negro on East St. Louis." *The Survey* 38 (August 18, 1917): 448.

Felder, Cain Hope, ed. *Stony the Road We Trod: African American Biblical Interpretation.* Minneapolis, MN: Fortress Press, 1991.

Fletcher, Samuel. *Black Samson: A Narrative of Old Kentucky.* Munro's Ten Cent Novels. New York: George Munro, 1867.

Flowers, Sandra Hollin. "Solving the Critical Conundrum of Jean Toomer's 'Box Seat.'" *Studies in Short Fiction* 25.3 (1988): 301–5.

Forbes, George Washington. "Requiem Dirge for Atlanta's Slain." Reprinted in Jesse Max Barber, "The Atlanta Tragedy." *The Voice of the Negro* (November 1906): 479.

Fortune, Timothy Thomas. *Black and White: Land, Labor, and Politics in the South.* New York: Fords, Howard, and Hulbert, 1884.

Fulton, David Bryant [Jack Thorne]. *Hanover, or, The Persecution of the Lowly: A Story of the Wilmington Massacre.* New York: M.C.L. Hill, 1900.

Gafney, Wil. "Black Samson and White Women on the History Channel." (March 11, 2013.) http://bit.ly/GafneySamson.

Garrison, William Lloyd. "The Mask Entirely Removed." *Liberator* 23 (December 16, 1853): 196.

Garvey, Marcus. "The Future as I See It." Pages 73–78 in *The Philosophy and Opinions of Marcus Garvey Or, Africa for the Africans.* Compiled by Amy Jacques Garvey. Dover, MA: Majority Press, 1986.

Gibbs, Jenna M. *Performing the Temple of Liberty: Slavery, Theater, and Popular Culture in London and Philadelphia, 1760–1850.* Baltimore: Johns Hopkins University Press, 2014.

Giovanni, Nikki. "The True Import of Present Dialogue, Black vs. Negro (For Peppe, Who will Ultimately Judge our Efforts)." Pages 11–12 in Nikki Giovanni, *Black Feeling, Black Talk.* New York: Distributed by Nikki Giovanni, 1968.

Giovanni, Nikki. "Black Poems, Poseurs and Power." *Negro Digest* 18.8 (June 1969): 30–34.

Giovanni, Nikki. *My House: Poems by Nikki Giovanni.* New York: William Morrow, 1972.

Gray, Thomas R. *The Confessions of Nat Turner: The Leader of the Late Insurrection in Southampton, Va., as Fully and Voluntarily Made to Thomas R. Gray, in the Prison Where He was Confined, and Acknowledged by Him to be Such, When Read before the Court of Southampton: with the Certificate, under Seal of the Court Convened at Jerusalem, Nov. 5, 1831, for His Trial.* Richmond: T. R. Gray, 1832.

Gregory, Carole Clemmons. "Love Letter." *Conditions: Five—The Black Woman's Issue* 2.2 (Autumn 1979): 64.

Gregory, Carole Clemmons. "Revelation." *Conditions: Five—The Black Woman's Issue* 2.2 (Autumn 1979): 61–63.

Gregory, Carole Clemmons. "A Freedom Song for the Black Woman." Pages 188–90 in *Black Sister: Poetry by Black American Women, 1746–1980.* Edited by Erlene Stetson. Bloomington: Indiana University Press, 1981.

Gross, Linda. "'Back Samson': Walks Softly, Carries Staff." *Los Angeles Times* (September 11, 1974): G14.

Gunn, David. *Judges.* Blackwell Bible Commentaries. Oxford: Blackwell, 2005.

Halloran, Fiona Deans. *Thomas Nast: The Father of Modern Political Cartoons.* Chapel Hill: University of North Carolina Press, 2012.

Harlan, Louis R., ed. *The Booker T. Washington Papers.* Vol. 3. Urbana: University of Illinois Press, 1974.

Harland, Marion. *Judith: A Chronicle of Old Virginia.* New York: Scribner, 1883.

Harper, Francis Ellen Watkins. *Iola Leroy, or Shadows Uplifted.* Philadelphia: Garrigues, 1892.

Harrison, Herbert H. *The Negro and the Nation.* New York: Cosmo-Advocate, 1917.

Harvey, Robert C. "Withdrawing the Color Line: The First Famous African American Cartoonist." Pages 86–97 in Robert C. Harvey, *Insider Histories of Cartooning: Rediscovering Forgotten Famous Comics and Their Creators.* Jackson: University Press of Mississippi, 2014.

Heard, Josephine D. (Henderson). "The Black Samson." Pages 88–89 in *Morning Glories.* Philadelphia: Publisher unidentified, 1890. Reprinted in *The Colored American Magazine* 12.4 (April 1, 1907): 251.

Heidler, David Stephen. *Pulling the Temple Down: The Fire-eaters and the Destruction of the Union.* Mechanicsburg, PA: Stackpole Books, 1994.

Helwig, Timothy Wade. "Race, Nativism, and the Making of Class in Antebellum City Mysteries." PhD dissertation. University of Maryland, 2006.

Herford, Oliver. "Uncle Samson and Delilah." *Life* 80 (November 9, 1922): 3.

Hickman, Rev. W. H. "Black Samson and the American Republic." *Manual of the Methodist Episcopal Church* 8 (1888): 76.

Higginson, Thomas W. *Travellers and Outlaws: Episodes in American History.* Boston: Lee and Shepard, 1889.

Holtz, Allan. "Ink-Slinger Profiles: Wilbert Holloway." Strippers Guide. Last modified February 13, 2012. http://bit.ly/HoltzHolloway.

Honey, Maureen. "Introduction." Pages xxxiii–lxviii in *Shadowed Dreams: Women's Poetry of the Harlem Renaissance*. 2nd edition. Edited by Maureen Honey. New Brunswick, NJ: Rutgers University Press, 2006.

hooks, bell. "Altars of Sacrifice: Re-membering Basquiat." *Art in America* 81.6 (June 1993): 68–75.

Hopkins, Dwight N. *Down, Up, and Over: Slave Religion and Black Theology*. Minneapolis, MN: Fortress, 2000.

Hopkins, Pauline Elizabeth. "Winona: A Tale of Negro Life in the South and Southwest." Serialized in *Colored American Magazine* 5.1–6 (March to October 1902).

Horton, Luci. "The Legacy of Phillis Wheatley: Women Poets Honor American's First Black Woman of Letters at Mississippi Festival." *Ebony* 29.5 (March 1974): 94–96, 98–100, 102.

Houdmann, S. Michael. "Is The History Channel's 'The Bible' Mini-Series Biblically Accurate." Blogos, March 3, 2013. http://bit.ly/HoudmannBlogos.

Howison, Robert R. *A History of Virginia*. 2 vols. Philadelphia: Carey and Hart, 1846.

Hughes, Langston. "Union." *New Masses* 7.4 (September 1931): 12.

Hughes, Langston. "On the Road." *Esquire* (January 1935): 92, 154.

Irmscher, Christoph. *Public Poet, Private Man: Henry Wadsworth Longfellow at 200*. Amherst: University of Massachusetts, 2009.

Jackson, Tim. *Pioneering Cartoonists of Color*. Jackson: University Press of Mississippi, 2016.

Jenkins, Betty. *Black Separatism: A Bibliography*. Westport, CT: Greenwood, 1976.

Johnson, James Weldon. *An Autobiography of an Ex-Colored Man*. Boston: Sherman, French, 1912.

Johnson, Sylvester A. *African American Religions, 1500–2000: Colonialism, Democracy, and Freedom*. New York: Cambridge University Press, 2015.

Jones, Absalom, and Richard Allen. *A Narrative of the Proceedings of the Black People, during the Late Awful Calamity in Philadelphia, in the Year 1793: And a Refutation of Some Censures, Thrown upon Them in Some Late Publications*. Philadelphia: William W. Woodward, at Franklin's Head, 1794.

Jones, LeRoi, and Larry Neal, eds. *Black Fire: An Anthology of Afro-American Writing*. New York: William Morrow, 1968.

Junior, Nyasha. *An Introduction to Womanist Biblical Interpretation*. Louisville: Westminster John Knox, 2015.

Junior, Nyasha. *Reimaging Hagar: Blackness and Bible*. New York: Oxford University Press, 2019.

Keller, Morton. *The Art and Politics of Thomas Nast*. New York: Oxford University Press, 1968.

Kennedy, John. *The Natural History of Man; or Popular Chapters on Ethnography*. London: J. Cassell, 1851.

King, Martin Luther, Jr. *Strength to Love*. New York: Harper and Row, 1963.

King, Martin Luther, Jr. *Where Do We Go from Here: Chaos or Community?* Boston: Beacon, 1967.

King, Martin Luther, Jr. "Draft of Chapter IV 'Love in Action.'" Pages 486–95 in *The Papers of Martin Luther King, Jr.* Vol. 6: *Advocate of the Social Gospel, September*

1948–March 1963. Edited by Clayborne Carson (senior editor), Susan Carson, Susan Englander, Troy Jackson, and Gerald L. Smith. Berkeley: University of California Press, 2007.

King, Martin Luther, Jr. "Levels of Love." Pages 437–45 in *The Papers of Martin Luther King, Jr.* Vol. 6: *Advocate of the Social Gospel, September 1948–March 1963*. Edited by Clayborne Carson (senior editor), Susan Carson, Susan Englander, Troy Jackson, and Gerald L. Smith. Berkeley: University of California Press, 2007.

King, Martin Luther, Jr. "Love in Action I." Pages 405–7 in *The Papers of Martin Luther King, Jr.* Vol. 6: *Advocate of the Social Gospel, September 1948–March 1963*. Edited by Clayborne Carson (senior editor), Susan Carson, Susan Englander, Troy Jackson, and Gerald L. Smith. Berkeley: University of California Press, 2007.

Lackey, Michael, ed. *The Haverford Discussions: A Black Integrationist Manifesto for Racial Justice*. Charlottesville: University of Virginia Press, 2013.

Lawrence, Novotny, and Gerald R. Butters, Jr., eds. *Beyond Blaxploitation*. Detroit: Wayne State University Press, 2016.

Lester, Julius. "James Baldwin—Reflections of a Maverick." *The New York Times Book Review* (May 27, 1984). Reprinted as pages 35–53 in *James Baldwin: The Last Interview and Other Conversations*. New York: Melville House, 2014.

Lewis, Ida. "Forward." Pages ix–xv in Nikki Giovanni, *My House: Poems by Nikki Giovanni*. New York: William Morrow, 1972.

Lincoln, Abraham. "Address before the Young Men's Lyceum of Springfield, Illinois." Pages 1:108–15 in *The Collected Works of Abraham Lincoln*. 9 vols. Edited by Roy P. Basler. New York: Abraham Lincoln Association, 1953.

Lindsay, Vachel. "How Samson Bore Away the Gates of Gaza (A Negro Sermon)." Pages 124–27 in Vachel Lindsay, *The Chinese Nightingale and Other Poems*. New York: Macmillan, 1917.

Lippard, George. *Blanche of Brandywine: Or, September the Eighth to Eleventh, 1777. A Romance of the American Revolution. The Scenes Are Laid on the Battleground of Brandywine*. Philadelphia: G. B. Zieber, 1846.

Lippard, George, *Legends of Mexico*. Philadelphia: T. B. Peterson, 1847.

Lippard, George. *Washington and His Generals, or, Legends of the Revolution by George Lippard; with a Biographical Sketch of the Author, by C. Chauncey Burr*. Philadelphia: T. B. Peterson, 1847.

Lipscomb, Terry W., ed. *Journal of the Commons House of Assembly of South Carolina, November 21, 1752–September 6, 1754*. Columbia: University of South Carolina Press, 1983.

Lockard, Joe. "'Earth Feels the Time of Prophet-Song': John Brown and Public Poetry." Pages 69–87 in *The Afterlife of John Brown*. Edited by Andrew Taylor and Eldrid Herrington. New York: Palgrave Macmillan, 2005.

Logan, Rayford. *The Negro in American Life and Thought: The Nadir, 1877–1901*. New York: Dial, 1954.

Lomax, Louis. *When the Word Is Given: A Report on Elijah Muhammad, Malcolm, and the Black Muslim World*. Cleveland: World, 1963.

Longfellow, Henry Wadsworth. *Voices of the Night*. Cambridge: John Owen, 1839.

Longfellow, Henry Wadsworth. *Poems on Slavery*. Cambridge: John Owen, 1842.

Longfellow, Henry Wadsworth. "Paul Revere's Ride." *The Atlantic Monthly* 7.39 (January 1861): 27–29.

Longfellow, Samuel, ed. *Life of Henry Wadsworth Longfellow: With Extracts from His Journals and Correspondence.* 2 vols. Boston: Ticknor, 1886.

Lossing, Benson John. *Pictorial Field-book of the Revolution; or, Illustrations, by Pencil and Pen, of the History, Biography, Scenery, Relics, and Traditions of the War for Independence.* New York: Harper and Brothers, 1851.

Lyman, Darius. *Leaven for Doughfaces; or, Threescore and Ten Parables. By a Former Resident of the South.* Cincinnati: Bangs, 1856.

Majors, M. A. "Jack Johnson Is Crucified for His Race." *Chicago Defender* (July 5, 1913): 1.

McCutcheon, John T. "Uncle Samson and Delilah." Reprinted in *The Literary Digest* 40.8 (August 25, 1917): 10.

McGilligan, Pat. "'Black Samson' at Saxon." *Boston Globe* (August 22, 1974): 61.

McKay, Claude. "Samson." *Workers' Dreadnought* (January 10, 1920): 1602.

McKay, Claude. "The Racial Question: The Racial Question in the United States." *International Press Correspondence* 2 (November 21, 1922): 817.

McKay, Claude. "Negro Author Sees Disaster If the Communist Party Gains Control of Negro Workers." *New Leader* (September 10, 1938): 5.

McKay, Claude. "Socialism and the Negro." Pages 50–54 in *The Passion of Claude McKay: Selected Poetry and Prose, 1912–1948.* Edited by Wayne F. Cooper. New York: Schocken, 1973. Originally published in *Workers' Dreadnought* (January 31, 1920): 1–2.

McKay, Claude. "Travail." Page 139 in Claude McKay, *The Complete Poems.* Edited by William J. Maxwell. Urbana-Champaign: University of Illinois Press, 2008. Originally published in *Workers' Dreadnought* (January 10, 1920): 1601.

McPherson, Grace H. "Letter to the Editor." *Life* 63.7 (August 18, 1967): 19.

Miles, Henry Downes. *Pugilistica: The History of British Boxing Containing Lives of the Most Celebrated Pugilists; Full Reports of their Battles from Contemporary Newspapers, with Authentic Portraits, Personal Anecdotes, and Sketches of the Principal Patrons of the Prize Ring, Forming a Complete History of the Ring from Fig and Broughton, 1719–40, to the Last Championship Battle between King and Heenan, in December 1863.* 3 vols. London: Weldon, 1880.

Moody, Christina. *A Tiny Spark.* Washington, DC: Murray Brothers Press, 1910.

Moody, Loring. *The Destruction of Republicanism the Object of the Rebellion: The Testimony of Southern Witnesses.* Boston: Emancipation League, 1863.

Morrison, Toni. *The Bluest Eye.* New York: Plume, 1993. Originally published as Morrison, Toni. *The Bluest Eye.* New York: Holt, Rinehart and Winston, 1970.

Muhammad, Elijah. *The Theology of Time: The Secret of Time.* Phoenix: Secretarious, 2002.

Nast, Thomas. "The Modern Samson." *Harper's Weekly* 12.614 (October 3, 1868): 632.

Neal, Larry. "The Black Arts Movement." *The Drama Review* 12.4 (1968): 28–39.

Newhall, Fales Henry. *The Conflict in America: A Funeral Discourse Occasioned by the Death of John Brown of Ossawattomie, who Entered into Rest, from the Gallows, at Charlestown, Virginia, Dec. 2, 1859, Preached at the Warren St. M.E. Church, Roxbury, Dec. 4.* Boston: J. M. Hewes, 1859.

Newton, Huey P. *Revolutionary Suicide.* New York: Penguin Books, 1973.

Odell, Margaretta Matilda, ed., *Memoir and Poems, a Native African and a Slave.* Boston: George W. Light, 1834.

Odum, Howard Washington. "Religious Folk-Songs of the Southern Negroes." PhD dissertation. Clark University, 1909. Reprinted in the *American Journal of Religious Psychology and Education* 3 (July 1909): 265–365.

Page, Thomas Nelson. *The Negro: The Southerner's Problem*. New York: C. Scribner's Sons, 1904.

Paine, Albert Bigelow. *Thomas Nast: His Period and His Pictures*. New York: Macmillan, 1904.

Panger, Daniel. *Ol' Prophet Nat*. Winston-Salem: John F. Blair, 1967.

Parks, Gordon. "What Their Cry Means to Me: A Negro's Own Evaluation." *Life* 54.22 (May 31, 1963): 31–32, 78–79.

Parks, Gordon. "Violent End of a Man Called Malcolm X." *Life* 58.9 (March 5, 1965): 26–31.

Patten, Dominic. "History's 'The Bible' & 'Vikings' Rise in Week 3." Deadline.com (March 19, 2013). http://bit.ly/PattenWeek3.

Patton, William Weston. *The Execution of John Brown: A Discourse, Delivered at Chicago, December 4th, 1859, in the First Congregational Church*. Chicago: Church, Goodman and Cushing, 1859.

Peters, Madison C. "What Shall We Do with the Negro?" *Christian Observer* (December 23, 1903): 1.

Peters, Madison C. *The Distribution of Patriotism in the United States*. New York: The Patriotic League, 1918.

Poe, Edgar Allan. "The Pit and the Pendulum." Pages 133–51 in *The Gift: A Christmas and New Year's Present, 1843*. Edited by Eliza Leslie. Philadelphia: Carey and Hart, 1842.

Pogrebin, Letty Cottin. "Anti-Semitism in the Women's Movement." *Ms.* (June 1982): 45–48, 62–72.

Powery, Emerson B., and Rodney S. Sadler, Jr. *The Genesis of Liberation: Biblical Interpretation in the Antebellum Narratives of the Enslaved*. Louisville, KY: Westminster John Knox Press, 2016.

Putnam Weale, B. L. "The Conflict of Color IV: The World's Black Problem." *The World's Work* 19 (November 1909–April 1910): 12327–32.

Rampersad, Arnold. "Introduction to the 1992 Edition." Pages vii–xx in Arna Bontemps, *Gabriel's Revolt: Virginia 1800*. Boston: Beacon, 1992.

Redpath, James. *Roving Editor: Or, Talks with Slaves in Southern States*. New York: A. B. Burdick, 1859.

Redpath, James. *The Public Life of Captain John Brown, with an Autobiography of His Childhood and Youth*. London: Thickbroom and Stapleton, 1860.

Reed, Justin. *Samson: Blessed Savior of Israel, the Remastered Edition*. New York: Published by Justin Reed, 2012.

Reese, George H., ed. *Journal of the Council of the State of Virginia, Vol. IV (December 1, 1786–November 10, 1788)*. Richmond: Virginia State Library, 1967.

Reid, Whitelaw. *After the War: A Southern Tour (May 1, 1865 to May 1, 1866)*. London: Samson Low, Son, and Marston, 1866.

Repplier, Agnes. "Uncle Samson and Delilah." *Life* 80 (November 9, 1922): 3.

Richardson, Harry J. *A Selection of Dialect Poems; Written on the Rail, and Dedicated to the "Army of the Gripsack."* Boston: Travelers, 1884.

Sanborn, Franklin Benjamin. "John Brown and His Friends." *Atlantic Monthly* 30 (July 1872): 50–61.

Sanborn, Franklin Benjamin. *Memoirs of John Brown, Written for Rev. Samuel Orcutt's History of Torrington, Ct., by F. B. Sanborn, with Memorial Verses by William Ellery Channing*. Concord: J. Munsell, 1878.

Sanborn, Franklin Benjamin, ed. *The Life and Letters of John Brown: Liberator of Kansas, and Martyr of Virginia*. Boston: Roberts Brothers, 1885.

Sanborn, Franklin Benjamin. *Recollections of Seventy Years*. Boston: R. G. Badger, 1909.

Savage, Kirk. "Molding Emancipation: John Quincy Adams Ward's 'The Freedman' and the Meaning of the Civil War." *Art Institute of Chicago Museum Studies* 27.1 (2001): 26–39, 101.

Schipper, Jeremy. "'On Such Texts Comment Is Unnecessary': Biblical Interpretation in the Trial of Denmark Vesey." *Journal of the American Academy of Religion* 85 (2017): 1032–49.

Schipper, Jeremy. "'Misconstruction of the Sacred Page': On Denmark Vesey's Biblical Interpretations." *Journal of Biblical Literature* 138 (2019): 23–38.

Schipper, Jeremy. *Denmark Vesey's Bible*. Princeton: Princeton University Press, forthcoming.

Schulte Nordholt, Jan Willem. *The People That Walk in Darkness*. Translated by M. B. van Wijngaarden. London: Burke, 1960.

Schulte Nordholt, Jan Willem. "The People That Walk in Darkness: Sea of Blood and Tears." *Chicago Defender* (December 10, 1962): 11.

Shanks, Julia Hicks. "Whenever I See Old Glory: Flag Day 1933." *The Baltimore Afro-American* (June 17, 1933): 24.

Shanks, Julia Hicks. "Where Was the Negro on the Fourth of July?" *The Baltimore Afro-American* (July 1, 1933): 7.

Sherwin, W. T. *Memoirs of the Life of Thomas Paine, with Observations on His Writings, Critical and Explanatory. To Which is Added, an Appendix, Containing Several of Mr. Paine's Unpublished Pieces*. London: R. Carlile, 1819.

Skinner, Charles M. *Myths and Legends of Our Own Land*. 2 vols. Philadelphia: J. P. Lippincott, 1896.

Smith, Welton. "Malcolm." Pages 283–91 in *Black Fire: An Anthology of Afro-American Writing*. Edited by LeRoi Jones and Larry Neal. New York: William Morrow, 1968.

Snelling, William J. "Song, Supposed to Be Sung by Slaves in Insurrection." *The Liberator* 29 (November 4, 1859): 176.

Sorett, Josef. *Spirit in the Dark: A Religious History of Racial Aesthetics*. New York: Oxford University Press, 2016.

Stevens, John. "Reflections in a Dark Mirror: Comic Strips in Black Newspapers." *Journal of Popular Culture* 10.1 (1976): 239–44.

Steward, Austin. *Twenty-Two Years a Slave, and Forty Years a Freeman; Embracing a Correspondence of Several Years, While President of Wilberforce Colony, London, Canada West*. Rochester: William Alling, 1857.

Stowe, Harriet Beecher. *Uncle Tom's Cabin; or, Life among the Lowly*. Boston: John P. Jewett, 1852.

Stowe, Harriet Beecher. *Dred: A Tale of the Great Dismal Swamp*. 2 vols. Boston: Phillips, Sampson, 1856.

Stowe, Harriet Beecher. Untitled editorial reprinted as "Mrs. Harriet Beecher Stowe." *The Principia* 2.45 (September 21, 1861): 770.

Styron, William. *The Confessions of Nat Turner*. New York: Random House, 1967.

Styron, William. "Nat Turner Revisited." *American Heritage* (October 1992): 65–73.

Tolson, Melvin B. "Rendezvous with America." Pages 3–12 in Melvin B. Tolson, *Rendezvous with America*. New York: Dodd, Mead, 1944.

Toomer, Jean. "Reflections on the Race Riots." *New York Call* (August 2, 1919): 8.

Toomer, Jean. *Cane*. New York: Boni and Liveright, 1923.

Tourgée, Albion W. *Bricks without Straw: A Novel*. New York: Fords, Howard and Hulbert, 1880.

Trowbridge, John Townsend. *The South: A Tour of Its Battlefields and Ruined Cities, a Journey through the Desolated States, and Talks with the People: Being a Description of the Present State of the Country—Its Agriculture—Railroads—Business and Finances*. Hartford, CT: L. Stebbins, 1866.

Van Gelder, Lawrence. "'Black Samson' from Film Netherworld." *New York Times* (August 15, 1974): 25.

Vander Stichele, Caroline, and Hugh S. Pyper, eds. *Text, Image, and Otherness in Children's Bibles: What's in the Picture?* Atlanta: Society of Biblical Literature, 2012.

Varnum, Joseph B., Jr. "The Seat of Government of the United States." *The Merchant's Magazine* 18.2 (February 1848): 142–51.

Villard, Oswald Garrison. *John Brown, 1800–1859: A Biography Fifty Years After*. Boston: Houghton Mifflin, 1910.

Vinson, J. Chal. *Thomas Nast: Political Cartoonist*. Athens: University of Georgia Press, 1967.

Von Holst, Hermann. *John Brown*. Edited by Frank Preston Stearns. Translated by Phillippe Marcou. Boston: DeWolfe, Fiske, 1888.

Wagner, Jean. *Black Poets of the United States: Paul Laurence Dunbar to Langston Hughes*. Translated by Kenneth Douglas. Urbana: University of Illinois Press, 1973.

Ward, Geoffrey C. *Unforgiveable Blackness: The Rise and Fall of Jack Johnson*. New York: Knopf, 2004.

Warren, Robert Penn. *John Brown: The Making of a Martyr*. New York: Payson and Clarke, 1929.

Washington, Linn. "MOVE: A Double Standard of Justice?" *Yale Journal of Law and Liberation* 1 (1989): 67–82.

Weisenfeld, Judith. *New World A-Coming: Black Religion and Racial Identity during the Great Migration*. New York: New York University Press, 2017.

Werden-Greenfeild, Ariella Y. "Warriors and Prophets of Livity: Samson and Moses as Moral Exemplars in Rastafari." PhD dissertation. Temple University, 2016.

Wells-Barnett, Ida B. *Southern Horrors: Lynch Law in All Its Phases*. New York: New York Age Print, 1892.

Wells-Barnett, Ida B. *The East St. Louis Massacre: The Greatest Outrage of the Century*. Chicago: Negro Fellowship Herald, 1917.

West, Cornel. *Prophesy Deliverance!: An Afro-American Revolutionary Christianity*. Philadelphia: Westminster, 1982.

Wheatley, Phillis. *Poems on Various Subjects, Religious and Moral*. London: Archibald Bell, 1773.

Wheatley, Phillis. "Letter to Samson Occum." *The Connecticut Gazette* (March 11, 1774).

Wilkerson, Isabel. *The Warmth of Other Suns: The Epic Story of America's Great Migration*. New York: Vintage, 2010.

Wilkerson, Isabel. "Where Do We Go from Here?" *Essence* 45.10 (January 2015): 88.

Williams, James. *Narrative of James Williams, an American Slave, Who was for Several Years a Driver on a Cotton Plantation in Alabama*. Boston: American Anti-Slavery Society, 1838.

Wilson, August. *Ma Rainey's Black Bottom: A Play in Two Acts*. New York: New American Library, 1985.

Wimbush, Vincent L., ed. *African Americans and the Bible: Sacred Texts and Social Textures*. New York: Continuum, 2000.

Winter, Kari J., ed. *The Blind African Slave, or, Memoirs of Boyrereau Brinch, Nicknamed Jeffrey Brace*. Madison: University of Wisconsin Press, 2004.

Wright, Richard. "Fire and Cloud." *Story* 12 (March 1938): 9–41.

Wright, Richard. "I Tried to Be a Communist." *Atlantic Monthly* 159 (August 1944): 61–70.

Songs

Spiritual, "Gawd's a-Gwineter Move All de Troubles Away."

Spiritual, "My Soul Is a Witness to My Lord."

"If I Had My Way I'd Tear the Building Down" recorded by Reverend T. E. Weems (1927).

"If I Had My Way" recorded by Reverend T. T. Rose (1927).

"If I Had My Way I'd Tear the Building Down" recorded by Blind Willie Johnson (1927).

Hymn. Charles Austin Miles. "The Cloud and Fire" published by the Hall-Mack Company (1900).

No Author Listed

13th. Directed by Ava DuVernay. 2016. Internet Movie Database, http://www.imdb.com/title/tt5895028/.

"A 20th Century Negro: Will the Negro of that Century be an Improvement as Compared with a Negro of this Day and Generation? Let's Hope So." *Plain Dealer* 1.33 (August 18, 1899): 1.

The Bible. 2013. Internet Movie Database. http://www.imdb.com/title/tt2245988/.

"Black Is Beautiful! by DAL: How Aware Are You?: Gabriel Prosser (1776–1800)." *Philadelphia Tribune* (September 28, 1968): 19.

Black Samson. Directed by Charles Bail. 1974. Internet Movie Database. https://www.imdb.com/title/tt0071226.

"The Black Samson Asleep." *Freeman* (October 5, 1889): 4.

"'Black Samson' Fights Mob with Ancient Art Kindo." *Baltimore Afro-American* (September 7, 1974): 11.

"Black Samson to Open in Black Areas." *Chicago Metro News* (August 17, 1974): D5.

"Black Sampson." *The Broad Ax* (October 15, 1921): 2.

"Black Sampson—Fall of the Chair Factory Ruins." *The Baltimore Sun* (May 15, 1874): 1.

"The Buffaloes: A First-Class Colored Regiment by One of Its Battalion Staff Officers Lieutenant O. E. McKaine with an Introduction by Its Commander, Colonel James A. Moss." *The Outlook* (May 22, 1918): 144–47.

"Conn. Fascist Pigs Vamp on Panthers." *The Black Panther* 2.18 (August 23, 1969): 7.

"D. A. R. Representative Gets Lesson in History." *Philadelphia Tribune* (October 9, 1930): 8.

"Dr. E. J. Scott Addresses Vets at Legion Confab: Howard University Official Pleads for New Deal." *Chicago Defender* (October 7, 1933): 4.

"Dr. Fry Insists Racial Crisis May Get Worse and Not Better." *Atlanta Daily World* (January 28, 1968): 2.

"Dr. Peters Praises Negro: Progress Has Been Rapid in South, Where He Is Best Treated." *The Baltimore Sun* (May 18, 1903): 7.

"Dr. Thirkeild Delivered a Lecture on the 'Black Samson.'" *Savannah Tribune* 14.34 (June 3, 1899): 2.

"Editorial Notes." *Western Christian Advocate* 67 (October 24, 1900): 1346.

"Editorial Notes." *Western Christian Advocate* 68 (July 2, 1902): 31.

The Great Debaters. 2007. Directed by Denzel Washington. Internet Movie Database. https://www.imdb.com/title/tt0427309/.

"Have We a War Policy?" *Weekly Anglo African* (April 27, 1861): No page numbers.

In Memoriam: Frederick Douglass. Philadelphia: John C. Yorston, 1897.

"Insurrection of the Blacks." *Niles' Weekly Register* 40 (August 27, 1831): 455.

Invincible 6 (October 2003). https://imagecomics.com/comics/series/invincible (accessed January 3, 2018).

Invinciible 112 (June 2014).

"Jack Johnson Still Nagged by Great White Hopes." *Philadelphia Tribune* (August 7, 1915): 4.

"John Arthur Johnson Still Holds the Championship Belt of the World." *Broad Ax* (July 9, 1910): 1.

"Marvels of Strength: 'Jimmy' Golden Is Called the 'Black Samson.'" *Boston Daily Globe* (July 4, 1908): 8.

"Meet to Honor Leader: With a Spirit to Pay Homage to One Whom They Loved Young and Old Pay Respectful Tribute." *The Chicago Defender* (November 27, 1915): 3.

"The Moral of Statistics." *The New Englander* 13 (May, 1855): 183–207.

"My Mamma Done Told Me." *Philadelphia Tribune* (April 11, 1942): 1, 3.

"No Colored Members in Delaware D.A.R: White Sons of Revolution Never Heard of Negro Heroes of 1776." *Baltimore Afro-American* (October 4, 1930): 3.

"Our Solider Boys Are Busy." *Cleveland Gazette* (June 22, 1918): 1.

"A Page from History." *Our Colored Missions* 26.7 (July 1, 1930): 109.

"Racial Violence Assailed by Dr. Luther King." *Los Angeles Times* (June 16, 1962): 11.

"Reading." *Baltimore Afro-American* (June 4, 1932): 5.

"Report of the Special Committee Authorized by Congress to Investigate the East St. Louis Riots: 65th Congress, 2nd Session, House of Representatives, Document 1231." Pages 1–22 in *Congressional Edition*: Volume 7444 (Washington, DC: US Government Printing Office, 1918).

"Report of UNIA Meeting." Pages 305–20 in *The Marcus Garvey and Universal Negro Improvement Association Papers*. Vol. 2: *27 August 1919–31 August 1920*. Edited by Robert Abraham Hill. Berkeley: University of California Press, 1983.

"Report of the UNIA Delegation to Liberia." Pages 246–60 in *The Marcus Garvey and Universal Negro Improvement Association Papers* Vol. 10: *Africa for the Africans, 1923–1945*. Edited by Robert Abraham Hill. Berkeley: University of California Press, 2006.

"Samson Gets His Hair Back." *Philadelphia Tribune* (March 31, 1938): 4.

"School Decision Freedom Quest's Most Significant Step, Dr. Mays Tells Emancipation Observance: Morehouse President Traces Struggle of the Negro Race." *Atlanta Daily World* (February 13, 1963): 1.

"Southern Outrages: Baptist Ministers Discuss Them in the Pulpits." *Plaindealer* (October 25, 1889): 2.

"The State of Affairs in Lilliput." *The Gentlemen's Magazine* 8 (June 1738): 283–88.

"Views of the Afro-American Press on the Johnson-Jeffries Fight." *Baltimore Afro-American* (July 16, 1910): 4.

"What Is a Communist?" *New York Amsterdam News* (November 4, 1925): 12.

"What Will Samson Do?" *Pittsburgh Courier* (November 19, 1941): 6.

"Yorty Assails Boast of Black Muslim Chief: Death of 130 in French Air Disaster Hailed in Tape Recording of Negro's Talk." *Los Angeles Times* (June 7, 1962): A1.

Unforgiveable Blackness: The Rise and Fall of Jack Johnson. Directed by Ken Burns. 2005. https://www.pbs.org/kenburns/unforgivable-blackness/.

Index

For the benefit of digital users, indexed terms that span two pages (e.g., 52–53) may, on occasion, appear on only one of those pages.

Figures are indicated by *f* following the page number